WomenHeart's
ALL HEART
Family Cookbook

Featuring the 40 Foods Proven to Promote Heart Health

Kathy Kastan, LCSW, MA ED, and Suzanne Banfield, PhD,

with Wendy.Leonard and the members of WomenHeart: The National Coalition
for Women with Heart Disease

Produced by The Philip Lief Group, Inc.

RODALE

This WomenHeart cookbook is dedicated to our eight million heart sisters and their families throughout the country. WomenHeart members have used their inspiration, perspiration, and creativity in developing this cookbook to give women and their families an excellent food guide that will help all of us to live well and thrive.

Copyright © 2008 by The National Coalition for Women with Heart Disease

All rights reserved. No part of this publication may be reproduced or transmitted in any form or by any means, electronic or mechanical, including photocopying, recording, or any other information storage and retrieval system, without the written permission of the publisher.

Rodale books may be purchased for business or promotional use or for special sales. For information, please write to: Special Markets Department, Rodale Inc., 733 Third Avenue, New York, NY 10017

Printed in the United States of America

Rodale Inc. makes every effort to use acid-free ∞, recycled paper ♻.

Photographs by Alexandra Rowley

Book design by Christina Gaugler

Library of Congress Cataloging-in-Publication Data

Kastan, Kathy.
    WomenHeart's all heart family cookbook : featuring the 40 foods proven to promote heart health /
Kathy Kastan, Suzanne Banfield, with Wendy Leonard and the members of WomenHeart: the National Coalition for
Women with Heart Disease.
        p.   cm.
    Includes index.
    ISBN-13 978–1–59486–796–5 hardcover
    ISBN-10 1–59486–796–8 hardcover
    1. Heart—Diseases—Diet therapy—Recipes. 2. Heart—Diseases—Prevention—Popular works. 3. Women—Diseases—
Prevention—Popular works. I. Banfield, Suzanne. II. Leonard, Wendy. III. WomenHeart. National Coalition for Women with
Heart Disease. IV. Title. V. Title: All heart family cookbook.
RC684.D5K37   2008
641.5'6311—dc22   2007038217

Distributed to the trade by Macmillan

2   4   6   8   10   9   7   5   3   1 hardcover

LIVE YOUR WHOLE LIFE™

We inspire and enable people to improve their lives and the world around them

For more of our products visit **rodalestore.com** or call 800-848-4735

CONTENTS

FOREWORD..v

INTRODUCTION vii

Part I: **The 40 Heart Healthy Foods**

Nutrient Spotlights 2

Apples 7

Asparagus 9

Avocados 10

Bananas 11

Beans 13

Berries... 14

Bran 16

Carrots.. 18

Chocolate, Dark 19

Cruciferous Vegetables 21

Flaxseed and Flaxseed Oil 23

Garlic 24

Grapes and Cherries 26

Greens, Dark Leafy 27

Herbs and Spices................................... 28

Kiwifruit 30

Lemons and Limes................................. 32

Lentils... 33

Mushrooms, Shiitake 34

Nuts 36

Oats 38

Olives and Olive Oil 39

Onions, Scallions, and Shallots............ 41

Oranges 42

Peppers, Bell 44

Peppers, Chile 46

Potatoes, Sweet...................................... 48

Quinoa.. 49

Salmon 51

Sea Vegetables 53

Seeds... 54

Soy Products 55

Spinach 58

Squash, Winter 59

Tea 61

Tomatoes... 63

Tropical Fruits 66

Whole Grains... 67

Wine, Red 70

Yogurt 72

Part II: 175 Family-Pleasing, Heart-Protecting Recipes

Chapter 1: Good Mornings 76

Chapter 2: Super Soups 95

Chapter 3: A Salad a Day 105

Chapter 4: Fruit and Vegetables at Every Meal....................................131

Chapter 5: The Great Grains 145

Chapter 6: Bean Cuisine and Meatless Mains 156

Chapter 7: Pasta and Noodles Galore...170

Chapter 8: Selections from the Sea 186

Chapter 9: Please 'Em with Poultry...201

Chapter 10: Accent with Meat..219

Chapter 11: Snack to Your Heart's Content 232

Chapter 12: Just for Dessert 242

Chapter 13: Dressings, Salsas, Sauces, and Spreads.............................258

Chapter 14: Party Hearty 267

INDEX 283

CONVERSION CHART...302

Y ou have heart disease." Hearing those words spoken can strike an anxious chord in the heart of any person. The WomenHeart community understands your apprehension, but we also know that with proper treatment of risk factors, a healthy diet, and exercise, you can reduce heart disease problems by 82 percent. It's important to remember that if you have heart disease, it doesn't mean you've lost all control—you can control what you eat, whether or not you smoke, and how much physical activity you fit into your day. In fact, WomenHeart created this book to help you take heart healthy control over your life.

In the past few decades, there have been great strides in cardiovascular care. New medicines and less invasive medical procedures help control heart disease and risk factors and improve quality of life. While we are pleased with the great progress in treatment, WomenHeart wants to do more for you. We want to teach you what you can do for yourself: how you can live—and thrive—with heart disease.

You have the power to reduce your risk for heart disease and even eliminate certain risk factors. By choosing the right foods to put in your body, staying physically active, and being proactive about your health care, you can have a positive effect on your heart health and on family members' health as well. And if you have been diagnosed with heart disease, you may be able to help manage it with these new food choices. Remember, though, before embarking on any dietary changes or fitness plans, it is important to consult with your doctor to determine what is best for your personal health needs.

One of the most important ways you can be proactive about your heart health is by making new dietary choices, and this book will help you do just that by introducing you to the 40 foods scientifically proven to promote heart health.

Almonds, avocados, cherries, beans, dark chocolate, olives, garlic, salmon, oatmeal, nuts. . . . Some of the 40 foods may surprise you, but each one we've included here is backed by scientific evidence that shows it can help control or greatly reduce at least one of the many risk factors of heart disease—factors such as high blood pressure, high cholesterol, diabetes, and obesity.

The good news this book brings is that taking control of your diet for better heart health doesn't mean you have to abandon appetizing food and flavors. The 175 recipes included here prove heart healthy eating can be delicious. For some of the recipes, we turned to our WomenHeart community leaders and asked them to share their favorites—recipes they have prepared for their own families and friends. The other recipes were developed by professional nutritionists and food writers. Almost every recipe in the book contains at least three of the 40 heart healthy foods and follows the most recent American Heart Association guidelines (look for the ♥ symbol in the ingredients list). And each recipe provides other nutritional information so you can plan your meals accordingly.

In this book you will also learn about nutrition and how it affects heart disease. You will discover how foods that are high in fiber (pinto beans, for instance) can fight the plaque buildup that threatens your arteries; how the unsaturated fats found in avocado can reduce your blood cholesterol levels; and how the omega-3 fatty acids in salmon can lower your triglyceride levels. You'll also learn that a diet low in salt but rich in fruits and vegetables can reduce your blood pressure and that the antioxidants found in broccoli and blueberries can stabilize your glucose levels and prevent diabetes.

As women, we have a tendency to think of ourselves last. At WomenHeart, experience has taught us that we need to reprioritize our lives—for ourselves and for our families. You *can* take control of your heart health. This book is a tool to help you get started. You can do something today, right in your own kitchen, to start making a difference. Begin now to make heart health a priority in your life—and the life of your family.

—SUSAN K. BENNETT, MD
Clinical Director
Women's Heart Program, George Washington University Hospital, Washington, DC

From the Heart

Our WomenHeart's message to you is positively simple: Eating for a healthy heart is not about what you *can't* eat, it's about all the wonderful, sublimely delicious foods you *can* eat. Who knew that foods that promote heart health and healing are the kinds of food women love—like strawberries and chocolate? We've got the science to prove it. And now, so do you!

This amazing collection of recipes will help you give your family (and you) the gift of health—every single day. The recipes reflect dietary guidelines based on the most recent scientific findings, and you will quickly see that you can enjoy a delicious variety of foods and still be heart healthy. Heart healthy food is meant to be celebrated. So, from our hearts to yours, enjoy.

A Word to the Wise

Pretty much everyone knows what the risk factors are for heart disease: high blood cholesterol, high blood pressure, smoking, obesity/overweight, diabetes, a sedentary lifestyle, age, family history, and genetics. There's no denying that the last three risk factors are beyond our control. Age: For women, the chance of developing heart disease rises after age 55; for men, that increase happens after 45. Family history: A woman whose mother or sister was diagnosed with heart disease before age 65 and a man whose father or brother was diagnosed before 55 are also at increased risk. Genetics: Two 2007 studies published in the journal *Science* identified two genetic variations (on chromosome 9p21) associated with an increased risk of heart disease.

But there's good news. Even if you have some risk factors that you can't change, you *can* (and frankly, should) do something to prevent or reduce the other major risk factors that lead to heart disease. Do it for yourself, your partner, and your entire family.

40 Heart Healthy Foods: What Can Chocolate and Cranberries Do for You?

For more than 80 years, heart disease has been the leading cause of death for both women and men in the United States—and that's been the case for all races and ethnicities. Sobering as that fact is, that's not the end of the story—far from it. Ready to feel better?

Based upon decades of evidence-based research, scientists have identified 40 foods that can help

According to the most recent government figures, slightly more than one out of every 10 women and men (11.6 percent and 11.4 percent, respectively) has been diagnosed with a cardiovascular condition.

reduce, prevent, and even reverse heart disease. From apples to avocados, chocolate to cranberries, red wine to whole wheat, this cookbook was specifically created to help you prepare meals that promote heart health and prevent heart disease in very specific ways.

Eating certain foods can, for example, reduce plaque buildup in your arteries, block the absorption of cholesterol, increase "good" HDL cholesterol, lower "bad" LDL cholesterol, lower blood pressure, stabilize sugar levels, and even reduce the risk of diabetes. Here's how.

ANATOMY OF A PLAQUE ATTACK

Healthy coronary arteries are pliable, elastic tubes that are about the width of a single strand of spaghetti. The interior walls of coronary arteries are supposed to be slippery, unobstructed passageways that allow blood, under pressure, to flow without interruption. However, if you have developed coronary artery disease (CAD), one or more of the arteries supplying blood to your heart has become obstructed in some way. The most common culprit is atherosclerosis (pronounced ATH-er-o-skler-O-sis).

From the Greek words *athero* (meaning "gruel" or "paste") and *sclerosis* ("hardness"), atherosclerosis is the thickening and hardening of the artery walls due to plaque buildup. This buildup can (1) narrow the arteries—called stenosis—which means the heart is not getting a sufficient amount of blood and oxygen; (2) totally block the arteries, which means that the heart isn't getting any blood and oxygen; or (3) cause the formation of blood clots—globular, jellylike masses that can further block the blood and oxygen supply to the heart.

What exactly is plaque? Either hard and stable or soft and unstable, plaque is made of cholesterol, fat, calcium, and other substances in the blood. Hard, stable plaque causes the artery walls to thicken, narrow, and harden. Soft, unstable plaque usually "breaks off," causing blood clots (although hard plaques can break off, too). Fortunately, you can fight plaque and its buildup by enjoying foods that contain high amounts of fiber, such as dried beans, oats, barley, fruits—notably, apples, berries, and citrus—and many vegetables.

When you eat high-fiber foods, the fiber binds onto dietary cholesterol in the gastrointestinal tract—and doesn't let it go—which helps your body eliminate the cholesterol rather effortlessly. This process helps reduce blood cholesterol levels, which, in turn, reduces the potential for cholesterol deposits to build up, harden, and thicken the walls of your arteries. Think of it this way: Just like your teeth need brushing and flossing every day, your arteries need fiber to promote and maintain optimal heart health. It's just that simple.

Types of Heart Disease

Heart disease is an umbrella term for any disorder that affects your heart's ability to function normally. Types of heart disease include:

CORONARY ARTERY DISEASE (CAD)

The leading cause of heart attacks, this is the most common type of heart disease. With this disease, the eventual plaque buildup, which we've just discussed (atherosclerosis), causes both narrowing and hardening of the arteries. As a result, your heart isn't getting as much blood as it needs. Having CAD can lead to angina and a heart attack.

Angina

From the Latin word *angere,* which means "to choke or throttle," angina of the heart is the all-too-familiar painful pressing, squeezing, elephant-on-your-chest feeling many people experience prior to having a heart attack. For some people, the pain may also be in the shoulders, arms, neck, jaw, or back; for others, angina might feel like a stomachache or indigestion.

Why is angina so often painful? Your heart is desperately trying to let you know it is literally starving for oxygen (technically called ischemia) as a result of atherosclerosis choking off the blood supply—and therefore the vitally important oxygen supply—to your heart. This lack of oxygen can cause significant damage as well as death of heart muscle tissue, which is why it's so important that you get to a hospital or emergency care facility as soon as possible. If started quickly enough, medical treatments such as clot-busting medications, stenting, or cardiac catheterization with angioplasty can stop more damage from happening.

How quickly is quickly enough? Called the golden hour by the medical community, a 60-minute window offers the best scenario for restoring bloodflow to your heart after a heart attack.

Angina is not a heart attack, but it increases your risk of having one or signals that you're about to have one. So if you are experiencing *any* of the symptoms of angina or know someone who is, seek medical attention right away. Don't put it off or wait for the symptoms to just go away. The sad reality is that more than half of women who've suffered heart attacks report having previously experienced one or more symptoms, which are generally more vague in women and all too often dismissed as "nothing to worry about." (See "Subtle Symptoms in Women" on page x.)

Heart Attack

Here's a very to-the-point definition to remember: Whether an artery is totally or severely blocked, you're having a heart attack if your heart doesn't get the blood it needs for more than 20 minutes. The medical term for heart attack is myocardial infarction (MI):

WEIGHING IN ON HOMOCYSTEINE

Homocysteine is a building block of protein (an amino acid) that circulates in your blood. A number of studies suggest a possible association between high levels of homocysteine and atherosclerosis, but a direct causal link has yet to be established. That being said, while the scientific jury is still out as to whether lowering your homocysteine levels directly reduces your risk for heart disease, foods high in folate (folic acid) and other B vitamins do lower homocysteine levels and definitely lower blood pressure. So you may as well include foods that are high in folate—which are usually delicious.

Myocardium is from the Greek words *myo,* which means "muscle," and *kardia,* which means "heart." *Infarction* is from the Latin word *infarcire,* which means to "cram, stuff, or plug up."

Not to be redundant, but if you believe someone is having a heart attack, get emergency attention (call 911) immediately. Time is extremely precious.

HEART FAILURE

Contrary to popular perception, heart failure doesn't mean your heart has stopped. What it does mean is that its ability to pump blood to other organs has become diminished. The most common signs of heart failure include:

- A feeling of extreme tiredness or fatigue
- A feeling like you can't get enough air in your lungs
- Shortness of breath (called dyspnea)
- Swollen ankles, legs, and/or feet

HEART ARRHYTHMIAS

Any disorder that changes the normal rhythm of your heart—your heartbeat—is called an arrhythmia (as in, "not in rhythm").

- Tachycardia: Your heart is beating faster than normal (more than 100 beats per minute).
- Bradycardia: Your heart is beating too slowly (less than 60 beats per minute).
- Atrial fibrillation: The atrial chambers are quivering instead of pumping correctly.
- Ventricular arrhythmia: The ventricles (the two primary pumping chambers) are sending erratic, disorganized signals. This is the most severe form of arrhythmia because blood circulation can stop.

SUBTLE SYMPTOMS IN WOMEN

Women often experience very different warning signs of a heart attack when compared to men. In fact, many women don't experience any symptoms at all or the symptoms may be vague and come and go—so a woman may erroneously believe there is no cause for concern or need for immediate medical attention. See your doctor if you experience:

- Unusual tiredness, anxiety, or weariness
- Back and shoulder pain
- Shortness of breath
- Indigestion or nausea
- Profuse sweating

The Big Four Risk Factors

This is only a test: For which of the following heart disease risk factors is there solid, scientific evidence that certain foods may help control, reduce, prevent, or even eliminate it?

A. High cholesterol

B. Hypertension (high blood pressure)

C. Diabetes

D. Overweight or obesity

E. All of the above

Correct! It's E—all of the above.

Now, if you would be so kind, please read the following two sentences twice: "The difference I can make in my own health and the health of my loved ones is undeniable. The choice is mine to make."

CHOLESTEROL: "GOOD" AND "BAD"

Nowadays, it's common knowledge that having high cholesterol increases your risk for heart disease. But what does that mean? What are you supposed to do about it? And what the heck is cholesterol, anyway?

Cholesterol is a type of fat. Your body actually needs a certain amount of cholesterol—but only a very small amount—to help it perform many important functions, such as producing hormones, vitamin D, and bile (the acid that helps digest fat). There are two types of cholesterol: low-density lipoprotein (LDL) and high-density lipoprotein (HDL). Lipoproteins are the "packages" that circulate lipids (fat) throughout your body by way of your bloodstream.

So why all the hubbub about cholesterol? If your bloodstream has too much of the cholesterol that's packaged in low-density lipoproteins, the surplus is dumped into your arteries—which, as you know, narrows and eventually may entirely plug up the interior walls of your arteries, causing atherosclerosis. That's why LDL cholesterol is considered bad.

On the other hand, the cholesterol that's carried by high-density lipoproteins actually helps remove artery-clogging cholesterol from the bloodstream. Thus, HDL cholesterol is considered good.

The Cholesterol–Food Connection
Saturated versus Unsaturated Fats

To be clear, not all fats are bad. In fact, some of them are not only good, they're necessary for your body to function at its best. For instance, without fats, your body can't process vitamins A, D, E, and K. The key

---

KNOW YOUR NUMBERS

Total cholesterol is a measure of the cholesterol in all of your lipoproteins, including LDL and HDL. Frankly, knowing your "total" numbers isn't that helpful. When you get your cholesterol levels tested, tell your doctor you want the specific breakdown of LDL and HDL. Note: Cholesterol levels are measured in milligrams (mg) of cholesterol per deciliter (dL) of blood—hence, the "mg/dL."

Just what numbers should you shoot for when it comes to your cholesterol?

Total Cholesterol Level	Category	LDL Cholesterol Level	Category
Less than 200 mg/dL	Desirable	Less than 100 mg/dL	Optimal (ideal)
200 to 239 mg/dL	Borderline high	100 to 129 mg/dL	Near optimal
240 mg/dL and above	High	130 to 159 mg/dL	Borderline high
		160 to 189 mg/dL	High
		190-plus mg/dL	Very high

HDL Cholesterol Level

Less than 40 mg/dL is a major risk factor for heart disease.

60 mg/dL or higher is protective.

---

is to choose the right kinds of fats and avoid the wrong kinds. Simply put, saturated fats (which are solid at room temperature) are bad because they increase cholesterol in your blood, and unsaturated fats (monounsaturated and polyunsaturated) are good because they decrease cholesterol levels.

Foods with bad artery-clogging saturated fat (most of which comes from animal sources) include:

- Fatty cuts of meat
- Beef
- Lamb
- Pork
- Poultry with skin
- Whole and 2 percent milk
- Butter
- Cheese
- Lard

A high content of bad saturated fat can also be found in a few plant-based foods, including:

- Palm kernel oil
- Palm oil
- Coconut oil
- Cocoa butter

HIGH BLOOD PRESSURE (AKA HYPERTENSION)

We've all had our blood pressure taken with one of those cuffs that wrap around the arm and inflate when a rubber bulb is squeezed. But most of us don't know exactly what blood pressure is. Let's remedy that right now: Blood pressure is the force of your blood pushing against the walls of your arteries.

With each heartbeat, the pressure rises, causing your heart to pump blood into your arteries. This is called systolic (sis-TOL-ik) pressure. In between beats, when your heart is essentially resting, the pressure falls. That's called diastolic (di-a-STOL-ik) pressure.

If your blood vessels have become narrowed due to plaque buildup, that increases your blood pressure.

KNOW YOUR TRIGLYCERIDES

Triglycerides are another type of fat that contributes to the hardening and narrowing of your arteries. Most of your stored body fat is in the form of triglycerides, and only a small amount is supposed to circulate in your bloodstream. One of your best ways to lower your triglyceride levels is to eat a diet rich in omega-3 fatty acids, found in fish and flaxseed oil (as well as in supplements, if your doctor determines you need additional omega-3s).

A simple blood test will tell you what your triglyceride levels are. You want them to be below 150. Levels above 200 are considered high, putting you at risk of having a heart attack.

Triglyceride Level	Category
Less than 150 mg/dL	Normal
150 to 199 mg/dL	Borderline high
200 to 499 mg/dL	High
500 mg/dL	Very high

How? Imagine water running through a garden hose. Now imagine squeezing the end of the hose with your thumb. What happens? The water pressure increases. That's how plaque raises blood pressure.

Blood pressure readings are usually given as two numbers: systolic pressure over diastolic pressure. But what do those numbers mean?

- 120/80 or lower: normal blood pressure
- 140/90 or higher: high blood pressure
- 120 to 139 for the top number or 80 to 89 for the bottom number: prehypertension

Known as the silent killer, high blood pressure usually creates no symptoms. Your heart could be working harder, your arteries could be taking a beating, and your chances of having a heart attack (as well as a stroke and kidney problems) could be significantly increasing, and you wouldn't even know it.

According to the National Heart, Lung, and Blood Institute (NHLBI), when high blood pressure isn't discovered and treated, it can cause an enlarged heart, which may lead to heart failure, aneurysm (AN-ur-ism) formation in your blood vessels, and hardening of the arteries (which can cause a heart attack or stroke), among a host of other problems.

Clearly, you don't want to ignore high blood pres-sure. Fortunately, you can control it with diet, exercise, and medications, if necessary. Evidence-based studies have established again and again that you can lower your blood pressure by reducing your sodium (salt) intake and eating a diet that's low in saturated fat, cholesterol, and total fat, as well as rich in fruits, vegetables, and low-fat or fat-free milk and milk products.

The High Blood Pressure–Food Connection

So if lowering your sodium intake is the first defense against high blood pressure, what's the problem with that? Chances are that most of your sodium intake comes from processed foods that often don't actually taste salty, so we're not even aware of the sodium. For

---

PHYSICAL ACTIVITIES AND CALORIES BURNED

Just how many calories do you burn when you do your favorite exercise? The exact number depends on many factors. For example, people who weigh more generally burn more calories during exercise than people who weigh less. That being said, to give you some working guidelines, here's how many calories are burned during 30 minutes of various physical activities.

Moderate Activities	130-Pound Woman	154-Pound Man	Vigorous Activities	130-Pound Woman	154-Pound Man
Hiking	175	185	Running/jogging		
Dancing	132	165	(5 mph)	236	295
Light gardening/			Bicycling (>10 mph)	236	295
yard work	118	165	Swimming		
Golf (walking and			(slow freestyle laps)	206	255
carrying clubs)	132	165	Aerobics	206	240
Bicycling (<10 mph)	118	145	Walking (4½ mph)	185	230
Walking (3½ mph)	112	140	Weight lifting		
			(vigorous effort)	177	220

Before engaging in any new physical activities, be sure to consult your doctor or health care provider to help you design a program that's right for you.

---

example, a large plain bagel has about 700 milligrams of sodium; 1 cup of canned tomato soup, nearly 750. Canned chicken noodle soup has over 1,100 milligrams!

Shake the Salt Habit

To get a handle on your salt intake, what should you do? First of all, whenever possible, choose fresh foods over processed (think homemade tomato sauce, not from a jar; fresh fruits and veggies, not canned) and skip the salt shaker. Second, if you must purchase processed foods, look for low-salt/low-sodium versions. Check labels carefully and aim for less than 2,400 milligrams of sodium a day—that's about 1 teaspoon of salt. However, if you already have high blood pressure, diabetes, or kidney disease; are older than 50; or are African American, it's advised that you consume less than 1,500 milligrams—just a hair over $\frac{1}{2}$ teaspoon of salt.

The Power of Potassium

The mineral potassium is an electrolyte that your body—especially your heart—needs to function properly. If you're low on potassium, your salt balance gets out of whack and spikes too high. And too much salt leads to high blood pressure. According to the NIH's National Library of Medicine, consuming the recommended 4.7 grams or more of potassium does indeed lower blood pressure.

THE DE-SODIUM CODE

What do all those sodium claims on food packages mean? To help you navigate the sometimes less than straightforward language on labels, you may want to copy the following list and keep it with you when shopping until you can remember it . . . by heart.

- **Sodium free and salt free:** contains less than 5 milligrams per serving
- **Very low sodium:** 35 milligrams or less per serving
- **Low sodium:** 140 milligrams or less per serving
- **Low-sodium meal:** 140 milligrams or less per 3½-ounce (100-gram) serving
- **Reduced or less sodium:** at least 25 percent less sodium than regular version
- **Light in sodium:** 50 percent less sodium than regular version
- **Unsalted or no salt added:** no salt *added* during processing; not necessarily a sodium-free food

Here's a partial list of foods that are high in potassium:

Apricots (dried)	Oranges and orange juice
Avocados	Peanuts (dry roasted, no salt)
Bananas	
Beets (cooked)	Pears
Brussels sprouts (cooked)	Potatoes (baked, flesh and skin)
Cantaloupe	Prunes and prune juice
Dates (dried)	
Figs (dried)	
Honeydew melon	Raisins
Kiwifruit	Spinach (cooked)
Lima beans	Tomato products
Milk (fat-free)	Winter squash
Nectarines	Yogurt (fat-free plain)

DIABETES MELLITUS

Technically called diabetes mellitus, diabetes is not a new disease. In fact, it was around the second century AD that Aretaeus of Cappadocia is believed to have first coined the term *diabetes*, derived from the Greek word *diabainein*, meaning "to siphon" or "to run through"—perhaps because the two most noticeable symptoms of the disease are excessive thirst (so you drink a lot) and excessive urination.

Now we know that if you have diabetes, you have too much glucose (sugar) in your blood. The two main types of diabetes are type 1 (insulin dependent) and type 2 (non–insulin dependent). Most people (95 percent) have type 2. While anybody can develop type 2 diabetes, you're at greater risk if you have high blood pressure and are overweight or obese (especially if you carry extra weight around your middle) and have a family history of diabetes. According to the NHLBI, diabetes is also particularly prevalent among African Americans, Asians, and Native Americans.

So what does having diabetes have to do with heart disease? Excess glucose in your blood damages your blood vessels, including the coronary arteries of the heart. In fact, almost 75 percent of people with diabetes develop heart and blood vessel diseases, according to the NIH. And women with diabetes are nearly four times more likely to die of coronary heart disease than women who don't have diabetes.

The Diabetes–Food Connection

If you have diabetes, you know better than anyone the enormous impact different foods have on blood glucose levels. You also know that the food choices you make (if you've been reading this chapter in order) have a profound impact on your blood pressure and on the level of lipids (fats) in your blood. Plus, the brain's only food is glucose—so maintaining healthy blood sugar levels isn't only key to your heart's health; it's also key to your brain's health.

Fiber

Studies have shown that foods high in fiber can lower LDL cholesterol. Fiber can also help control diabetes by enhancing glycemic control and improving insulin resistance—all of which also lower your risk of heart disease. Fiber-rich foods should be high on anyone's heart healthy grocery list.

Antioxidants

One of the things that can increase your risk of developing type 2 diabetes—or worsen an existing case—

is oxidative stress, which is also believed to be a culprit in hypertension, atherosclerosis, and cancer.

What's oxidative stress? It's easy to spot in our environment—silver tarnishing, iron rusting, and sliced apples turning brown are all examples of oxidation. In our bodies, it's the accumulation of destructive molecules called free radicals. Oxidative stress damages arteries, as well as tissues, cells, and organs. Eating more antioxidant-rich foods (generally easy to spot as they're plentiful in colorful fruits and vegetables) has been scientifically shown to reduce oxidative stress.

OVERWEIGHT AND OBESITY

There's no magic bullet to weight loss. It takes time and commitment. It's not easy, but it's not impossible,

MEAL MAKEOVER TIPS

To make healthier meals, consider the following advice from the National Heart Lung Blood Institute. Begin by choosing foods that are low in saturated fat, sodium, and calories.

- Try fat-free or 1 percent milk.
- Buy only reduced-fat or fat-free cheese.
- Eat fruits and vegetables without butter or sauce.
- Serve brown rice, beans, and whole grains.
- Choose lean cuts of meat, fish, and skinless turkey and chicken.
- Buy low- or reduced-sodium or no-salt–added versions of foods whenever possible.

Revamp recipes with these substitutions.

- Use two egg whites for each whole egg, or use cholesterol-free egg substitutes (¼ cup equals 1 egg).
- Use olive oil instead of butter.
- Use light mayonnaise instead of the full-fat version.
- Use fat-free yogurt or sour cream instead of the regular version.
- Use reduced-fat cheese instead of regular varieties.
- Use 1 percent or fat-free milk instead of whole.
- Use fresh poultry, fish, and lean meat rather than canned or processed types.

Rethink preparation and serving habits.

- Make meat loaf and meatballs with lean ground turkey.
- Make tacos with skinless chicken breast.
- Cool soups and gravies and skim off the fat before reheating.
- Top a baked potato with salsa instead of butter.
- Make spicy baked fish seasoned with green pepper, onion, garlic, oregano, lemon, or cilantro.
- Bake, broil, or grill foods instead of frying.
- Eat fruit instead of pie or cake for dessert.

---

either. If you're reading this book, you are already on the road to making healthier food choices and preparing them in a healthier fashion; but the hard part is realizing that the portions you may be used to are probably way out of proportion. It's not your fault. Besides jumbo portions and all-you-can-eat buffets, we have plates, cups, and bowls that have enlarged dramatically over the years. For example, the standard size of a restaurant dinner plate just 30 years ago was 9 inches across. Now it's 12 inches—yes, a full foot. No wonder we're in the midst of a weight crisis.

Being overweight or obese not only increases your risk for heart disease, it can increase your chance of getting high blood pressure, type 2 diabetes, and abnormally high levels of blood fats (including cholesterol), each of which may significantly raise your risk of heart disease even higher.

As for family concerns, studies clearly show that overweight kids are more likely to become overweight or obese adults, who are then at a substantially increased risk of all of the aforementioned diseases and conditions.

During your regular checkups, talk frankly with the doctor about all of your health concerns—including weight—and discuss the steps that need to be taken.

Food for Thought

Heart disease is a problem you can do something about. And that's a blessing. How amazing is it to know that you can gain control. You *can* get the upper hand. By eating heart healthy foods and getting regular exercise, you can slow the progression of heart disease and even reverse many of its effects. And if you don't already have heart disease, you might prevent it.

Have you wondered why there aren't walkathons or telethons to fund scientific research to figure out what causes heart disease? That's because we *know* the risk factors that lead to heart disease. We have effective medicines and surgical interventions that can add years to our lives. And we can eat the foods that will make our hearts and cardiovascular systems healthier.

It's all about choice. So when it comes to heart healthy eating, we suggest you make your choice . . . simply delicious.

The *40*

Heart Healthy

Foods

NUTRIENT SPOTLIGHTS

A number of nutrients are particularly good for your heart and thus are present in many of the 40 Heart Healthy Foods recommended later in this chapter. Let's begin with a quick rundown of these heart health powerhouses, including omega-3 fatty acids, fiber, antioxidants (including carotenoids, flavonoids, and vitamin C), B vitamins, and potassium, and why they're important to your daily diet.

However, just like it's wise to talk to your doctor before starting a new fitness regimen, the same is true about starting a new diet. This is particularly true if you are on any medications such as blood thinners, channel blockers, or diuretics because some foods, despite their heart healthy capabilities, may impact the effectiveness. So together with your doctor, review all of the medications you're taking, to be sure you fully understand what foods and nutrients may need to be limited, avoided, or even increased.

SPOTLIGHT: OMEGA-3S

Technically known as omega-3 essential fatty acids, omega-3s are polyunsaturated fatty acids. They're called essential because we can't manufacture them in our bodies, which means we have to eat them. Polyunsaturated fats are easy to identify because they're liquid at room temperature.

Omega-3s can help prevent, reverse, or lower your risk for heart disease. They lower your "bad" LDL cholesterol levels (and other bad fats, such as triglycerides), increase your "good" HDL cholesterol levels, lower your blood pressure, and reduce plaque from building up in arteries. It's really quite amazing,

when you think about it: By simply enjoying salmon once a week; adding some nutty, crunchy flaxseed to yogurt or cereal; or switching to flaxseed oil when making salad dressing, you can proactively reduce your risk for heart disease.

Science backs this up: In a study published in 2006, researchers found that consuming as little as 25 to 57 grams (1 to 2 ounces) of omega-3s a week decreased the risk of cardiovascular disease, as well as heart attacks and sudden cardiac death.

The AHA on Omega-3s

For healthy adults without a history of heart disease, the American Heart Association (AHA) recommends eating fatty fish such as salmon and whitefish at least twice a week. A recent study found that young, healthy adults who ate 4½ ounces of salmon a day for 4 weeks enjoyed a 4 percent drop in blood pressure, a 15 percent drop in triglycerides, a 7 percent drop in LDL levels, and a 5 percent increase in HDL levels. Overall, they reduced their risk of developing heart disease by 25 percent.

Numerous other studies confirm the heart healthy and even heart *mending* properties of fish oil. See Salmon (page 51) for more information.

> **OMEGA-3 SUPERSTARS:** flaxseed, salmon, walnuts
>
> **THE RUNNERS-UP:** bell peppers, quinoa, sea veggies, soy products, spinach, winter squash

SPOTLIGHT: FIBER

Frankly speaking, when it comes to heart health, the importance of getting enough fiber in your diet cannot be overstated. Fiber not only soaks up artery-clogging LDL cholesterol, it also inhibits blood sugar spikes and facilitates moving things gently and effectively through your system.

Fiber exists in two forms—soluble and insoluble—and for optimal health, you need both. Whole grains provide both types, though they all tend to have a lot more of one than the other. For example, oats have more soluble fiber than all other grains. Additional grains with a high proportion of soluble fiber include barley, millet, rice, and rye. Wheat grains and corn are high in insoluble fiber.

Fruits and vegetables are also good sources of soluble fiber, and insoluble fiber is found in dark leafy greens, fruit skins, and root vegetable skins.

Fiber Makes a Huge Difference

Now, some compelling study results: In a 19-year study of nearly 10,000 men and women, researchers

> **FIBER SUPERSTARS:** beans, berries, bran, flax, lentils, oats, quinoa, soy, whole grains
>
> **THE RUNNERS-UP:** apples, asparagus, bananas, bell peppers, carrots, cruciferous vegetables, dark leafy greens, grapes and cherries, kiwifruit, lemons and limes, onions, oranges, sea vegetables, shiitake mushrooms, spinach, sweet potatoes, tomatoes, tropical fruits

found that those who ate more than 4 grams of fiber a day had a 15 percent lower risk of coronary heart disease (CHD) and 24 percent lower mortality from CHD, compared with men and women who consumed less than 1.3 grams of fiber a day.

And a 6-year study of 39,876 female health professionals with no known cardiovascular disease revealed that women who had a high intake of dietary fiber were at lower risk for both developing heart disease and having a heart attack. Interestingly, in this study, consuming a "high-fiber" diet was defined as eating an average of 26.3 grams a day—slightly more than the fiber guidelines recommended by National Academy of Science's Institute of Medicine (see "How Much of a Good Thing?").

It gets better: Clinical studies have shown that you can reduce cholesterol levels an incredible 0.5 to 2 percent for every gram of soluble fiber eaten per day. For example, by just eating one bowl of oatmeal, you'll get 4 grams of fiber. Add 1 cup of raspberries (with an impressive 8.4 grams) and not only will you have hit nearly half of your total fiber needs for the

---

HOW MUCH OF A GOOD THING?

The National Academy of Sciences' Institute of Medicine, which provides the national dietary guidelines, recommends the following for total daily fiber intake.

- Women 50 years old and younger: 25 grams
- Women 51 and older: 21 grams
- Men 50 and younger: 38 grams
- Men 51 and older: 30 grams

day, you could potentially lower your cholesterol up to 24 percent.

SPOTLIGHT: ANTIOXIDANTS

Antioxidants are powerhouse nutrients that neutralize much of the artery-damaging effects of free radicals, thereby lowering cholesterol and blood pressure in one fell swoop.

To really appreciate antioxidants, it's important to understand that cholesterol isn't inherently bad. Your body naturally produces it (and, of course, you eat foods that contain cholesterol). What makes cholesterol turn bad (literally) is when the free radicals in your blood grab on to it and oxidize it, much like oxygen causes iron to rust. The problem with cholesterol "rusting" is that it is rendered very sticky and tends to attach to artery walls. Antioxidants, on the other hand, neutralize free radicals, rendering them harmless and unable to do oxidative damage in the first place. That's why antioxidants are such a big deal and why you want to be sure to include a lot of them in your diet every day.

Important antioxidants include the carotenoids (such as beta-carotene, lutein, and lycopene), flavonoids (quercetin, resveratrol, and rutin), and vitamin C, which are each discussed below. Allicin, found in garlic, is another important antioxidant; see Garlic (page 24) for more information.

Carotenoids and Heart Disease

The antioxidant family that provides plants their bright red, orange, and yellow colors also provides amazing heart-protective benefits. Beta-carotene is probably the best-known carotenoid; it's found in carrots, dark leafy greens, sweet potatoes, and winter

---

A SUPPLEMENTAL WORD OF CAUTION

When you eat carotenoid-rich foods—specifically, beta-carotene, which is found in foods like squash, carrots, and bananas—your body does this amazing thing: It transforms those carotenoids into vitamin A on an as-needed basis. And that's key.

But (and this is a big "but") taking man-made supplements impedes your body's ability to naturally regulate vitamin A—which means it can build up in your body and reach toxic levels. Be sure to check with your doctor before taking any supplements.

---

squash. Alpha-carotene, lycopene, and lutein are also important to heart health. You may already be familiar with heart superstar lycopene, the nutrient that provides the bright red color of tomatoes and other red fruits; see Tomatoes (page 63) for more information.

A large study of 73,286 nurses examined the relationship between dietary carotenoids and the risk of CHD in women. Over the course of 12 years, there were 998 incidents of CHD (including 718 nonfatal heart attacks) and 280 deaths. The women who had the highest intake of alpha-carotene had a 20 percent lower risk of CHD, and those with the highest intake of beta-carotene had a 26 percent lower risk.

CAROTENOID SUPERSTARS: carrots, dark leafy greens, sweet potatoes, tomatoes, winter squash

THE RUNNERS-UP: cherries, tropical fruits

Another well-reported study examining heart attack risk and carotenoids confirms that vegetables are a powerful heart health ally. In an unusual design, researchers looked at blood samples of 25,802 heart patients 7 to 14 years before their first heart attack (they got the samples from a blood bank). The researchers tested each sample for blood levels of four carotenoids (beta-carotene, lutein, lycopene, and zeaxanthin). The men and women who had the highest levels of beta-carotene had a 55 percent lower risk of suffering a heart attack, compared with those with the least.

Flavonoids and Heart Disease

Flavonoids (often called bioflavonoids) are another group of plant chemicals with impressive antioxidant abilities, a few of which deserve special mention: Quercetin is a very potent, heart healthy flavonoid found in apples, onions, and red wine (see Onions, Scallions, and Shallots, page 41). Red wine also has another powerful flavonoid called resveratrol, which has been shown to reduce blood clots (see Red Wine, page 70). And hesperitin, the primary flavonoid in oranges, does something few other antioxidants can: It can actually *reactivate* the antioxidant powers of vitamin C. See Oranges (page 42) for more information.

A comprehensive 14-year study in Finland—with an impressive 26-year follow-up period—investigated a possible association between flavonoid intake and CHD. Researchers followed over 5,000 men and women between the ages of 30 and 69 who, at the start, showed no signs of heart disease. It turned out that the women who ate the fewest flavonoid-rich foods were significantly more likely to develop artery-

FLAVONOID SUPERSTARS: apples, blueberries and other berries, onions, oranges, red wine, tea

THE RUNNERS-UP: asparagus, cherries and grapes, cruciferous vegetables, dark chocolate, kiwifruit

clogging plaque (atherosclerosis) and die from CHD. The same link was seen in men, but the connection was not quite as strong. Thus, this study concluded that people with very low dietary intakes of flavonoids are at increased risk for heart disease, while people with high intakes experience a protective effect.

It seems the news about flavonoids is especially good for those who already have heart disease: Another study of almost 35,000 male health professionals also investigated the relationship between flavonoid intake and CHD over a 6-year period. The researchers concluded that eating flavonoid-rich foods may indeed protect men with preexisting heart disease.

Vitamin C and Heart Disease

Okay, we all know that vitamin C is good for preventing colds, but it's important to know that it's good for your heart as well! This powerful antioxidant can prevent, reduce, and reverse the damaging effects of atherosclerosis—which, among other benefits, helps to lower your blood pressure. Studies repeatedly demonstrate that eating foods high in vitamin C reduces the risk of all causes of death—including heart disease.

A large-scale 2007 study investigated the role of free radicals and antioxidants in health and disease. The study authors clearly explain that antioxidants neutralize much of the damage caused by highly destructive free radicals. In fact, this study highlights the fact that vitamin C is one of the two principal antioxidants thought to "protect the body against the destructive effects of free radicals." The authors further expound that free radical damage is one of the primary underlying mechanisms that lead to diabetes, heart disease, heart attacks, high blood pressure, and atherosclerosis (narrowing of the arterial walls caused by plaque buildup), which reduces bloodflow to the heart.

SPOTLIGHT: FOLATE (AND OTHER B VITAMINS)

Folate, a water-soluble form of vitamin B_9, helps lower, prevent, and reverse high blood pressure—but exactly

how it does this is still being studied. Researchers suspect that folate eases bloodflow, relaxes the blood vessels, and lowers homocysteine levels.

A large-scale study with a $12\frac{1}{2}$-year follow-up investigated whether foods rich in B vitamins, such as folate (B_9) and pyridoxine (B_6), and omega-3 essential fatty acids might lower the incidence of blood clots. The study participants included almost 15,000 black and white middle-aged adults (6,709 men and 8,253 women) from the Atherosclerosis Risk in Communities (ARIC) study. At the beginning of the study, 12 percent had diabetes, and 68 percent were overweight or obese.

The participants who consumed more than $2\frac{1}{2}$ servings of fruits and vegetables a day (with B_6, B_9, and omega-3s) were associated with a 27 to 53 percent lower risk of blood clots. Of note, those who ate more than $1\frac{1}{2}$ servings of red and processed meat a day had twice the risk of developing blood clots.

Another interesting study, this one with 171 patients under age 80 at three separate hospitals, investigated the possible association between dietary folate intake and nonfatal heart attacks. The men and women who had diets high in folate from natural plant sources—particularly oranges, peppers, dark leafy greens, green beans, and lettuce—had significantly less risk of suffering a heart attack. In fact, the study authors posit that dietary folate intake may be an independent protective factor for heart attacks.

SPOTLIGHT: POTASSIUM

Potassium should be a hypertension patient's best friend. This mineral helps your body get rid of the excess sodium that causes high blood pressure.

In fact, studies show that by reducing sodium levels over the long term, you can lower your risk of suffering a heart attack by 25 to 30 percent.

Between 1987 and 1990, two especially important studies focused on the effects of dietary sodium on high blood pressure. Participants had prehypertension and ranged in age from 30 to 45 years old. Some were assigned to sodium-reduced diets, and others were not. The studies showed that following a reduced-sodium diet can prevent hypertension because it lowers blood pressure.

A follow-up study with the same participants next examined the diet's long-term effects on heart health. The results were stunning: There was a 25 to 30 percent lower risk of cardiovascular events for people assigned the low-sodium diet. Clearly, choosing to increase your potassium intake to help rid your body of excess sodium is an excellent, heart healthy choice.

> **POTASSIUM SUPERSTARS:** bananas, broccoli, cantaloupe, chile peppers, kiwifruit, tomatoes, sweet potatoes
>
> **THE RUNNERS-UP:** asparagus, avocado, beans, bell peppers, berries, carrots, dark leafy greens, flaxseed, grapes and cherries, lentils, onions, oranges, soy, spinach, tropical fruits, winter squash, yogurt

APPLES

How fabulous is it to sink your teeth into a wonderfully sweet (or sweet-tart, if you prefer) apple? That perfect "snap" at your first bite . . . the refreshing juice that gently drips down your chin . . . Thank you, Johnny Appleseed.

These delicious members of the rose family, *Malus domestica*, provide not one, not two, but three heart healthy benefits. First of all, apples contain flavonoids that have powerful antioxidant properties. Second, apples are an excellent source of fiber. And third, they even have some potassium.

This tempting fruit (apologies to Adam, Eve, and Snow White) contains an average of 4 grams of fiber, 160 milligrams of potassium, virtually no fat (0.4 gram), and only about 80 calories. Thus, eating a medium apple (a little under 3 inches across) every day certainly merits its reputation for keeping the doctor away. And with over 7,500 known varieties, you're sure to find one—if not many—to your liking.

QUINTESSENTIAL QUERCETIN

Whether your apple of choice is red or green, either has more heart healthy quercetin than any other fruit. What is quercetin? It's one of many pigment-causing flavonoids that numerous scientific studies have shown to have impressive antioxidant and anti-inflammatory properties.

APPLE PICKING

There's a whole wide world of apple varieties out there. What's the best for baking a pie? Or making applesauce? Or if you just want to take a big bite out of a juicy crisp one?

Best for eating: Braeburn, Empire, Fuji, Granny Smith, Red Delicious, Red Rome, Royal Gala, Winesap

Best for pies and applesauce: Empire, Fuji, Golden Delicious, Granny Smith, Newtown Pippin

Best for baking whole: Braeburn, Cortland, Golden Delicious, McIntosh, Newtown Pippin, Red Rome

PEEL APPEAL

For optimal heart health benefits, eat your apple with the peel. Otherwise, you'll cheat yourself of nearly half the antioxidant and flavonoid benefits, as well as the insoluble fiber. That said, keep in mind that 80 percent of an apple's soluble fiber comes from the pectin (the fleshy white part). If the only way you can get your kids to eat apples is to peel them, then so be it. The pectin is responsible for the nice, gradual release of the apple's sugar into the blood—instead of a sudden spike. It also soaks up unwanted cholesterol in the blood.

APPLE RECIPES

- Apple and Jicama Slaw (page 108)
- Apple-Cranberry Crisp (page 248)
- Baked Oatmeal Pudding (page 86)
- Carrot and Sweet Potato Puree (page 140)
- Fat-Free Applesauce Oatmeal Cookies (page 237)
- Fruit with Creamy Chocolate Dip (page 234)
- Healthy Chef's Salad (page 126)
- Quick No-Bake Apple-Cherry Crisp (page 234)
- Sautéed Bitter Greens (page 134)
- Toasted Trail Mix (page 233)
- Warm Kale Salad (page 109)

HEART HEALTH BENEFITS

- Lowers total cholesterol
- Lowers "bad" LDL cholesterol
- Raises "good" HDL cholesterol
- Lowers blood pressure

ASPARAGUS

Once so revered by the Egyptians that spears were presented as offerings to the gods, asparagus is one of the earliest harbingers of spring. A visual delight, the delicately long, pencil-thin, apple-green stalks—with their lovely blush of purple kissing the tips of their scalelike leaves—are a joy to behold at the market. Indeed, these proud members of the lily family (*Asparagus officinalis*) have a stunningly long culinary heritage: There's even an asparagus recipe in a 4th- or 5th-century Roman cookbook called *Apicius*.

Asparagus is one of the premier sources of folate (folic acid) and potassium, both of which help reduce high blood pressure. It's also a very good source of fiber, which helps your body get rid of artery-clogging cholesterol. And on top of that, asparagus is tops in antioxidants, say researchers. In 2003, the department of public health at the University of Parma, Italy, investigated the antioxidant capacity of a large variety of plant foods. Of all of the vegetables tested, asparagus had the greatest antioxidant capacity. Pretty impressive. Plus, one spear weighs in at only about 4 calories (yes, you read that right: 4 calories each), is very low in sodium, and has essentially zero fat.

So mark your calendar: Asparagus season runs from February until early June. Be sure you and your family don't miss out on enjoying the heart healthy benefits of asparagus.

IT HAPPENS IN A DAY

Did you know that you can practically watch asparagus grow? The time between a spear's first emergence from the ground (under ideal growing conditions) to when it reaches a height of 10 inches can be as short as 24 hours!

ASPARAGUS RECIPES

- Apricot Asparagus and Carrots (page 133)
- Asparagus Frittata (page 79)
- Asparagus Salad with Goat Cheese (page 111)
- Beef and Asparagus Stir-Fry (page 224)
- Chicken and Vegetables in Cream Sauce (page 204)

HEART HEALTH BENEFITS

- Lowers total cholesterol
- Lowers "bad" LDL cholesterol
- Raises "good" HDL cholesterol
- Lowers blood pressure
- Lowers homocysteine levels

AVOCADOS

Decadent, buttery, and *luxurious* are all words that come to mind when thinking about indulging in the gorgeous, yellow-green, creamy-smooth flesh of an avocado. But you can also add another phrase: *heart healthy.*

Avocados are packed with monounsaturated fats, which can substantially improve cholesterol levels. They're also rich in potassium and folate, both of which lower blood pressure. And avocados are a good source of insoluble and soluble fiber, which soaks up artery-clogging cholesterol, helps with glycemic control, and helps keep you regular.

GOOD NEWS, GREAT NEWS

The avocado's enticing texture comes from its abundance of fat—a fact that gave avocados the undeserved reputation of being a bad-for-you food. Yes, the avocado is indeed full of fat; the particular type is oleic acid, the same type of fatty acid that gives olive oil its star status in the heart health world. Thus, it's no surprise that scientific studies suggest avocados can hold their own when it comes to providing heart health benefits.

For example, researchers asked men and women with moderate to high cholesterol levels to eat avocado every day for 1 week. In those 7 days, the study participants lowered their LDL cholesterol by 22 percent and raised their HDL levels by an amazing 11 percent. So, if you've been passing on the avocados, go ahead and indulge. They're good—make that *great*—for you.

ADDED BENEFITS

A study published in the *Journal of Nutrition* in 2005 found that avocados enhance the body's ability to absorb, use, and store a type of antioxidant called carotenoids.

For the study, fresh sliced avocado was added to two different carotenoid-rich test meals. One was a salad of romaine lettuce, shredded carrots, and baby spinach; the other was a store-bought "thick and chunky" salsa. The researchers found that whether adding a whole avocado (150 grams) or just half (75 grams), the carotenoid bioavailability was "significantly enhanced" in both the salad and the salsa.

Nevertheless, avocados are fattening, right? Well, a research study investigated just that. Both men and women were asked to replace about 30 fat grams per

---

OPTIMIZING YOUR AVOCADO EXPERIENCE

- Selecting: Choose firm, solid, heavy-for-their-size avocados that are free of soft spots, holes, or other outward damage.

- Storing: Keep avocados at room temperature for several days until they ripen (the leathery skin will darken, and the fruit will easily give to a gentle press of your thumb). Once ripe, store in the refrigerator.

- Preserving: To help protect their lovely color, sprinkle freshly cut slices with lime juice if not eating them immediately.

---

day from other dietary fats (such as margarine) with 30 fat grams from two avocados. Not only did the participants' heart healthy oleic acid levels improve significantly, but both the men and women had significant drops in percentage of body fat, body mass, and body mass index!

Rich, seductive, sumptuous, heart healthy . . . and diet-friendly. Now that's justice.

AVOCADO RECIPES

- Better-for-You Black Bean Chili (page 163)
- Soy Delicious Guacamole (page 265)
- Spiced Salmon Tacos (page 192)
- Turkey Cutlets with Avocado Salsa (page 214)

HEART HEALTH BENEFITS

- Lowers total cholesterol
- Raises "good" HDL cholesterol
- Lowers "bad" LDL cholesterol
- Lowers blood pressure
- Lowers homocysteine levels
- Enhances absorption of carotenoid antioxidants

BANANAS

The sublimely smooth and creamy texture of a perfectly ripe, sweet, and fragrant banana is an unrivaled, mouth-satisfying delight for children and adults alike.

A true standout for its heart healthy benefits, one whole medium banana has nearly 3 grams of artery-scrubbing fiber; 467 milligrams of hypertension-lowering, plaque-reducing, and blood clot–inhibiting potassium; 96 IU free radical–neutralizing carotenoids (vitamin A); and less than 1 gram each of sodium and fat—all perfectly "packaged" for your eating pleasure and with only about 100 calories.

THE POWER OF BANANAS

Bananas contain carotenoids, powerful antioxidants that can neutralize the artery-damaging effects of free radicals and lower your LDL cholesterol as well

RIPEN BANANAS LICKETY-SPLIT

If you need your bananas to ripen in a jiffy, place them in your common-variety brown paper bag—along with an apple or a tomato—and keep it out of direct sunlight. The apple or tomato gives off ethylene gas, which speeds the ripening process.

FOR ULTIMATE BANANA PLEASURE

Bananas, which are members of the *Musaceae* family, are actually giant herbs that share the same lineage as orchids, lilies, and palms. Interestingly, bananas are one of the only fruits that actually ripen better if cut from the plant while still green. If left to ripen on the banana plant, the fruit's texture becomes cottony instead of forming the lovely, rich, and smooth texture we know and love.

To make the most of this wonderful fruit, try these tips.

- Choose bananas that are beautifully yellow, with no signs of green and just a few brown speckles, for peeling and eating.
- Sauté or grill slightly green bananas to transform the already creamy fruit into an indescribably luxurious treat. Cooking caramelizes the natural sugars, adding to the seductive allure and optimizing taste and texture.
- Peel and freeze dark, speckled, overripe bananas to make luscious smoothies. When they're past their peel-and-eat prime, that's the absolute best time to make homemade banana bread and muffins!

---

as your blood pressure—all of which have been shown to have the ability to prevent, reduce, and even reverse heart disease.

But bananas are probably best known for being an excellent source of potassium, a mineral that can lower high blood pressure (hypertension), thus reducing the formation of blood clots, artery-clogging plaque, and aneurysms—all of which are precursors to heart disease. Potassium accomplishes all that by helping your body get rid of excess sodium that can raise blood pressure.

BANANA RECIPES

- Berry Smoothie (page 94)
- Frozen Berry Pops (page 240)
- Fruit with Creamy Chocolate Dip (page 234)
- Tropical Fruit Pops (page 240)
- Tropical Phyllo Cups (page 253)

HEART HEALTH BENEFITS

- Lowers blood pressure
- Lowers "bad" LDL cholesterol
- Raises "good" HDL cholesterol
- Reduces oxidative stress

BEANS

Once called a poor man's meat, beans are a heart healthy nutritional wonder. They're packed with fiber, potassium, folate, and alpha-linolenic acid. Beans are also low in both fat and sodium, contain zero cholesterol, and are rich in high-quality protein. What does that mean for your heart?

Beans can reduce your risk for developing heart disease. And if you already have heart disease, beans can help reverse it. And if you don't like some, remember there are hundreds of varieties to choose from. For example, garbanzo beans (chickpeas) have a lovely firm texture and a flavor that's somewhere between chestnuts and walnuts—which may be one of the reasons it's the most consumed bean in the world. Great Northern beans (of French cassoulet fame) have exceptionally thin skins and a mild, delicate flavor. And pinto beans—known for their gorgeous pink color with reddish-brown speckles—have more fiber content than any other bean.

A FEW BEANS = BIG BENEFITS

Eating ⅓ cup of cooked beans on a daily basis lowers heart attack risk by 38 percent. That's the impressive finding of a study of 2,118 men and women that investigated whether eating dried beans would protect against heart attack. Of note, the participants mostly ate black beans. However, according to the authors, the basic nutrient composition among dried beans is essentially the same.

Eating ⅓ cup of cooked beans at least 4 days a week cuts coronary heart disease (CHD) by 22 percent. So concluded the authors of a study of 9,632 men and women—with an impressive 19-year follow-up—on the effects of legumes (beans) on risk of heart disease. The authors stated that eating more legumes is "an important part of a dietary approach to the primary prevention of coronary heart disease in the general population."

GAS-FREE SOAKING METHOD

Beans contain a certain type of sugar (called an oligosaccharide) that the human body doesn't digest. However, you can avert the consequences (read: gas). The secret is to break down that sugar before you eat the beans—which is simple to do. According to the Centers for Disease Control and Prevention (CDC), you can break down 75 to 90 percent of the indigestible sugar by doing the following:

1. Place 1 pound of beans in a large stockpot and add 10 or more cups of water.
2. Boil for 2 to 3 minutes.
3. Take off the heat, cover the pot, and set aside overnight.
4. Pour off the water (which is now full of the unwanted sugar) and rinse the beans thoroughly. Cook and enjoy!

BEAN RECIPES

- Better-for-You Black Bean Chili (page 163)
- Black Bean Salad (page 120)
- Black Beans and Rice (page 155)
- Braised Lentils with Spinach (page 159)
- Broccoli Rabe and Chickpea Soup (page 101)
- Chicken Ragout (page 205)
- Curried Vegetables with Beans (page 162)
- Escarole and Bean Soup (page 100)
- Grandma's Baked Beans (page 164)
- Italian Three Bean Salad (page 122)
- Piled-High Nachos (page 281)
- Quick White Bean Stew (page 231)
- Quinoa Florentine (page 148)
- Slow-Cooked Chili Con Carne (page 279)
- Spicy Red Lentil Soup (page 99)
- Spinach and Cannellini Beans (page 160)
- Tex-Mex Beans and Rice (page 158)
- Vegetarian Gumbo (page 157)

HEART HEALTH BENEFITS

- Lowers total cholesterol
- Lowers "bad" LDL cholesterol
- Raises "good" HDL cholesterol
- Lowers blood pressure
- Lowers homocysteine levels
- Inhibits blood clot formation
- Inhibits ventricular fibrillation
- Improves glycemic control
- Improves insulin sensitivity

BERRIES

BLUEBERRIES • CRANBERRIES • BLACKBERRIES
RASPBERRIES • STRAWBERRIES

Ah, berries . . . Few foods can match the wholly satisfying experience of popping a peak-season berry and experiencing that divinely sweet or refreshingly tart burst of juice.

While pretty much all berries have heart healthy benefits, the latest research suggests that blueberries, cranberries, blackberries, raspberries, and strawberries are the standouts. The deeper the color, the better for protecting against cardiovascular disease. Why is that the case?

All of the aforementioned berries owe their superb antioxidant capabilities—which we know are cardio-protective—to a healthy dose of anthocyanin, the pigment-causing chemical behind their gorgeous blue and red colors. Further, blueberries, raspberries, and cranberries are all rich in a phytochemical called

Increasing your daily fiber intake is exceptionally heart smart, and berries are a fabulous source. How much fiber is in your favorite berry?

Fruit	Fiber (per cup)	Season
Raspberries	8.4 grams	May to November
Blackberries	7.6 grams	May to August
Cranberries	5 grams	September to November
Blueberries	3.9 grams	May to October
Strawberries	3.8 grams	May to June

For optimal enjoyment and succulent heart healthy benefits, remember to seek out the best of the best berries while they're in season.

resveratrol, which studies have shown can help prevent (yes, prevent) heart disease. And blackberries, raspberries, and strawberries are also rich in the phytochemical ellagitannin, which studies have shown can thwart the development of heart disease.

YOU SEE, IT'S NOT ONLY C

Berries used to be relatively dismissed for their health benefits because most don't pack the sizable wallop of vitamin C that citrus fruits offer—although strawberries do offer some.

The scientific community now has an incredible amount of evidence for the multitude of benefits that berries offer your heart. For example, a 2005 study found that simply eating 250 grams (about 1 cup) of blueberries a day can prevent the onset of heart disease. The authors suggest that these impressive results are likely due to blueberries' antioxidant capacity to reduce the amount of fats clogging up your arteries. Similarly, a 2002 study found that consuming antioxidant-rich cranberries and cranberry

juice can reverse atherosclerosis and that cranberries inhibit blood clots and LDL cholesterol.

Another long-term study (with a 16-year follow-up) investigated the possible association between diet and dying from cardiovascular disease. The participants included over 34,000 postmenopausal women from the Iowa Women's Health Study. Published in 2007, the study found that the women who enjoyed foods high in anthocyanins—the red/blue pigment antioxidant found in the healthiest berries—were far less likely to die from heart disease. That just about says it all, doesn't it?

A BERRY SMART PREP TIP

It's best to wash berries just prior to eating them. Washing ahead of time encourages spoiling, and berries readily soak up water, which dilutes their lovely flavor and makes them unpleasantly mushy—so wait to wash.

- Apple-Cranberry Crisp (page 248)
- Baked Oatmeal Pudding (page 86)
- Beef Tenderloin with Cranberry Port Sauce (page 221)
- Berry Smoothie (page 94)
- Chocolate Angel Food Cake (page 252)
- Chocolate Berry Crepes (page 256)
- Cran-Raspberry Ice (page 256)
- Fat-Free Applesauce Oatmeal Cookies (page 237)
- French Toast with Orange Cream (page 82)
- Frozen Berry Pops (page 240)
- Frozen Yogurt with Fruit Wine Sauce (page 274)
- Fruit and Bran Muffins (page 87)
- Fruit 'n' Nut Coffee Cake (page 249)
- Fruited Granola (page 83)
- Fruited Rice Pilaf (page 150)
- Gingered Fruit Salad (page 93)
- Greens with Strawberries and Kiwifruit (page 110)
- Harvest Cookies (page 236)
- Lemon Blueberry Muffins (page 89)
- Peach-Blueberry Shortcakes (page 244)
- Peach Melba Smoothie (page 94)
- Raspberry Buckle (page 248)
- Summer Fruit Compote (page 257)

HEART HEALTH BENEFITS

- Lowers total cholesterol
- Lowers "bad" LDL cholesterol
- Raises "good" HDL cholesterol
- Lowers blood pressure

BRAN

Abundant in fiber and surprisingly nutritious, bran is the husk (the hard outer layer) of cereal grains such as wheat, barley, millet, oats, rye, and corn. Foods with bran also include buckwheat, quinoa, and rice, but, technically speaking, those are not grains.

Even so, you might not often think to yourself, "Oh boy, I'd love to sink my teeth into some bran!" But perhaps after reading the following, you'll have a change of heart.

BOUNTIFUL BRAN STUDIES

A comprehensive research study investigated what role whole grains, bran, and germ might have upon reducing major risk factors associated with heart disease. Of the 938 participants, half were male health professionals ages 40 to 75, and half were female nurses ages 25 to 42.

The study showed that the men and women whose diets were high in whole grains (including the bran

ANATOMY OF WHOLE GRAINS

Whole grains, which are actually plant seeds, can be divided into three parts: bran, endosperm, and germ. The bran is the husk (outer shell), which contains most of the fiber and protects the seed from damage. It's also a rich source of B vitamins and trace minerals. The endosperm, sometimes referred to as the kernel, is essentially everything "inside" the grain and provides protein and carbohydrates. The germ is the baby plant (called an embryo) contained inside the seed. It's rich in antioxidants, vitamin E, and B vitamins such as folate. The germ also provides nourishment for the seed itself.

and germ) experienced improved glycemic control, lipid profiles, and homocysteine levels—which in turn reduced their risks of heart disease.

Another study of 42,850 male health professionals to evaluate the impact that whole grains had on heart disease produced even more impressive findings. Of note, the majority of the participants ate grains from cold breakfast cereals, brown rice, dark bread, and cooked oatmeal.

The study found that over 14 years the men who ate more than three servings of whole grain foods a day reduced their risk of heart disease by 20 to 30 percent! The authors concluded that the bran might play the biggest role in reducing heart disease risk.

BRAN (WHOLE GRAIN) RECIPES

- Baked Oatmeal Pudding (page 86)
- Barley Edamame Salad (page 119)
- Beef and Asparagus Stir-Fry (page 244)
- Beef and Vegetable Stroganoff (page 233)
- Black Beans and Rice (page 155)
- Broccoli-Barley Pilaf (page 154)
- Brown Rice with Greens and Feta (page 151)
- Curry Chicken and Rice Salad (page 127)
- Edamame Pilaf (page 150)
- Fat-Free Applesauce Oatmeal Cookies (page 237)
- Fruit and Bran Muffins (page 87)
- Fruited Granola (page 83)
- Green Tea–Oatmeal Pancakes (page 80)
- Lemon Blueberry Muffins (page 89)
- Peanut Bars (page 233)
- Quick and Easy Rice Pudding (page 243)
- Quinoa Florentine (page 148)
- Soba Noodle Salad (page 117)
- Sweet-and-Sour Shrimp Soup (page 102)
- Toasted Trail Mix (page 233)
- Vegetable Quinoa (page 146)

HEART HEALTH BENEFITS

- Lowers total cholesterol
- Lowers "bad" LDL cholesterol
- Lowers blood pressure
- Improves glycemic control

CARROTS

Sweet and crunchy when raw, creamy and even sweeter when cooked, carrots are a year-round delight . . . and they make perfectly charming noses for snowmen, too!

Owing its lovely orange color to the powerful antioxidant beta-carotene, this domesticated form of the wildflower Queen Anne's lace has been written about since the first century. By the 1500s, carrots were a kitchen staple. So how many heart healthy benefits can you reap from your classic, garden-variety, grocery-store carrot? You guessed it: a lot!

For starters, the profound antioxidant ability of carrots has been shown to prevent, reduce, and even reverse hypertension and hardening of the arteries. Carrots are an excellent source of the salt-reducing mineral potassium, which helps prevent, lower, and reverse high blood pressure. They're also a fine source of fiber, which lowers LDL cholesterol.

WHAT'S UP, DOC?

The scientific evidence about the benefits of eating carrots is beyond impressive and profound. For example, a study involving women ages 22 to 69 investigated what impact, if any, certain foods—including carrots—might independently have on the risk of suffering a heart attack.

The risk was indeed directly associated with cer-

RAW VERSUS COOKED: IS THERE A DIFFERENCE?

Whether raw or cooked, carrots' overall nutritional benefits are nearly identical—except when it comes to vitamin A. You need only eat ½ cup of raw carrots to reap 150 percent of the vitamin A you need in a day. Hard to beat . . . unless you cook them. Yes, if you cooked that same ½ cup of carrots, you'd reap 270 percent of your daily requirement! Heat makes the vitamin A more bioavailable (which means your body can more easily absorb it). But truly, whether you prefer raw carrots or cooked carrots, you can't go wrong.

tain foods. The biggest offenders were ham and salami. The two foods that had the greatest protective effect were carrots and fish.

Another study investigated the effects of different antioxidants on reducing heart attack risk and revealed that the people who ate beta-carotene–rich foods had the most protection against suffering a first heart attack. The authors concluded that people who eat beta-carotene–rich foods—specifically, carrots and green-leaf vegetables—can reduce their risk of a heart attack.

CARROT RECIPES

- Apricot Asparagus and Carrots (page 133)
- Braised Lentils with Spinach (page 159)
- Broccoli Rabe and Chickpea Soup (page 101)
- Carrot and Sweet Potato Puree (page 140)
- Creamy Carrot Soup (page 96)
- Creamy "Egg" Salad (page 114)
- Curried Vegetables with Beans (page 162)
- Edamame Pilaf (page 150)
- Gingered Carrot Loaf (page 92)
- Happy Heart Pasta Primavera (page 175)
- Herbed Bread Dressing (page 276)
- Orzo Pilaf (page 178)
- Soba Noodle Salad (page 117)
- Souped-Up Sloppy Joes (page 225)
- Spicy Red Lentil Soup (page 99)
- Sweet-and-Sour Shrimp Soup (page 102)
- Vegetable Quinoa (page 146)
- Zesty Clam Chowder (page 103)

HEART HEALTH BENEFITS

- Lowers total cholesterol
- Lowers "bad" LDL cholesterol
- Raises "good" HDL cholesterol
- Lowers blood pressure

CHOCOLATE, DARK

Sinfully smooth, decadently creamy, and visually lustrous, dark chocolate is loved by almost everyone. It's perfectly befitting that the scientific name for cocoa is *Theobroma cacao,* which is Latin for "food of the gods." And isn't it wonderful news that this heavenly food is good for your heart? Research has shown that dark chocolate can be beneficial to your cardiac health, thanks to antioxidants called flavonoids. (Note that the heart health benefits apply to dark chocolate with a cocoa content of 60 percent or more.)

Evidence-based studies have demonstrated that the flavonoids found in dark chocolate can increase HDL cholesterol; lower LDL, triglycerides, and blood pressure; and reduce the damaging effects of oxidative stress by scavenging free radicals—thereby reducing your risk for atherosclerosis and heart disease.

Additionally, dark chocolate has been shown to

CHOCOLATE FRUIT?

Cocoa "beans" are actually the seeds of the cacao tree. Weighing in at about 1 pound when ripe, your average cacao pod contains anywhere between 20 and 60 seeds. So technically speaking, chocolate is a fruit . . . but you may not want to share that bit of information with your kids.

have antiplatelet capabilities similar to aspirin. Dark chocolate also exhibits anti-inflammatory properties and improves insulin sensitivity, which is particularly helpful for preventing or managing type 2 diabetes.

A HEART SMART DRINK

A 15-year study investigated what effect, if any, regularly drinking flavonoid-rich cocoa might have on heart disease. The participants were 470 Dutch men between ages 65 and 84, and those who regularly enjoyed drinking cocoa had significantly lower blood pressure—which you know is a critically important factor for maintaining heart health.

But there's more to this story: Over the course of the study, 314 of the men died—152 of them as the result of heart disease. However, the cocoa drinkers were half as likely to have died from heart disease. That number was found to be even lower when the researchers factored in such variables as smoking, drinking, and physical activity levels, which further reinforces the idea that flavonoid-rich chocolate is a heart smart choice.

BLACK-AND-WHITE FINDINGS

A particularly interesting study examined the possible cardio-protective effects of eating flavanol-rich dark chocolate, compared with flavanol-empty white chocolate. Study participants who ate the white chocolate had no measurable results at all. Those who ate the dark chocolate, on the other hand, enjoyed decreased blood pressure and LDL levels, relaxed blood vessels, and improved insulin sensitivity—all of which are key elements for preventing, reducing, or reversing atherosclerosis and coronary heart disease.

Another study in 2005 led to similar conclusions. In brief, 15 healthy men and women, ranging in age from 26 to 41, participated. For the first 7 days, they abstained from consuming any form of chocolate, as well as other flavonoid-rich foods such as wine. Then, for the next 15 days, half of the participants ate one dark chocolate bar per day, and the other half ate a white chocolate bar every day. Upon completion, blood pressure and blood glucose levels were taken, followed by another 7-day chocolate-free period. The participants then switched chocolates: Those who had eaten dark now ate white and vice versa, then the same measurements were taken.

You already guessed the results: Those who ate the dark chocolate experienced a significant increase in insulin sensitivity and a decrease in blood pressure. The white chocolate—which is devoid of flavonoids—had no such heart healthy effects.

THAT COOL SENSATION

You know that "cool" sensation you get when a piece of fine chocolate begins to melt on your tongue? That happens because chocolate starts to melt at about 90°F, just slightly lower than the temperature in your mouth.

CHOCOLATE RECIPES

- Chocolate Almond Biscotti (page 239)
- Chocolate Almond Pudding (page 243)
- Chocolate Almond Scones (page 84)
- Chocolate Angel Food Cake (page 252)
- Chocolate Berry Crepes (page 256)
- Chocolate Snack Cake (page 282)
- Flavorful Fruit Tart (page 254)
- Flourless Chocolate Cake (page 251)
- Fruit with Creamy Chocolate Dip (page 234)
- Mocha Coffee (page 236)

HEART HEALTH BENEFITS

- Lowers "bad" LDL cholesterol
- Lowers triglycerides
- Raises "good" HDL cholesterol
- Lowers blood pressure
- Inhibits blood clot formation
- Reduces inflammation
- Reduces plaque buildup
- Improves insulin sensitivity

CRUCIFEROUS VEGETABLES

Called cruciferous because their white, four-petaled flowers resemble a cross, these vegetables are members of the *Brassicaceae* family and include some of the heart-healthiest vegetables on the planet. Cruciferous standouts include broccoli, Brussels sprouts, cabbage, and cauliflower.

Cruciferous vegetables are incredibly rich in the pigment flavonoids quercetin, beta-carotene, and

QUICKIE CRUCIFEROUS COOKING

Running short on ideas for preparing your favorite cruciferous veggies? Try these.

- Steam broccoli or cauliflower florets, then quickly sauté minced garlic in a little olive oil. Add the steamed veggies, toss once or twice, and serve.
- Season steamed broccoli with a squirt or two of fresh lemon juice and a sprinkle of sesame seeds.
- Roasted cauliflower is delicious! Cut into small to medium pieces and toss with olive oil and salt. Spread on a jelly-roll pan and roast at 400°F, turning the pieces occasionally, for about 30 minutes, or until browned.
- Sneak cauliflower into mashed potatoes (they'll never know!). Cook florets along with cut-up potatoes in boiling water until tender. Then continue with your mashed potato recipe as usual.

lutein. All three (called bioflavonoids by the media) are powerful antioxidants that have been scientifically shown to prevent, reduce, and even reverse high blood pressure and hardening of the arteries. Cruciferous vegetables are also powerful sources of vitamins A and C. For example, just 1 cup of steamed broccoli supplies over 205 percent of your daily requirement of vitamin C and over 150 percent of your vitamin A.

BRAVO FOR BROCCOLI

A large-scale study of 34,492 postmenopausal women with a 10-year follow-up investigated the association of flavonoid intake from fruits and vegetables and the risk of heart disease. The researchers discovered that women who ate the most flavonoids (between 18.7 and 22.8 milligrams a day) had a 38 percent reduc-

tion in coronary heart disease mortality! Broccoli had the strongest association, and the participants ate just under two servings a week (1.7).

CRUCIFEROUS VEGETABLE RECIPES

- Broccoli and Cheese Strata (page 77)
- Broccoli-Barley Pilaf (page 154)
- Broccoli Rabe and Chickpea Soup (page 101)
- Brussels Sprouts Amandine (page 136)
- Coleslaw with Lemon Dressing (page 106)
- Curried Vegetables with Beans (page 162)
- Curry-Roasted Cauliflower (page 141)
- Happy Heart Pasta Primavera (page 175)
- Orange-Glazed Broccoli (page 135)
- Quick Chicken Noodle Soup (page 104)
- Quick Vegetable Mac 'n' Cheese (page 172)

HEART HEALTH BENEFITS

- Lowers total cholesterol
- Lowers "bad" LDL cholesterol
- Raises "good" HDL cholesterol
- Lowers blood pressure
- Lowers homocysteine levels
- Reduces plaque buildup
- Improves glycemic control

FLAXSEED AND FLAXSEED OIL

Flax, also known as linseed, is a lovely plant with long, gray-green stems and baby blue flowers. And it's a heart healthy beauty: Its tiny seeds are a terrific source of omega-3 essential fatty acids (including alpha-linolenic acid, which studies have shown can prevent ventricular fibrillations, inhibit blood clots from forming, and reduce your chance of dying from a heart attack). Flaxseed also has a stunning amount of fiber, which we know soaks up artery-clogging LDL cholesterol. And there's plenty of potassium to help reduce blood pressure.

Historically, most of the ALA (alpha-linolenic acid) studies associated with lowering heart attack risk focused on men. However, a 10-year follow-up study of 76,283 female nurses (called the Nurses' Health Study) found that women who consumed an ALA-rich diet reduced their relative risk of fatal ischemic heart disease by 45 percent. Approximately 70 percent of their ALA intake came from plant sources, especially salad dressings. Another excellent source is fish.

A WORD ABOUT THE SEEDS

You need to first crush flaxseed's outer hull so that your body can process the omega-3s. A mortar and pestle or a coffee grinder works really well.

FLAXSEED IN YOUR DIET

Here's how you can incorporate ground flaxseed and flaxseed oil into your diet.

- Sprinkle ground flaxseed on top of muffins and cookies before baking.
- Sprinkle it on cereal, yogurt, cottage cheese, fresh fruit, and salads.
- Add to smoothies and hot cereal.
- Add to hamburger patties, meat loaf, meatballs, casseroles, stews, and soups.
- Mix into peanut butter, cheese spreads, and dips.
- Use half flaxseed oil and half olive oil when making vinaigrette.
- Use flaxseed oil as you would melted butter: Drizzle it on corn on the cob and other vegetables, or brush it on whole grain toast for breakfast.

Remember that whole flaxseed should be ground to release its omega-3s. And it's best to add ground flaxseed and flaxseed oil to foods *after* they're cooked because heat destroys many of the health benefits.

FLAXSEED RECIPES

- Asian Slaw with Chicken (page 123)

- Cherry Corn Muffins (page 90)

- Fruited Granola (page 83)

- Greens with Strawberries and Kiwifruit (page 110)

- Peanut Bars (page 233)

- Quick Arugula and Shrimp Salad (page 126)

- Spicy Oven-Fried Chicken (page 206)

- Tortellini Salad (page 118)

- Zesty Succotash Salad (page 107)

HEART HEALTH BENEFITS

- Lowers total cholesterol

- Lowers "bad" LDL cholesterol

- Raises "good" HDL cholesterol

- Lowers blood pressure

- Inhibits blood clot formation

- Inhibits ventricular fibrillation

- Improves glycemic control

GARLIC

Considered so sacred by the ancient Egyptians, it was placed in the tombs of Pharaohs. Believed to be so powerful by the Greeks and Romans, they ritually consumed it prior to going to war. So loved by the Israelites, they pined for it when wandering the desert.

Of what are we speaking? Garlic, of course.

Hippocrates and Pliny the Elder strongly encouraged the consumption of garlic because of its profound health virtues.

Indeed, the "stinking rose" (and a member of the lily family) has a long history of offering a veritable cornucopia of heart healthy benefits—a reputation that it absolutely deserves.

Thanks to garlic's rich antioxidant content in the form of allicin, plus vitamins A and C, study after study has shown that regularly eating garlic can lower LDL and raise HDL cholesterol levels, as well as prevent, reduce, and even reverse the development of atherosclerosis. Garlic is also a terrific source of salt-lowering potassium, which in turn reduces blood pressure. And it's rich in folate, which lowers blood pressure and homocysteine levels, relaxes blood vessels, and improves bloodflow. Plus, garlic has been shown to reduce blood sugar levels, help prevent the formation of blood clots, and stave off heart disease—and reduce the risk of suffering a heart attack.

HEART HELPER EXTRAORDINAIRE

A study investigated how garlic might benefit 30 people with preexisting coronary heart disease. Each day for 3 months, participants consumed 1 gram of peeled and crushed raw garlic. The results showed a significant reduction in total cholesterol and triglycerides and a significant increase in HDL. The study also concluded that garlic successfully inhibits the formation of blood clots.

Another study investigating whether eating garlic might help reduce blood clots followed men ranging in age from 40 to 50 who ate one clove of garlic (approximately 3 grams) each day for 16 weeks. Tested 6 months after their last daily clove, the men, on average, reduced their cholesterol levels by 20 percent and reduced their serum thromboxane—a lipid in your blood that encourages clot formation—by a dramatic 80 percent!

Then there was a study investigating garlic's impact on moderately high cholesterol levels. Every day for 6 months, 56 men ages 32 to 68 consumed 7.2 grams of pure garlic extract. On average, they achieved a 6 to 7 percent reduction in total cholesterol, a 4.6 percent reduction in LDL cholesterol, and a 5.5 percent decrease in blood pressure.

GARLIC RECIPES

- Beef and Vegetable Stroganoff (page 223)
- Better-for-You Black Bean Chili (page 163)
- Braised Lentils with Spinach (page 159)
- Cilantro-Broiled Chicken Breasts (page 203)
- Creamy Garlic Dressing (page 259)
- Escarole and Bean Soup (page 100)
- Garlic Smashed Potatoes (page 144)
- Garlicky Hummus (page 266)
- Garlic-Roasted Sweet Potatoes with Arugula (page 143)
- Happy Heart Pasta Primavera (page 175)
- Linguine with Walnut Pesto (page 180)
- Mediterranean Pasta with Shrimp (page 184)
- Quick White Bean Stew (page 231)
- Quinoa Florentine (page 148)
- Roast Chicken and Vegetables (page 209)
- Sautéed Bitter Greens (page 134)
- Scallops Fra Diavolo (page 190)
- Sesame-Seared Tofu (page 165)
- Slow-Cooked Chili Con Carne (page 280)
- Spaghetti with Puttanesca Sauce (page 179)
- Tandoori Chicken (page 202)
- Tex-Mex Beans and Rice (page 158)
- Tofu and Bok Choy Stir-Fry (page 166)
- Vegetarian Gumbo (page 157)
- Warm Artichoke Dip (page 270)
- Warm Kale Salad (page 109)

HEART HEALTH BENEFITS

- Lowers "bad" LDL cholesterol
- Lowers triglycerides
- Raises "good" HDL cholesterol
- Lowers blood pressure
- Lowers homocysteine levels
- Inhibits blood clot formation
- Reduces plaque buildup
- Improves bloodflow
- Lowers blood sugar
- Improves glycemic control

GRAPES AND CHERRIES

Simply bursting with sweet and juicy goodness, grapes and cherries are refreshing, delightfully crunchy fruits the whole family can enjoy. And when it comes to heart health, these two fruits are hard to beat.

The number and variety of the heart healthy components in grapes and cherries are staggering.

First, they're good sources of potassium (288 milligrams and 260 milligrams, respectively) and vitamin C. They're also really good sources of fiber, which helps reduce the risk of coronary heart disease (CHD).

And last, but certainly not least, both cherries and grapes are loaded with the flavonoids anthocyanin, quercetin, and resveratrol, as well as the carotenoids beta-carotene, lutein, and zeaxanthin. All of these amazing pigment-causing phytochemicals are super-powerful antioxidants that can appreciably lower bad cholesterol and raise good cholesterol levels.

A CORNUCOPIA OF HEART HEALTH BENEFITS

Preliminary lab studies in mice have demonstrated that anthocyanin, which is abundant in cherries and grapes, not only significantly increases the production of insulin (by 50 percent!) but prevents glucose intolerance. The mice also had a 24 percent decrease in weight gain.

Another researcher was interested in learning if grapes would exert a cardio-protective effect in both premenopausal and postmenopausal women. The participants were given 36 grams of freeze-dried grapes that were made into a powder and mixed in water to be drunk every day for 4 weeks. All of the women experienced significant drops in LDL cholesterol and oxidative stress (determined by a specialized biomarker test). Additionally, the premenopausal women's triglycerides dropped 15 percent, and the postmenopausal women's triglycerides dropped 6 percent. Thus, the study authors concluded, grapes do offer an overall protective effect against CHD.

KID-FRIENDLY GRAPE JUICE WINS

You know the 100 percent grape juice you loved as a kid? The stuff that left a telltale purple mustache? That's Concord grape juice. A recent study compared the antioxidant capacity of 13 of the most popular juices available at the supermarket—and Concord took top honors!

GRAPE AND CHERRY RECIPES

- Cherry Corn Muffins (page 90)
- Curried Chicken Salad (page 213)
- Flavorful Fruit Tart (page 254)
- Grape and Fennel Salad (page 109)
- Orange Pistachio Cake (page 247)
- Quick and Easy Rice Pudding (page 243)
- Quick No-Bake Apple-Cherry Crisp (page 234)
- Summer Fruit Compote (page 257)
- Toasted Trail Mix (page 233)

HEART HEALTH BENEFITS

- Lowers "bad" LDL cholesterol
- Lowers triglycerides
- Raises "good" HDL cholesterol
- Lowers blood pressure
- Lowers homocysteine levels
- Inhibits blood clot formation
- Reduces plaque buildup
- Improves bloodflow
- Lowers blood sugar
- Improves glycemic control

GREENS, DARK LEAFY

Simply referred to as greens south of the Mason-Dixon Line, dark leafy vegetables such as kale, Swiss chard, and collard greens have astonishingly high amounts of vitamins A and C and nearly as impressive amounts of potassium, folate, fiber, as well as some omega-3 fatty acids—which is why they're considered among the most nutritious, heart healthiest vegetables. For example, 1 cup of boiled kale, Swiss chard, or collard greens offers over 100 percent of your RDA of vitamin A and over 50 percent of vitamin C!

Plus, dark leafy greens are outstanding sources of the profoundly heart healthy antioxidants beta-carotene and lutein, which have the ability (both individually and collectively) to neutralize much of the artery-damaging effects of oxidative stress caused by free radicals. In fact, kale and collard greens (as well as spinach) contain more lutein than any other fruit or vegetable.

And let's not forget potassium. Kale, Swiss chard, and collard greens have ample amounts of this mineral, which helps your body get rid of excess salt to help lower high blood pressure.

AMAZING GREENS

Here's a guide to dark leafy greens: If you love mild, smoky flavors, try collard greens. If you appreciate earthy flavor, go for the kale. And if you enjoy dishes that are slightly salty and bitter, then you absolutely must try Swiss chard.

IMPRESSIVE FIBER

Clinical studies have shown that you can reduce your cholesterol levels an incredible 0.5 percent to 2 percent for every gram of soluble fiber eaten per day—and dark leafy greens provide ample amounts. For example, just 1 cup of delicious, mildly smoky, steamed collard greens nets you 5 grams of fiber. Add 1 cup of delightfully complementary (and classic) Great Northern beans (a whopping 16 grams of fiber) and, depending upon your age and sex, you'll have achieved between 56 and 100 percent of your total fiber intake needs for the day. And if you do the math, 21 grams of fiber means you could potentially be on the road to lowering your cholesterol levels up to 42 percent.

DARK LEAFY GREENS RECIPES

- Brown Rice with Greens and Feta (page 151)
- Greens with Strawberries and Kiwifruit (page 110)
- Sautéed Bitter Greens (page 134)
- Warm Kale Salad (page 109)
- Warm Steak and Orange Salad (page 128)

HEART HEALTH BENEFITS

- Lowers "bad" LDL cholesterol
- Raises "good" HDL cholesterol
- Lowers blood pressure
- Lowers homocysteine levels
- Reduces plaque buildup
- Improves bloodflow
- Lowers blood sugar
- Improves glycemic control

HERBS AND SPICES

You know how certain smells—like a sudden whiff of apple pie (with cinnamon, of course) baking in the oven—instantly make you feel comforted and happy? That's called Proustian memory—named after 20th-century novelist Marcel Proust, who in *Swann's Way* magnificently describes the rush of memories experienced after smelling a madeleine pastry dipped in lime-blossom tea.

Beyond making you feel emotionally good (which has heart health value in and of itself), many herbs and spices can contribute to a healthy heart as well. So hey, just because it's wise to limit your salt intake, that certainly doesn't mean you have to limit your spice pleasure. Perish the thought!

Studies have shown that these herbs and spices have the healthiest heart benefits.

Cinnamon (*Cinnamomum verum*): lowers LDL cholesterol, lowers triglycerides, raises HDL cholesterol, improves glycemic control and insulin sensitivity

Ginger (*Zingiber officinale*): reduces formation of blood clots

Ground red pepper (*Capsicum frutescens*): lowers LDL, lowers triglycerides, reduces formation of blood clots, helps dissolve clots

Mustard seed (*Brassica juncea*): lowers LDL, lowers triglycerides, raises HDL

Lemon balm (*Melissa officinalis*): lowers LDL

Oregano (*Origanum vulgare*): lowers LDL, raises HDL

Peppermint (*Mentha piperita*): lowers LDL

Sage (*Salvia officinalis*): lowers LDL, raises HDL

Thyme (*Thymus vulgaris*): lowers LDL, raises HDL

Turmeric (*Curcuma longa*): lowers LDL, enhances insulin sensitivity

ÜBERANTIOXIDANT HERBS

A recent study investigated the contribution of dietary antioxidants from culinary and medicinal herbs by way of some highly sophisticated assays (tests). A total of 85 herb varieties and species were tested. Incredibly high concentrations of antioxidants were found in dried oregano, sage, peppermint, garden thyme, lemon balm, clove, allspice, and cinnamon. The study authors state that in a normal diet, "intake of herbs may therefore contribute significantly to the total intake of plant antioxidants, and be an even better source of dietary antioxidants than many other food groups such as fruits, berries, cereals, and vegetables."

SUPER CINNAMON

A study investigated what benefits cinnamon might confer on 60 men and women ages 45 to 58 with type 2 diabetes. For 40 days, the participants consumed a daily total of either 1 gram (about $\frac{1}{4}$ teaspoon), 3 grams (just over $\frac{1}{2}$ teaspoon), or 6 grams (about $1\frac{1}{4}$ teaspoons) of cinnamon right after meals. All three amounts of cinnamon reduced the mean fasting serum glucose (blood sugar) levels by 18 to 29 percent, LDL by 7 to 27 percent, triglycerides by 23 to 30 percent, and total cholesterol by 12 to 26 percent.

The study authors noted that since only a $\frac{1}{4}$ teaspoon of cinnamon a day provided such substantive benefit, perhaps even a smaller amount might prove helpful.

TREMENDOUS TURMERIC

A study investigated what role turmeric (curcumin) might play on the cholesterol levels of 10 healthy people (for example, no indication of heart disease or diabetes). The study participants consumed 500 milligrams (about $\frac{1}{8}$ teaspoon) of curcumin every day for a week. After those 7 days, they had a significant (29 percent) increase in HDL and a 12 percent decrease in total cholesterol.

HEART HEALTH BENEFITS (DEPENDING ON THE SPICE)

- Lowers total cholesterol
- Lowers "bad" LDL cholesterol
- Lowers triglycerides
- Raises "good" HDL cholesterol
- Lowers blood pressure

- Inhibits blood clot formation
- Improves bloodflow
- Improves glycemic control
- Improves insulin sensitivity

KIWIFRUIT

Don't you wonder who was the first person to think, "Hey, let me try a bite of this fuzzy little egg-shaped brown thing"? Just imagine her look of sheer delight when she discovered that inside was beautifully translucent, emerald-green flesh with perfectly concentric circles of tiny black seeds—and that it tasted like an exotic combination of a strawberry, pineapple, melon, and banana! Even more appealing: its impressive amounts of vitamin C. Ounce for ounce, no fruit (except the guava) provides more vitamin C.

Kiwis are also rich in a variety of flavonoids, such as the pigments beta-carotene and lutein, and in sodium- and blood pressure–lowering potassium; and they offer a fine amount of the B vitamin folate.

Similar to frequently nibbling dark chocolate, regularly eating kiwis has been shown to help lower the risk of developing blood clots. And let's not forget that kiwis are a rich source of vitamin E, another known free radical–scavenging, LDL-lowering, HDL-improving antioxidant, as well as a really good source of fiber (both soluble and insoluble).

Good things really do come in small—albeit funny-looking—packages!

CARDIO-PROTECTIVE KIWIFRUIT

A recent study investigated whether eating kiwifruit would have a beneficial effect on people who don't already have heart disease. Specifically, would it impact lipid levels (LDL cholesterol and triglycerides) and reduce the formation of blood clots? The methodology was rather straightforward: Half of the participants ate two or three kiwis a day for 1 month; the other half didn't eat any. Compared with the kiwi abstainers, the kiwi eaters had a 15 percent reduction in lipid levels and an 18 percent reduction in clots.

Another study further investigated kiwis' heart healthy impact on reducing oxidative stress, compared with consuming a vitamin C solution. The results were clear: Eating kiwi was far more effective. The authors conclude that because of the cardioprotective properties demonstrated in kiwis, more fruits and vegetables should be tested in this way.

SELECTING, PREPARING, AND ENJOYING

First, a quick fun fact: Kiwi is one of only a handful of fruits that are actually green when ripe. (Another is the avocado.)

When selecting kiwis at the market, choose those that are plump, heavy for their size, and unbruised. Kiwis are ready to eat when they yield slightly to gentle pressure. Some people eat these funny little orbs skin and all; others rub off the fuzz. However, most people peel them with a paring knife and then slice them. Another terrific method is to slice the whole, unpeeled fruit in half and scoop out the sweet green flesh with a spoon, eating it as you would a soft-cooked egg.

KIWIFRUIT RECIPES

- Flavorful Fruit Tart (page 254)
- Gingered Fruit Salad with Yogurt (page 93)
- Greens with Strawberries and Kiwifruit (page 110)
- Peach-Blueberry Shortcakes (page 244)

HEART HEALTH BENEFITS

- Lowers total cholesterol
- Lowers "bad" LDL cholesterol
- Raises "good" HDL cholesterol
- Lowers blood pressure
- Lowers homocysteine levels
- Inhibits blood clot formation
- Improves glycemic control
- Improves insulin sensitivity

LEMONS AND LIMES

Don't you just love the zing of lemons and limes? Now, think about the one-of-a-kind olfactory experience that always happens nanoseconds after you first slice into a lemon or lime. Exactly! That fabulous scent is both fun and sophisticated. Lemons and limes enhance so many dishes, from drinks to appetizers to main meals to desserts. In short, these versatile citrus fruits are an absolute, must-have kitchen staple. And nutritionally? Well, you know that they're winners. Lemons and limes are terrific sources of vitamin C and have a respectable amount of fiber, making these lovely fruits a wise, heart healthy choice.

C IS FOR CARDIOVASCULAR HEALTH

Lemons and limes pack in the vitamin C: Just ¼ cup of lemon juice has 28 milligrams—that's almost half of your daily requirement. And lime juice is almost as good, with 18 milligrams, or 30 percent of the vitamin C you need every day. Vitamin C is a particularly powerful antioxidant that can prevent, reduce, and reverse the damaging effects of atherosclerosis—which, among other benefits, helps to lower blood pressure. Scientific studies repeatedly demonstrate that eating foods high in vitamin C reduces the risk of all causes of death—including heart disease.

LEMON AND LIME RECIPES

- Apple and Jicama Slaw (page 108)
- Apple-Cranberry Crisp (page 248)
- Arugula Tabbouleh (page 153)
- Barley Edamame Salad (page 119)
- Citrus Vinaigrette (page 260)
- Coleslaw with Lemon Dressing (page 106)
- Corn Salsa (page 265)
- Curry Chicken and Rice Salad (page 127)
- Frozen Yogurt with Fruit Wine Sauce (page 274)
- Garlicky Hummus (page 266)
- Greens with Strawberries and Kiwifruit (page 110)
- Grilled Shrimp with Mango Salsa (page 195)
- Herb-Dijon Vinaigrette (page 262)
- Italian Three Bean Salad (page 122)
- Lemon-Lime Pudding Cake (page 246)
- Linguine with Walnut Pesto (page 180)
- Mediterranean Pasta with Shrimp (page 184)
- Quick Arugula and Shrimp Salad (page 126)
- Soy Delicious Guacamole (page 265)
- Spicy Fajitas (page 222)
- Vegetable Noodle Bowl (page 182)
- Warm Kale Salad (page 109)

HEART HEALTH BENEFITS

- Lowers total cholesterol
- Lowers "bad" LDL cholesterol
- Raises "good" HDL cholesterol
- Lowers blood pressure
- Improves glycemic control

LENTILS

Dating back to the Stone Age (the Neolithic period), lentils are delicious little lens-shaped legumes that come in a beautiful array of colors, ranging from yellow to pink to orange to green to brown to black. They offer a fabulous variety of flavors and textures, too. More important, they are a treasure trove of folate and fiber and also provide respectable amounts of magnesium and potassium.

By eating just 1 cup of cooked lentils, you get an incredible 90 percent (358 micrograms) of your DV of folate, which helps to lower, prevent, and reverse high blood pressure; ease bloodflow; relax blood vessels; and lower homocysteine levels, which have also been linked with atherosclerosis. You also get 63 percent (16 grams) of your daily fiber. As a bonus, the fiber in lentils isn't just the insoluble kind; it's also a super source of soluble fiber.

Plus, that same cup of cooked lentils provides you with 18 percent (71.3 milligrams) of your DV of magnesium, which studies show may significantly reduce the risk of developing heart disease. And you get 21 percent (731 milligrams) of your daily potassium, which helps lower blood pressure by getting rid of excess salt in your body. And no fruit or vegetable (except soybeans) has more protein than lentils.

THE LEGUME STUDIES

A huge, 25-year, seven-country study investigated the associations in middle-aged men between the intake of particular food groups and dying from coronary heart disease (CHD). In the study, CHD was defined as sudden coronary death or fatal heart attack. The results demonstrated that eating a diet high in legumes (such as lentils) was associated with a stunning 82 percent reduction in the risk of dying from CHD.

Another study investigated what consuming a powder comprised of 66.6 percent whole grains, 22.2 percent legumes, 5.6 percent seeds, and 5.6 percent vegetables (in place of refined white rice) might have on lipid profiles (that is, LDL and HDL), homocysteine levels, and insulin sensitivity. The study participants were 78 men with CHD. For 16 weeks, half the patients ate their usual diet with refined white rice. The other half ate their usual diet but, instead of rice, had whole grain and legume powder that they dissolved in a glass of water and drank.

The powder had significant beneficial effects on blood sugar levels, insulin sensitivity, and homocysteine concentrations, as well as decreased LDL and increased HDL levels. The rice group enjoyed none of these heart healthy benefits.

JUST ONE-THIRD CUP!

- According to a US study, eating just ⅓ cup of cooked beans (such as lentils) daily results in a 38 percent lower risk of a heart attack.
- And according to a similar study, eating ⅓ cup of cooked beans (such as lentils) just 4 days a week results in a 22 percent reduction in coronary heart disease.

LENTIL RECIPES

- Braised Lentils with Spinach (page 159)
- Spicy Red Lentil Soup (page 99)

HEART HEALTH BENEFITS

- Lowers total cholesterol
- Lowers "bad" LDL cholesterol
- Raises "good" HDL cholesterol
- Lowers blood pressure
- Lowers homocysteine levels
- Inhibits blood clot formation
- Improves glycemic control
- Improves insulin sensitivity

MUSHROOMS, SHIITAKE

Having a delectable smoky-earthy flavor and a satisfying meaty texture, shiitake mushrooms have been a symbol of longevity for centuries. Once considered an exotic and rare delicacy in the United States, shiitake mushrooms are now readily available both fresh and dried in markets across the country.

Shiitake mushrooms are rich in vitamin C, eritadenine, and L-ergothioneine (powerful antioxidants that can help prevent, reduce, and reverse atherosclerosis and high blood pressure) and are an excellent source of fiber. Shiitake mushrooms also offer linoleic acid, an essential fatty acid that must be obtained from foods because our bodies cannot manufacture it.

THE SHIITAKE STUDIES

One study found that people with high cholesterol levels who consumed 9 grams of dried shiitake mushrooms a day experienced a 7 to 10 percent decrease in serum cholesterol levels. In a similar study, people age 60 and over with high lipid (fat) content in their blood who consumed 90 grams of fresh shiitake mushrooms for just 7 days experienced a 9 to 12 percent decrease in total cholesterol and a 6 to 7 percent decrease in triglycerides.

PLEASE DON'T WASH THE MUSHROOMS

Fresh mushrooms soak up water like porous little sponges, which makes them soggy and gross. To clean them, either use a mushroom brush (yes, there is such a thing) or gently wipe them with a soft paper towel or a clean cloth towel. If you must use water, slightly moisten the towel.

On the other hand, dried mushrooms must be soaked in a liquid before you can eat or cook with them. In that case, washing and then soaking in water is fine. However, a better idea is to reconstitute dried mushrooms with other more flavor-enhancing liquids, such as low-sodium chicken broth or wine.

For the past 10 years, there have also been extensive animal studies investigating the heart health impact of shiitake mushrooms. One study found that feeding rabbits shiitakes significantly inhibited the buildup of artery-clogging plaque. Another found that regularly feeding shiitakes to hypertensive lab animals significantly lowered their cholesterol levels (especially triglycerides). A nearly identical study found that feeding hypertensive lab rats a diet containing 5 percent shiitake powder reduced their LDL levels and lowered their blood pressure.

And still another study found that feeding lab animals the antioxidant eritadenine significantly

---

SHIITAKES BEAT LIVER!

One of the best sources of the antioxidant L-ergothioneine is chicken liver (a decidedly heart *un*healthy food). But here's great news: An American research team recently presented findings that mushrooms—specifically, shiitakes—have an average of 13 milligrams of L-ergothioneine in a 3-ounce serving, which is at least four times more than chicken liver offers.

---

lowered their cholesterol levels, including triglycerides, regardless of which types of fats the lab animals were fed.

SHIITAKE RECIPES

- Beef and Vegetable Stroganoff (page 223)
- Coquilles St. Jacques (page 187)
- Herbed Bread Dressing (page 276)
- Makeover Veal Marsala (page 226)
- Penne with Roasted Autumn Vegetables (page 174)
- Piled-High Nachos (page 281)
- Sautéed Mushrooms and Spinach (page 138)
- Sugar Snap Peas with Shiitakes (page 139)
- Sweet-and-Sour Shrimp Soup (page 102)
- Tofu and Bok Choy Stir-Fry (page 166)
- Tuna Tetrazzini (page 197)
- Vegetable Noodle Bowl (page 182)
- Vegetable Quinoa (page 146)

HEART HEALTH BENEFITS

- Lowers "bad" LDL cholesterol
- Lowers triglycerides
- Raises "good" HDL cholesterol
- Lowers blood pressure
- Lowers homocysteine levels
- Improves blood clot formation
- Reduces plaque buildup
- Improves bloodflow
- Lowers blood sugar
- Improves glycemic control

NUTS

If you love nuts, have we got great news for you: Those crunchy, buttery, savory little delights are incredibly (yes, incredibly!) heart healthy.

Nuts are packed with fiber, which soaks up artery-clogging cholesterol, and jam-packed with phytosterols, compounds that help block cholesterol from being absorbed in your intestines. They're also rich in monounsaturated fatty acids (the same heart healthy fat as olive oil), which means that eating nuts can improve bloodflow by smoothing the inside walls of blood vessels.

A HANDFUL OF NUT STUDIES

Contrary to popular belief, eating fat-filled nuts can actually help you lose weight. A 28-month study of 937 men and women found that those who ate nuts two or more times a week had a 31 percent lower risk of weight gain than those who rarely or never ate nuts—who, in fact, actually gained weight! So, when it comes to nuts, even though they are loaded with fat, you can have your cardio-protection and lose weight too!

Another huge study with a 14-year follow-up investigated the relationship between coronary heart disease (CHD) and eating nuts. The study participants were 86,016 women ranging in age from 34 to 59, with no previously diagnosed CHD. Over the 14 years, 861 women had nonfatal heart attacks, and 394 died of CHD. The women who ate 5 or more ounces of nuts a week had a 35 percent lower risk of CHD

and heart attack. Five ounces of nuts a week translates into a small handful a day, adding up to just over 1 cup a week.

A similar large-scale study of 31,208 women and men found that people who ate nuts more than four times a week reduced their risk of suffering both fatal and nonfatal heart attacks by 50 percent.

Not that nutty about nuts? Consider just a few. Another study of 34,111 postmenopausal women investigated whether eating nuts often would reduce the risk of death due to CHD. Over the course of 12 years, 657 women died from CHD. The women who ate two or more 28.5-gram servings of nuts per week (that's only about 5 nuts a day) reduced their relative risk by 43 percent.

WALNUTS AND OMEGA-3S

Walnuts, in particular, are rich in omega-3 fatty acids, which lower LDL cholesterol levels (and other bad fats, such as triglycerides), increase desirable HDL levels, lower blood pressure, and reduce plaque buildup in arteries.

In fact, eating as little as 1 to 2 ounces of walnuts (or other foods high in omega-3s, like flaxseed) a week decreases the risks of heart disease, both fatal and nonfatal heart attacks, sudden cardiac death, and all causes of death.

NUT RECIPES

- Asparagus Salad with Goat Cheese (page 111)
- Baked Oatmeal Pudding (page 86)
- Brussels Sprouts Amandine (page 136)
- Bulgur-Stuffed Roasted Peppers (page 169)
- Chocolate Almond Biscotti (page 239)
- Chocolate Almond Pudding (page 243)
- Chocolate Almond Scones (page 84)
- Chocolate Snack Cake (page 282)
- Cinnamon-Raisin Quick Bread (page 91)
- Curried Chicken Salad (page 213)
- Curried Couscous (page 149)
- Flavorful Fruit Tart (page 254)
- Flourless Chocolate Cake (page 251)
- Fruit and Bran Muffins (page 87)
- Fruit 'n' Nut Coffee Cake (page 249)
- Fruited Granola (page 83)
- Fruited Rice Pilaf (page 150)
- Gingered Carrot Loaf (page 92)
- Grape and Fennel Salad (page 109)
- Harvest Cookies (page 236)
- Linguine with Walnut Pesto (page 180)
- Orange Pistachio Cake (page 247)
- Peanut Bars (page 233)
- Peanut Noodle Salad (page 116)
- Pumpkin Pie in Nut Crust (page 277)
- Quick and Easy Rice Pudding (page 243)
- Simple Salmon with Almonds (page 190)
- Spinach Salad with Warm Onion Dressing (page 112)
- Toasted Trail Mix (page 233)
- Tropical Phyllo Cups (page 253)
- Turkey Picadillo (page 217)
- Wild Rice with Almonds and Currants (page 151)

HEART HEALTH BENEFITS

- Lowers "bad" LDL cholesterol
- Lowers triglycerides
- Raises "good" HDL cholesterol
- Lowers blood pressure
- Lowers homocysteine levels
- Reduces plaque buildup
- Lowers blood sugar
- Improves glycemic control

OATS

It's one of the ultimate comfort foods: a piping hot bowl of creamy, satisfying oatmeal. Whether you prefer classic rolled oats (the kind that come in the cardboard canister) or the more gourmet steel-cut oats (with a chewier texture and a decidedly nuttier flavor), oats abound with fantastic heart healthy nutrients. Teeming with both soluble and insoluble fiber, oatmeal also offers the antioxidant avenanthramide.

Oats, oatmeal, and oat bran all contain a particularly heart healthy type of soluble fiber called beta-glucan, which behaves like a thirsty sponge, soaking up artery-clogging LDL in your blood.

Soluble fiber also slows down your body's absorption of glucose (sugar from carbohydrates), which inhibits sudden, unwanted spikes in blood sugar.

THE FACTS ON OATMEAL

A 6-week study of 75 men and women with high cholesterol investigated whether the fiber in oats, called beta-glucan, would appreciably improve lipid profiles by reducing LDL. For 6 weeks, half of the participants were given 6 grams per day of concentrated oat beta-glucan; the other half received placebos. The results? Those given beta-glucan significantly lowered their LDL levels.

A 3-year study of 229 postmenopausal women with coronary heart disease investigated whether eating cereal fiber and whole grains would slow the progression of atherosclerosis, which reduces blood-flow to the heart. The study found that those women who ate at least 3 grams of cereal fiber per week, as well as those women who ate at least 6 servings of whole grains, slowed their existing atherosclerosis.

OAT RECIPES

- Baked Oatmeal Pudding (page 86)
- Fat-Free Applesauce Oatmeal Cookies (page 237)
- Fruited Granola (page 83)
- Green Tea–Oatmeal Pancakes (page 80)
- Lemon Blueberry Muffins (page 89)
- Peanut Bars (page 233)
- Toasted Trail Mix (page 233)

HEART HEALTH BENEFITS

- Lowers total cholesterol
- Lowers "bad" LDL cholesterol
- Lowers blood pressure
- Improves glycemic control

OLIVES AND OLIVE OIL

Drizzled over perfectly ripened tomatoes or hot, crusty bread; used to gently sauté fresh broccoli and garlic—these are just a few of the nearly endless ways you can enjoy the fresh, fragrant, fruity, and buttery notes of a really good olive oil. And the best part? Olive oil and olives are rich in three different classes of antioxidants (simple phenols, secoiridoids, and lignans) and in monounsaturated fats and polyunsaturated fats—which means it eases bloodflow by reducing friction in the interior surfaces of every blood vessel in your body—from your capillaries to your heart.

SIGNIFICANT HEART PROTECTION

A study of 700 men and 148 women investigated whether olive oil has protective capabilities with regard to the risk of heart disease in general and acute coronary syndrome (a sudden rupture of plaque inside the coronary arteries) in particular. Researchers found that both men and women who used olive oil exclusively reduced their risk of acute coronary syndrome by 47 percent. The study authors conclude that choosing olive oil (over other fats or oils) in food preparation provides "significant protection against CHD (coronary heart disease)."

Another hospital-based study looked into whether olive oil reduces a person's risk of having a first non-fatal heart attack. The participants with the highest olive oil consumption (just under 4 tablespoons daily) reduced their risk by an astounding 82 percent! And those who took in about 2 tablespoons a day enjoyed a 64 percent reduction in first heart attack.

But when it comes to the different types of oil, it seems extra-virgin olive oil may be the most heart

WHAT CONSTITUTES A "GOOD" OLIVE OIL?

Olive oils are like wines. Their flavors, undertones, nuances, complexity, body, balance, acidity, color, mouthfeel, etc., vary tremendously, depending upon many factors, including the country of origin. And like wine, what constitutes a "good" olive oil is a matter of personal preference. Fortunately, many upscale gourmet stores offer olive oil tastings. Some shops will open different varieties for you to taste if you ask. If you don't have that luxury available, simply buy a couple of small bottles of different olive oils and have your own private tasting.

You could even host a tasting party in your home! Ask guests to bring one bottle of olive oil from a different location, such as Spain, Italy, Greece, Turkey, France, Portugal, Morocco, or the United States, and supply a nice variety of oils yourself, of course. Offer various dipping foods, such as some lovely breads, cherry tomatoes, and blanched asparagus, for taste-testing the different oils.

For optimal heart health, olive oil needs to be extra-virgin. But beyond that, what makes any olive oil "good" is that *you* like it. Find one (or two) that you love—perhaps a cheaper olive oil for cooking, a more expensive one for drizzling—and you're set.

healthy. Researchers in five European countries compared the heart healthy capabilities of different grades of olive oil in 200 men with no known cardiovascular disease. Over a 3-month period, each of the men included 25 milliliters a day (about 5 teaspoons) of the different grades of olive oil in his diet. The extra-virgin olive oil provided the best heart healthy results, which was defined as a decrease in LDL cholesterol and triglycerides and an increase in HDL. The study authors posit that the higher levels of polyphenols (antioxidants) found in extra-virgin versus lower grades is probably the reason it performed better.

OLIVES PREDATE THE FLOOD

Olive oil (and olives, of course) is absolutely antediluvian: The earliest surviving olive oil amphorae (those beautiful two-handled ceramic vases) date back to 3500 BC, during the Minoan period. There's even evidence that olives were regularly gathered as early as the Neolithic period (about 8500 BC). And, of course, it was an olive branch that the dove brought back to Noah after the flood, signifying dry land.

OLIVE RECIPES

- Arugula Tabbouleh (page 153)
- Chicken Ragout (page 205)
- Greek-Inspired Pasta (page 177)
- Spaghetti with Puttanesca Sauce (page 179)
- Tofu Citrus Salad (page 113)
- Turkey Picadillo (page 217)
- Warm Steak and Orange Salad (page 128)

And, of course, many other recipes feature extra-virgin olive oil.

HEART HEALTH BENEFITS

- Lowers total cholesterol
- Lowers "bad" LDL cholesterol
- Lowers triglycerides
- Raises "good" HDL cholesterol
- Lowers blood pressure
- Improves bloodflow
- Reduces plaque buildup
- Reduces all-cause mortality

ONIONS, SCALLIONS, AND SHALLOTS

It was historian/poet/novelist Carl Sandburg (1878–1967) who wrote, "Life is like an onion." But did he know that this indispensable vegetable promotes life, too?

Onions, scallions, and shallots are all heart healthy members of the *Allium* family. Scientific studies have demonstrated that these pungent, sometimes tear-causing vegetables can help lower LDL cholesterol and triglycerides and raise HDL—thanks to their high levels of the antioxidants vitamin C and quercetin. They've also been shown to improve glucose tolerance, lower insulin levels, and lower blood sugar—thanks to their chromium and fiber. Further-more, onions have been shown to lower blood pressure and homocysteine levels—thanks to folate. And if that weren't enough, onions help remove excess sodium (which lowers your blood pressure)—thanks to potassium.

With all these impressive heart healthy *Allium* family attributes, it's no wonder that study after study has shown that regularly eating onions can help prevent atherosclerosis, heart disease, and heart attacks.

QUERCETIN MAKES A BIG IMPACT

Onions are an excellent source of the very potent, heart healthy antioxidant flavonoid quercetin. For example, a comprehensive 14-year study with a 26-year follow-up investigated a possible association between flavonoid intake and coronary heart disease (CHD). More than 5,000 men and women between the ages of 30 and 69 who had no previous indications of heart disease participated. Over the course of the study, nearly 500 people died of CHD. The participants who had high dietary intakes of flavonoids experienced a protective effect against the onset of CHD, while those who had very low intakes were at increased risk of heart disease. How big of a role did onions play? Approximately 95 percent of all the flavonoids eaten by the study participants were gleaned from quercetin-rich onions and apples.

WHAT'S CHROMIUM?

Chromium is a mineral that our bodies need in trace amounts. According to the National Institutes of Health, chromium enhances the action of insulin. For example, studies have demonstrated that people with type 1, type 2, gestational, and steroid-induced diabetes can improve glycemic control and insulin metabolism and reduce many diabetes symptoms (including fatigue, thirst, and frequent urination) with chromium. By eating just 1 cup of raw onions (not so hard to do if you love fresh salsa), you'll fulfill 20 percent of your daily requirement for chromium.

ONION, SCALLION, AND SHALLOT RECIPES

- Barley Edamame Salad (page 119)
- Corn Salsa (page 265)
- Creamy Potato Salad (page 274)
- Edamame Pilaf (page 150)
- Garlic Smashed Potatoes (page 144)
- Mashed Root Vegetables (page 278)
- Peppered Couscous (page 149)

- Piled-High Nachos (page 281)
- Soba Noodle Salad (page 117)
- Spinach Salad with Warm Onion Dressing (page 112)
- Stuffed Mushrooms (page 271)
- Sweet-and-Sour Shrimp Soup (page 102)
- Tofu Citrus Salad (page 113)
- Vegetable Noodle Bowl (page 182)

HEART HEALTH BENEFITS

- Lowers "bad" LDL cholesterol
- Lowers triglycerides
- Raises "good" HDL cholesterol
- Lowers blood pressure

- Lowers homocysteine levels
- Reduces plaque buildup
- Lowers blood sugar
- Improves glycemic control

ORANGES

When's the last time you sat down and peeled a fabulously sweet and juicy orange? If it's been a while, it's time to start treating yourself again to this lovely citrus fruit—on a regular basis! Oranges are an incredible source of heart healthy benefits due to the abundance of antioxidants, fiber, folate, and potassium.

NUTRIENTS GALORE

Oranges have an amazing amount and variety of cardio-protective antioxidants, including the pigment-causing carotenoid phytochemicals lutein, beta-cryptoxanthin, and zeaxanthin and the bioflavonoid hesperitin, to name just a few. And, of course, oranges

are *the* classic source of the powerhouse antioxidant vitamin C and also an excellent source of vitamin A.

Hesperetin, a chemical abundant in oranges, has quite an unusual quality: It can actually reactivate the antioxidant powers of vitamin C. After the vitamin C flowing in your blood has done its job of neutralizing many of the free radicals it encounters,

BETTER THAN 100 PERCENT

The average orange (about 2⅝ inches in diameter) provides you with 116 percent of your daily requirement of vitamin C—and it has only 62 calories!

its powers are depleted. But hesperetin allows the free radical–scavenging task to begin again!

However, it's important to note that hesperetin is found only in the peel and white pulp of the orange, so you need to eat the whole fruit, not just the juice to get this heart healthy benefit.

As if the antioxidant benefits weren't enough, your average orange has over 3 grams of fiber, plus about 40 micrograms of folate and 237 milligrams of potassium. What does that mean for your heart health? Well, the potassium helps to remove excess salt and sodium from your body, which lowers high blood pressure, which in turn reverses the formation of blood clots, artery-clogging plaque, and aneurysms. The folate helps lower, prevent, and reverse high blood pressure; eases bloodflow; relaxes the

blood vessels; and lowers homocysteine levels, which have also been linked with atherosclerosis. And the fiber soaks up artery-clogging LDL cholesterol, inhibits blood sugar spikes, and helps move things gently and effectively through your system.

APPLES AND ORANGES

Hercules' 12th and final labor was to steal the "golden apple" from the Garden of Hesperides. But that golden apple was no apple. It was an orange—at least according to the writings of Juba, the king of Mauretania from the first century. He explains that oranges were actually called the apple of Hesperia back then; therefore, "apples of Hesperides" is clearly a misnomer.

ORANGE RECIPES

- Asian Slaw with Chicken (page 123)
- Carrot and Sweet Potato Puree (page 140)
- Citrus Vinaigrette (page 260)
- Cran-Raspberry Ice (page 256)
- Fruited Granola (page 83)
- Gingered Fruit Salad (page 93)
- Orange-Ginger Pork Chops (page 227)
- Orange-Glazed Broccoli (page 135)
- Orange Pistachio Cake (page 247)
- Orzo Pilaf (page 178)
- Peach Melba Smoothie (page 94)
- Tofu Citrus Salad (page 113)
- Tropical Fruit Pops (page 240)
- Warm Steak and Orange Salad (page 128)
- Wild Rice with Almonds and Currants (page 151)

HEART HEALTH BENEFITS

- Lowers "bad" LDL cholesterol
- Raises "good" HDL cholesterol
- Lowers blood pressure
- Lowers homocysteine levels
- Reduces plaque buildup
- Improves bloodflow
- Lowers blood sugar
- Improves glycemic control

PEPPERS, BELL

Dating back to South America circa 5000 BC, bell peppers come in an array of colors beyond green. And did you know that the green ones are actually unripe? That's why green peppers are tangier than, for instance, the wonderfully sweet orange bell peppers. You'll find a rainbow range of red, yellow, purple, brown, black, and even white ripe peppers.

COLOR ME BEAUTIFUL

You know what deep, beautiful jewel tones mean: superantioxidant, heart healthy, pigment-producing carotenoids! Which ones? It depends on the color of the pepper. They all have beta-carotene and quercetin, and most have lutein and zeaxanthin, but only red peppers have lycopene. But rest assured: What a pepper lacks in one carotenoid, it usually makes up for in quantity in another.

Bell peppers are also an incredible source of vitamin C, ranging from 200 to 569 percent of the DV, depending on the color. Red peppers have twice as much vitamin C as green peppers. In fact, red peppers have more vitamin C than oranges (the citrus fruits, not the peppers). Peppers, particularly red ones, are also a great source of vitamin A, with 4,666 IU in 1 cup chopped—that's 93 percent of your DV. Of course, you know that both vitamins A and C are powerful antioxidants that neutralize the artery-damaging effects of free radicals, lower bad cholesterol levels, and lower blood pressure.

SWEET VERSUS HEAT

It's well known that hot red peppers increase thermogenesis, or the process of heat production; in this case, by increasing the body's core temperature due to high levels of capsaicin (the same stuff in pepper spray). Why are we discussing thermogenesis in a heart health cookbook? Because it increases your metabolism—which means you burn more calories, and that helps you lose weight. Achieving and maintaining a healthy weight are incredibly cardio-protective, reducing two of the major risk factors of heart disease: being overweight and developing type 2 diabetes.

A study (you knew we'd back up this very cool—or, rather, hot—information with a study!) investigated how red bell peppers (which have almost no capsaicin) compare with red chile peppers in terms of thermogenesis. The study participants (healthy men and women ages 22 to 25) ate either a sweet or a hot pepper, chewing it 30 times before swallowing and downing it with about ¼ cup of water. Twenty minutes later, various tests revealed that the bell pepper significantly accelerated thermogenesis—and without breaking a sweat. The moral of this study: You can have your sweet and heat it, too!

RED TRUMPS ORANGE

Red peppers have more vitamin C than oranges! One cup of navel orange sections, without membrane or seeds, provides you with 97.5 milligrams of vitamin C, which is 163 percent of the Daily Value (DV). But 1 cup of chopped red pepper, without membrane or seeds, provides you with 190 milligrams, or 317 percent of the DV.

BELL PEPPER RECIPES

- Asparagus Salad with Goat Cheese (page 111)
- Balsamic-Rosemary Pork Kebabs (page 230)
- Beef and Vegetable Stroganoff (page 223)
- Better-for-You Black Bean Chili (page 163)
- Black Bean Salad (page 120)
- Black Beans and Rice (page 155)
- Bulgur-Stuffed Roasted Peppers (page 169)
- Chicken and Vegetables in Cream Sauce (page 204)
- Corn Salsa (page 265)
- Creamy Potato Salad (page 274)
- Curry-Roasted Cauliflower (page 141)
- Ginger-Roasted Pork with Sweet Potatoes (page 228)
- Happy Heart Pasta Primavera (page 175)
- Italian Three Bean Salad (page 122)
- Paella (page 189)
- Peanut Noodle Salad (page 116)
- Peppered Couscous (page 149)
- Piled-High Nachos (page 251)
- Quick White Bean Stew (page 231)
- Salmon Cakes (page 199)
- Scallops Fra Diavolo (page 190)
- Slow-Cooked Chili Con Carne (page 280)
- Souped-Up Sloppy Joes (page 225)
- Spaghetti with Puttanesca Sauce (page 179)
- Spicy Fajitas (page 222)
- Spicy Red Lentil Soup (page 99)
- Spinach and Cannellini Beans (page 160)
- Tex-Mex Beans and Rice (page 158)
- Turkey Picadillo (page 217)
- Vegetable Quinoa (page 146)
- Vegetarian Gumbo (page 157)
- Warm Artichoke Dip (page 270)
- Zesty Clam Chowder (page 103)

HEART HEALTH BENEFITS

- Lowers "bad" LDL cholesterol
- Lowers triglycerides
- Raises "good" HDL cholesterol
- Lowers blood pressure
- Lowers homocysteine levels
- Reduces plaque buildup
- Improves bloodflow
- Lowers blood sugar
- Improves glycemic control

PEPPERS, CHILE

From the rich and sweet ancho to the fiercely fiery habanero, chile peppers are a delicious (and sometimes eye-watering) way to heat up your ability to promote heart health.

And a little goes a long way when it comes to their heart health benefits: A $\frac{1}{2}$-cup serving of raw chile peppers provides you with 300 percent of the RDA of vitamin C and 20 percent of vitamin A—both of which are powerful antioxidants. Chile peppers are also an excellent source of potassium, which has hypertension-lowering, plaque-reducing, and blood clot–inhibiting capabilities.

But what makes the chile pepper a heart healthy standout is its capsaicin, the component that makes it hot.

WHERE'S THE HEAT?

Capsaicin lowers your risk of type 2 diabetes and helps stabilize your blood sugar. Even more, the fiery stuff reins in your appetite, gives you a sense of

PICK A PEPPER

Anaheim: Also called California green chile or long green chile, the Anaheim is one of the most commonly used chiles in the United States, especially for making stuffed peppers. The red or green chiles are long, slender, lobed, and very mild.

Cascabel: Rich and deeply flavored, these squat round red or green peppers range in heat from moderately hot (if you lose the seeds and the membrane) to pretty darn hot (if you use the whole thing). They are occasionally used fresh, but most cascabel chiles are dried. Fun fact: When dried, their skin turns a translucent red-brown color and their seeds rattle inside.

Cayenne: Also called long hots, cayennes are red when fully mature. The long (6 to 10 inches) thin peppers can add a fiery heat to any dish. However, if used in moderation, they'll lend a more subtle touch. In the spice aisle (and in this book), ground cayenne often goes by the generic name "ground red pepper."

Chipotle: Rich, smoky, and hot (but not searing), chipotles are red jalapeño chile peppers that have been slowly dried and wood smoked.

Guajillo: Smoky, rich, complex, and only moderately hot, these dried, smooth-skinned, beautiful, big, long, purple/black chile peppers are considered to be a backbone of Mexican cooking.

Habanero: These little orange, red, or green lantern-shaped peppers are incredibly hot. In fact, they're the hottest commercially grown pepper in the world. Their intense fiery flavor has a unique floral undertone. They're delicious (if you can stand the heat), but proceed with extreme caution.

Poblano: Large and juicy, poblano chile peppers are dark purple when fresh. Dried poblanos (aka ancho chiles) are flat, wrinkled, heart shaped, and almost black. Poblanos are rich and sweet, with a mild to moderate heat.

HOT SPICE IN MICE

Get this: Researchers in Canada injected capsaicin (from chile peppers) into mice with type 1 diabetes (in which the pancreas doesn't produce insulin at all). The results actually stunned the researchers: The pancreas started to work normally! And it continued to produce insulin for weeks. Of course, we're talking mice here, not people. But that's where most studies start.

satiety (makes you feel full), and increases your energy expenditure—which means it revs up your metabolism! So if you need to lose a few pounds, chiles might help speed things along.

Contrary to popular belief, the seeds aren't the source of the chile pepper's heat. It's the white membrane that fires things up. The seeds become fiery because they're in such close contact with the membrane. Flavorless, odorless capsaicin (the same stuff used in pepper spray and tear gas) acts upon pain receptors in your mouth. The amount of "heat" or "burning" you'll feel depends upon the pepper and, of course, your own sensitivity to heat. As a rule of thumb, the larger the pepper, the milder its heat.

Capsaicin also stimulates the release of endorphins, eliciting a sense of well-being and a general feeling that all is right in the world. Think of it as a mini brain vacation. Who couldn't use that?

In terms of antioxidant studies, a study published in the *British Journal of Nutrition* in 2006 investigated a possible association between eating a freshly chopped chile pepper blend (55 percent cayenne) and reducing free radical damage (which leads to hardening of the arteries). In just 4 weeks, the men and women who ate the chile blend significantly lowered the rate of free radical damage.

Another study found that regularly eating meals that contain chiles decreases the amount of insulin needed to lower blood sugar and helps with postprandial hyperinsulinemia—the postmeal blood sugar spike.

If you can take the heat, get into the kitchen—and start spicing up meals with chile peppers.

CHILE PEPPER RECIPES

- Better-for-You Black Bean Chili (page 163)
- Corn Salsa (page 265)
- Grilled Shrimp with Mango Salsa (page 195)

HEART HEALTH BENEFITS

- Lowers total cholesterol
- Lowers "bad" LDL cholesterol
- Raises "good" HDL cholesterol
- Lowers blood pressure
- Reduces plaque buildup
- Stabilizes blood sugar
- Increases metabolism

POTATOES, SWEET

Don't wait until Thanksgiving to enjoy sweet and luscious, moist and creamy sweet potatoes. Since sweet potatoes have been categorized as an "antidiabetic" food, they should become a staple in your heart healthy diet, too. Yes, recent studies have found that sweet potatoes help stabilize blood sugar levels and lower insulin resistance.

FOR YOUR SWEET HEART

Bursting with powerful antioxidants, just 1 cup of baked, skin-on sweet potatoes provides an astounding 23,017 micrograms of beta-carotene, 796 percent of the DV of vitamin A, and 65 percent of the DV of vitamin C. These powerful antioxidants neutralize the artery-damaging effects of free radicals. Sweet potatoes are also a great source of the mineral potassium (27 percent of DV) and a good source of vitamin B_6, which works with folate to help reduce homocysteine levels. Sweet potatoes are also a really good source of fiber (with 6.6 grams per cup, or 26 percent of the DV) and a source of betaine, a rarely talked about nutrient that studies have shown not only has heart healthy homocysteine-lowering properties but also is associated with less fatigue, greater strength and endurance, a sense of well-being, and increased desire for (and performance of) physical and mental work.

Also exciting is a 12-week study that investigated the possible value sweet potatoes might have for controlling type 2 diabetes. Recruited from the offices of general practitioners, the study participants were men and women in their fifties who had type 2 diabetes, and most were treated by diet alone.

Half of the participants consumed 4 grams of sweet-potato extract daily, while the other half consumed placebos. The results showed that those who consumed sweet potato had much lower blood sugar levels and significantly improved insulin sensitivity, without increasing insulin levels.

In addition, while not part of what the researchers were originally looking at, the participants who ate the sweet-potato extract had lower LDL cholesterol levels and clinically significant weight loss! Yes, they lost weight eating sweet potatoes. Now that's a super heart healthy "wow!"

A QUICK PRIMER ON INSULIN RESISTANCE AND DIABETES

Foods that you eat are broken down into glucose (a type of sugar), which is your body's main source of energy and your brain's only food. Without insulin (a hormone), your cells can't use the glucose in your blood. So instead of getting burned for energy, the glucose stays in your bloodstream and continues to rise—which explains how blood sugar levels can get too high.

Diabetes is characterized by hyperglycemia (high blood sugar levels) and insulin resistance: If you have type 2 diabetes, your body produces insulin but doesn't respond to it properly. With type 1, the body (specifically, the pancreas) doesn't make insulin at all.

SWEET POTATO RECIPES

- Better-for-You Black Bean Chili (page 163)
- Carrot and Sweet Potato Puree (page 140)
- Garlic-Roasted Sweet Potatoes with Arugula (page 143)
- Ginger-Roasted Pork with Sweet Potatoes (page 228)
- Mashed Root Vegetables (page 278)
- Oven-Fried Fish and Chips (page 200)
- Roast Chicken and Vegetables (page 209)

HEART HEALTH BENEFITS

- Lowers "bad" LDL cholesterol
- Lowers triglycerides
- Raises "good" HDL cholesterol
- Lowers blood pressure
- Lowers homocysteine levels
- Inhibits blood clot formation
- Reduces plaque buildup
- Improves bloodflow
- Improves glycemic control
- Improves insulin sensitivity

QUINOA

Fluffy, light quinoa is delightfully creamy and slightly crunchy, with a wonderfully subtle nutty flavor. It is usually referred to as a grain (it's actually a seed) and is supersimple to prepare—just boil it like rice. And guess what? It's heart healthy, too. Plus, if you have trouble digesting foods with gluten—and you seriously miss that pasta—quinoa is a good gluten-free substitute.

QUINOA NUTRITION: 1, 2, 3

First of all, quinoa is a very good source of magnesium, which relaxes blood vessels to help lower blood pressure. In fact, just 1 cup of quinoa has 357 milligrams, or a whopping 89 percent of the DV. A large-scale, 30-year study of 7,172 men ages 45 to 68, with no known heart disease, investigated what role dietary magnesium intake might have on future risk of heart disease.

There were 1,431 incidents of heart disease identified over the course of the study. By the end of the first 15 years, the incidence of age-adjusted coronary

THE MOTHER OF ALL GRAINS

The Incas believed quinoa to be a sacred crop, calling it *chisaya mama*, which means "mother of all grains." Each year, the emperor of the Incas had the honor of sowing the first quinoa seeds of the season—which he purportedly did with a special tool made of gold!

COOKING QUINOA

Before cooking quinoa, place it in a sieve and rinse well, until the water is clear. Then, cook it pretty much as you do rice: Bring 2 cups of water or broth to a boil and add 1 cup quinoa. Reduce the heat, cover, and simmer for about 20 minutes, or until all the water is absorbed.

heart disease "decreased significantly," write the authors, with just 50 to 186 milligrams of magnesium needed daily to confer this protective result.

Second, 1 cup (170 grams) of cooked quinoa provides 84 micrograms of folate—21 percent of your DV, which can work wonders for your heart health. Third, that cup of nutty, delicious quinoa has a whopping 10 grams of fiber, which is a champion at soaking up (and helping the body get rid of) artery-clogging LDL cholesterol and stabilizing blood sugar levels. Indeed, clinical studies show that every gram of soluble fiber you eat each day has the potential to lower your cholesterol levels by 0.5 to 2 percent. Let's see . . . A cup of cooked quinoa has 10 grams of fiber. Multiply that by 0.5, as well as by 2. So by regularly including a cup of quinoa in your diet, you could potentially lower your cholesterol levels by 5 to 20 percent.

QUINOA RECIPES

- Beef and Vegetable Stroganoff (page 223)
- Quinoa Florentine (page 148)
- Vegetable Quinoa (page 146)

HEART HEALTH BENEFITS

- Lowers "bad" LDL cholesterol
- Lowers triglycerides
- Raises "good" HDL cholesterol
- Lowers blood pressure
- Lowers homocysteine levels
- Reduces plaque buildup
- Improves bloodflow
- Lowers blood sugar
- Improves glycemic control

SALMON

Revered by Native Americans as a symbol for life, this heavenly, succulent, rich-tasting fish is a genuine survivor of the Ice Age! Salmon is simply gorgeous in color—ranging from pale pink to red to orange—and an exceptionally fantastic heart healthy food.

Salmon is an outstanding source of omega-3 fatty acids and monounsaturated and polyunsaturated fatty acids, all of which lower LDL cholesterol levels (and other bad fats, such as triglycerides), increase HDL, lower blood pressure, and prevent plaque from building up in the arteries. Salmon also offers some potassium and is a great source of magnesium, which studies have shown may significantly reduce the risk of developing heart disease. And despite its decadent luxuriousness and fat content, salmon has only 184 calories per 3-ounce serving (about half a fillet) and a mere 56 milligrams of sodium.

SUPERHEALTHY FISH OIL

Increasing your daily intake of omega-3s from fish oil sources—in addition to plant and nut oil sources—is arguably one of the best decisions you can make for your heart. According to the NIH, evidence from a multitude of studies confirms that eating more fish (and taking natural fish-oil supplements) lowers triglycerides and blood pressure and reduces risks of dangerous abnormal heart rhythm, strokes in people with hardening of the arteries, and heart attacks and death.

A caution: The NIH also states that a qualified health care provider should be consulted prior to taking fish oil supplements, because of a risk of bleeding.

A number of large studies have investigated omega-3 fatty acids (derived from fish oil) and their possible preventive impact on secondary prevention—meaning, whether fish-based omega-3s could help people who already have heart disease and/or experienced a cardiovascular event such as angina or a heart attack. That answer is a resounding yes: People with a history of heart attacks who regularly eat fish rich in omega-3s (such as salmon) reduce their risk of another heart attack (fatal or nonfatal), sudden death, and death from any cause. Most of the participants in these studies were also using conventional heart drugs; according to the NIH, that suggests that omega-3 fish oils may enhance the effects of other therapies.

OMEGA-3S AND FATTY FISH

The American Heart Association (AHA) recommends eating fish at least twice a week, particularly "fatty" fish that are rich in omega-3s. Here's the AHA's list.

- Anchovies
- Bluefish
- Carp
- Catfish
- Halibut
- Lake trout
- Mackerel
- Salmon
- Striped sea bass
- Tuna (albacore)
- Whitefish

The AHA also recommends plant-based sources (technically, alpha-linolenic acid), including tofu and soybeans, walnuts, and flaxseed oil.

For people with diabetes, another study investigated the possible benefits that small amounts of omega-3 fatty acids from fish oil might confer on people with type 2 (non-insulin-dependent) diabetes. Every day for 6 weeks, the participants consumed $2\frac{1}{2}$ grams of omega-3 fatty acids from fish oil. The results: significant decreases in platelet aggregation (formation of blood clots), triglyceride levels, and systolic blood pressure. The study authors concluded, "Small quantities of omega-3 fatty acids or dietary fish are safe and potentially beneficial in NIDDM [non-insulin-dependent diabetes mellitus] patients."

SALMON AND OTHER FATTY FISH RECIPES

- Chopped Niçoise Salad (page 125)
- Grilled Tuna with Wasabi Cream (page 196)
- Hoisin Halibut with Bok Choy (page 199)
- Salmon Cakes (page 199)
- Sesame Salmon with Spicy Cucumber Salad (page 191)
- Simple Salmon with Almonds (page 190)
- Spiced Salmon Tacos (page 192)
- Tuna Tetrazzini (page 197)

HEART HEALTH BENEFITS

- Lowers "bad" LDL cholesterol
- Lowers triglycerides
- Raises "good" HDL cholesterol
- Lowers blood pressure
- Inhibits blood clot formation
- Reduces plaque buildup
- Improves bloodflow
- Reduces all-cause mortality

SEA VEGETABLES

From Scotland to Iceland, from New Zealand to Japan, and from China to South America, sea vegetables have been a source of culinary enjoyment for more than 10,000 years. Not familiar with sea vegetables? Technically speaking, they're . . . seaweeds. And they're delicious as well as heart healthy.

NEPTUNE'S PRIDE

For starters, sea vegetables have two terrific antioxidants, beta-carotene and lignans, that have been shown to help lower LDL cholesterol and triglyceride levels and raise HDL cholesterol. Sea vegetables are also a fine source of folate, omega-3s, and polyunsaturated and monounsaturated fatty acids. Their fiber soaks up and helps you eliminate artery-clogging cholesterol.

In terms of research, it's worth noting that lignans, a subcategory of phytoestrogens, are naturally occurring chemicals found in both land and marine plants—including sea vegetables. Studies have found that people who regularly consume lignan-rich foods have a reduced risk of heart disease. Scientists believe this cardio-protective ability is due to lignans' antioxidant capabilities, which means they scavenge free radicals and reduce oxidative damage, thereby lowering LDL cholesterol and triglyceride levels.

Another large study with a 30-year follow-up investigated whether regularly consuming dietary magnesium might protect against developing coronary heart disease (CHD). Over 7,000 men, none of whom had any known CHD at the outset, participated. The men who consumed an average of 50 to 186 milligrams of magnesium-rich foods a day significantly reduced their risk of developing CHD. What's a terrific source of magnesium? You guessed it: sea vegetables.

TYPES OF SEA VEGETABLES

Arame: The sweetest and mildest of the bunch, this seaweed is emerald green when fresh, black-green when dried; it looks like a tumble of angel hair pasta.

Hijiki: This strongly flavored seaweed is brown but turns jet black when dried and is similar in texture and appearance to black spaghetti.

Kelp: Most often sold in flake form, this seaweed varies in color from dark green to tawny brown and, like all of the sea vegetables, has an "umami" flavor.

Nori: Best known for wrapping up sushi rolls, this seaweed is dark purplish-black (but turns green when toasted).

Ulva lactuca: Commonly called sea lettuce because of its ruffled edges and general "leafy" appearance, this lovely, spring-green seaweed is most often used in salads and soups.

Wakame: Best known for enhancing the flavor and appearance of Japanese miso and used in tofu salad, this very dark green seaweed is usually sold in sheets.

SEA VEGETABLE RECIPE

● Asian Slaw with Chicken (page 123)

HEART HEALTH BENEFITS

- Lowers "bad" LDL cholesterol
- Lowers triglycerides
- Raises "good" HDL cholesterol
- Lowers blood pressure

- Inhibits blood clot formation
- Reduces plaque buildup
- Improves bloodflow
- Improves glycemic control

SEEDS

What do the oldest known condiment to man (sesame seeds, circa 1600 BC), the innards of a jack-o'-lantern, and the beautiful studded center of a sunflower all have in common? With nearly identical nutritional profiles, these deliciously nutty, crunchy seeds are all super heart healthy!

GOOD THINGS COME IN SMALL PACKAGES

Well deserving of the moniker "healthy fats," sesame, pumpkin, and sunflower seeds are all rich in mono-unsaturated (oleic) and polyunsaturated (linolenic) fatty acids, which a number of clinical studies show lower total cholesterol, LDL cholesterol, and triglyceride levels; raise HDL cholesterol (which helps get rid of the "bad" cholesterol); and improve insulin sensitivity. Feel like grabbing a handful of dry-roasted pumpkin or sunflower seeds or maybe sprinkling some toasted sesame seeds on your next salad?

These seeds are rich in folate, which fights high blood pressure, eases bloodflow, relaxes blood vessels, and lowers homocysteine levels (which a Harvard study has linked with a reduced risk of developing heart disease). Their fiber helps soak up artery-clogging cholesterol, reduces blood pressure, provides a sense of satiety (helping weight control), and mediates the absorption of sugar in the bloodstream.

CHOLESTEROL-BLOCKING PHYTOSTEROLS

Sesame, sunflower, and pumpkin seeds are all terrific sources of cholesterol-blocking phytosterols. For every 3½ ounces (about 100 grams):

- Sesame seeds have 400 to 413 milligrams of phytosterols.
- Sunflower seeds have 270 to 289 milligrams.
- Pumpkin seeds have 265 milligrams.

Sesame, pumpkin, and sunflower seeds are also rich in lignans (naturally occurring estrogen-like chemicals called phytoestrogens), as well as beta-carotene and vitamins A, C, and E—all of which scavenge free radicals, which helps lower LDL cholesterol and blood pressure. Plus, they're all a super source of heart-protecting magnesium. For example, ¼ cup of sesame seeds has about 125 milligrams of magnesium, almost one-third of the DV. Sesame, pumpkin, and sunflower seeds are excellent sources of phytosterols, which help block cholesterol from being absorbed in your intestines.

SESAME, PUMPKIN, AND SUNFLOWER SEED RECIPES

- Fruited Granola (page 83)
- Sesame Salmon with Spicy Cucumber Salad (page 191)
- Sesame-Seared Tofu (page 165)

HEART HEALTH BENEFITS

- Lowers "bad" LDL cholesterol
- Lowers triglycerides
- Raises "good" HDL cholesterol
- Lowers blood pressure
- Lowers homocysteine levels
- Inhibits blood clot formation
- Reduces plaque buildup
- Improves bloodflow
- Improves glycemic control
- Improves insulin sensitivity

SOY PRODUCTS

People tend to have strong feelings about tofu. They either love it or won't touch it with a 10-foot pole. Fortunately (for those of you who aren't fans), the heart health benefits of soy-based foods extend beyond tofu.

You can also get the benefits of soy by drinking and cooking with creamy and delicious soy milk—which nowadays not only doesn't taste "beany" but also comes in luscious flavors like vanilla, chai, eggnog, and chocolate (as well as plain). Dry-roasted soy nuts are fun to crunch and munch. And beautiful bright green edamame (soybeans) have a wonderful fresh taste and firm yet soft texture. Bags of these lima-bean

GO SOY NUTS FOR FIBER

Looking for an easy way to get your fiber? Just 1 cup of delicious dry-roasted soy nuts provides a whopping 14 grams of fiber. For a woman over age 51, that's two-thirds of her daily requirement!

look-alikes are usually sold near the organic, vegetarian, or Asian foods in the freezer section.

(Personal note to tofu haters: Give edamame and soy nuts a try. They're both really good and bear no resemblance whatsoever to tofu. Promise.)

SOY, OH BOY!

Soy foods have an excellent amount of omega-3s as well as monounsaturated and polyunsaturated fats. Additionally, soy foods have a significant amount of phytoestrogens, which help lower LDL levels.

Soy foods are also a great source of potassium and folate, both of which help lower, prevent, and reverse high blood pressure. And some soy products are a super source of fiber, which soaks up artery-clogging fats and slows the absorption of sugar in the bloodstream.

As far as the impact soy foods can have on cholesterol, and thus heart disease, the results are clear. A 1-month dietary intervention study investigated what effect replacing lean meat with a soy product (specifically, tofu) might have on risk factors associated with coronary heart disease.

The study participants were 43 healthy men ages 35 to 62. One group ate 150 grams of lean meat per day, while the other group ate 290 grams of tofu each day instead of meat. (The diets were otherwise the same.) The tofu group had significantly reduced total cholesterol, triglyceride, and LDL cholesterol levels, compared with the meat eaters.

Another 1-month study looked at soybean's effects on women's cholesterol levels. The study participants, 120 university students, consumed either 6.26 grams of soybean protein, including 50 milligrams of soy

THE LABEL CONTROVERSY

The FDA's rules covering health claims on food labels are appropriately strict. In 1999, it was only after an extensive review of the plethora of sound, scientific evidence that the FDA authorized that the association between soy protein and "the reduced risk of coronary heart disease (CHD)" can be used on food labels. In 2006, the American Heart Association issued a statement discounting this. Their position seems to be that soy is useful in the diet to replace foods with higher fat and cholesterol but that some of the earlier claims have not held up.

phytoestrogens in pill form, or a placebo pill (with zero soy content) every day for a month. The women who got the soy version saw a significant reduction [an average of 242 (+/–17) to 220 (+/–25)] in their total cholesterol during that time.

Need more proof? Consider the 2-month study that investigated the effect different amounts of soy protein might have on people with high cholesterol. The participants (63 men and 54 women) consumed 15 or 25 grams of soy protein or a placebo every day. The people who had the soy had significant drops in their LDL cholesterol levels (up to 5 percent), but the results were twice as good in those who took 25 grams as in those who consumed 15 grams. Meanwhile, those who got the placebo actually had an unhealthy 3.6 percent *increase* in LDL. The study authors conclude that including 25 grams of daily soy protein "may effectively reduce serum cholesterol levels and therefore is likely to diminish the risk for cardiovascular disease."

SOY RECIPES

- Barley Edamame Salad (page 119)
- Bulgur-Stuffed Roasted Peppers (page 169)
- Cherry Corn Muffins (page 90)
- Creamy Carrot Soup (page 96)
- Creamy "Egg" Salad (page 114)
- Edamame Pilaf (page 150)
- Fruit and Bran Muffins (page 87)
- Gingered Carrot Loaf (page 92)
- Green Tea–Oatmeal Pancakes (page 80)
- Lemon-Lime Pudding Cake (page 246)
- Mocha Coffee (page 236)
- Peach Melba Smoothie (page 94)
- Penne with Alfredo Sauce (page 181)
- Quick and Easy Rice Pudding (page 243)
- Raspberry Buckle (page 248)
- Rich Tomato Soup (page 98)
- Sesame-Seared Tofu (page 165)
- Soy Delicious Guacamole (page 265)
- Tofu and Bok Choy Stir-Fry (page 166)
- Tofu Citrus Salad (page 113)
- Tofu Mayonnaise (page 259)
- Updated Cheese Sauce (page 263)
- Vegetable Noodle Bowl (page 182)
- Zesty Succotash Salad (page 107)

HEART HEALTH BENEFITS

- Lowers "bad" LDL cholesterol
- Lowers triglycerides
- Raises "good" HDL cholesterol
- Lowers blood pressure
- Lowers homocysteine levels
- Inhibits blood clot formation
- Reduces plaque buildup
- Improves bloodflow
- Improves glycemic control
- Improves insulin sensitivity

SPINACH

Nothing quite compares to the delicate, mildly sweet, slightly salty taste of fresh, crisp, delightful spinach. Fresh spinach is not to be confused with the slimy canned stuff of yesteryear or spinach that's been boiled until it's black and bitter. If that's the spinach you've tried before, then for all intents and purposes, you've never tried spinach.

After you read the compelling list of all the heart healthy benefits spinach has to offer, you may just want to give it another try. And if you already love spinach, you'll be doubly pleased.

THE INCREDIBLY COMPELLING LIST

Raw spinach weighs in at only 7 calories per 1-cup serving, so this is definitely your go-to veggie for: beta-carotene, lutein, and zeaxanthin; vitamins A, C, and E; folate; fiber; potassium; phytosterols; betaine; and omega-3 essential fatty acids. Pretty impressive list for fewer than 10 calories, right? To be even more amazed, consider the following: An animal study investigated whether spinach leaves possess any anti-hypertension capabilities. After just 4 hours of feeding the hypertensive lab animals a simple extract of spinach, there were already observable beneficial effects on high blood pressure!

Another fascinating study investigated the satiety effects (feeling full and satisfied) that spinach might confer when eaten with a normal meal, including a protein source and other vegetables, compared with a spinachless meal. The study participants were 10 healthy men. The spinach was steamed in a micro-wave, and the test portions were 150 grams (5.3 ounces) and 250 grams (8.9 ounces), which contain 4.3 and 7.2 grams of dietary fiber, respectively.

The study indicated that eating 250 grams of spinach with meals not only substantially increases satiety, it also helps control blood sugar levels. This is important information, because failure to maintain normal blood sugar levels over time can lead to persistent hyperglycemia, which, left unchecked, can lead to diabetes, a major risk factor for heart disease. So adding spinach to some of your meals is a great way to help you feel satisfied *and* help keep your blood sugar in check.

POPEYE LORE . . . OFF BY A DECIMAL

Remember how all Popeye had to do to get the better of Bluto was pop open and gulp a can of spinach? Well, that particular cartoon magic probably came about because of some scientific misinformation dating back to the late 1800s.

A scientist named Dr. E. von Wolf wrote a paper in 1870 that included the iron content of spinach. Unfortunately, when the paper was published, a decimal point was misplaced, erroneously listing the iron content of spinach as 10 times more than it really was! While spinach is a fine source of iron (2.5 milligrams in 3½ ounces), we're betting it was Popeye's love of Olive Oyl that did the trick!

SPINACH RECIPES

- Arugula Tabbouleh (page 153)
- Baked Pasta and Spinach (page 171)
- Braised Lentils with Spinach (page 159)
- Bulgur-Stuffed Roasted Peppers (page 169)
- Greek-Inspired Pasta (page 177)
- Quinoa Florentine (page 148)
- Sautéed Mushrooms and Spinach (page 138)
- Spinach and Cannellini Beans (page 160)
- Spinach Linguine with Fresh Tomatoes and Pork (page 185)
- Spinach Salad with Warm Onion Dressing (page 112)
- Sweet-and-Sour Shrimp Soup (page 102)

HEART HEALTH BENEFITS

- Lowers "bad" LDL cholesterol
- Lowers triglycerides
- Raises "good" HDL cholesterol
- Lowers blood pressure
- Inhibits blood clot formation
- Reduces plaque buildup
- Improves bloodflow
- Improves glycemic control
- Improves insulin sensitivity

SQUASH, WINTER

Ranging in flavors from nutty and peppery to downright honey sweet, the members of the *Cucurbitaceae* family (often called winter squash) include pumpkins and butternut, acorn, spaghetti, hubbard, and turban squashes. Hardly newcomers in the culinary timeline, archeological evidence suggests that these fruits were already being cultivated in Central America between 8,000 and 10,000 years ago. And the Central Americans were very wise to cultivate them because squashes have an extraordinary amount of heart healthy benefits. For example, 1 cup of cooked pumpkin has a whopping 5,135 micrograms of beta-carotene and 245 percent of the DV of vitamin A.

IT'S THE GREAT PUMPKIN

Linus was right: Pumpkins and their fellow squashes are truly great! Let's start with the carotenoids, pigment-causing phytochemicals that have amazing cardio-protective, antioxidant capabilities. Squashes are jam-packed with alpha-carotene, beta-carotene, lutein, and zeaxanthin, which help prevent, reduce, and even reverse high blood pressure and atherosclerosis. The latest research findings suggest that carotenoids may be beneficial to blood sugar regulation, which has promising implications for people with diabetes.

There are five more heart healthy aspects to

SOME DELICIOUS SQUASH CHOICES

- **Acorn squash:** With forest-green skin with patches of yellow and shaped like an acorn (no surprise there), its orange/yellow flesh has a sweet, nutty, peppery flavor.
- **Butternut squash:** With orange skin and shaped like a giant pear, its deep orange flesh tastes similar to a sweet potato.
- **Spaghetti squash:** Ivory to yellow-orange and shaped like a football, its bright orange flesh falls away like strands of spaghetti when cooked; it's delightfully crunchy with a touch of sweetness.
- **Pumpkin:** Usually orange on the outside (although there are white, red, and gray varieties), these generally oblong or ovoid squash have yellow-orange flesh that ranges in texture and flavor from grainy and not sweet to succulently creamy and sugar sweet.

squashes: One, they're rich in omega-3 fatty acids. Two, they're a great source of the mineral (and electrolyte) potassium, which helps lower your blood pressure. Three, they're rich in folate, which lowers homocysteine levels that are linked with atherosclerosis. Four, they're practically overflowing with vitamin A and have a super amount of vitamin C, two powerful antioxidants that help improve cholesterol levels. And five, they're an excellent source of fiber.

WINTER SQUASH RECIPES

- Harvest Cookies (page 236)
- Penne with Roasted Autumn Vegetables (page 174)
- Pumpkin Pie in Nut Crust (page 277)
- Roasted Winter Vegetables (page 141)

HEART HEALTH BENEFITS

- Lowers "bad" LDL cholesterol
- Lowers triglycerides
- Raises "good" HDL cholesterol
- Lowers blood pressure
- Lowers homocysteine levels
- Reduces plaque buildup
- Improves bloodflow
- Improves glycemic control
- Improves insulin sensitivity

What could be more welcome on a hot summer's day than a tall glass of iced tea filled with clinking, crackling ice cubes—perhaps a fragrant, steaming cup of hot tea on a cold winter's morning? The truth is, no matter when you drink it or how you stir it, tea is one heart healthy beverage.

Teas are rich in incredibly heart healthy phytochemicals (especially flavonoids) including quercetin, kaempferol, myricetin, epicatechin, epigallocatechin gallate (EGCG), and rutin, among others. Tea also has trace amounts of folate, potassium, magnesium, and omega-3 fatty acids.

Instead of detailing what each of these individual components can do for your heart (which would take pages and pages), let's dive right into the research.

THE ROTTERDAM STUDIES

A large-scale study with a 5-year follow-up investigated the association of tea and flavonoid intake with incidents of myocardial infarction (heart attack) in the general Dutch population. The study participants included 1,836 men and 2,971 women, 55 years and older, with no history of heart attacks. Over the course of the study, 146 first myocardial infarctions occurred, and 30 were fatal. The regular tea drinkers were not only less likely to suffer heart attacks, they were significantly less likely to die from one.

A follow-up study investigated the association of tea and atherosclerosis. The participants included 1,323 men and 2,131 women, age 55 or older, who were free of cardiovascular disease when the study

---

ONE AND THE SAME—SORT OF

Black, green, white, and oolong teas all come from the same perennial evergreen, *Camellia sinensis*. Their differences are the result of how they're processed.

- **Black:** Allowed to first air-dry for an hour or so (which ferments them, making them turn brownish-black), the tea leaves are then rolled and dried (called getting fired, which happens in a hot wok or with hot air). This is the most strongly flavored of the four teas.
- **Green:** Briefly steamed shortly after harvesting, the leaves are rolled and fired. This tea has a fresh "leafy" and slightly acerbic taste.
- **Oolong:** Leaves are fermented about half as long as black tea before being rolled and fired. Not unexpectedly, this tea is milder than black tea and richer than green tea.
- **White:** This is made from young leaves and buds that are steamed or fired immediately to prevent fermentation, then rolled and dried. White tea is subtle, complex, and mildly sweet.

---

began. The people who drank an average of 4 cups of tea a day reduced their risk of severe atherosclerosis by an astonishing 70 percent! And even those who averaged only a cup or two a day lowered their risk by 46 percent. The study authors point out that the protective effect was especially strong in women.

MORE TEA RESEARCH

Another interesting study investigated tea drinking and its possible link with endothelial function and heart disease. Endothelia are the smooth cells that line the inner surface of your blood vessels, including your arteries and veins, as well as the lining of the heart. Staying smooth is essential for unobstructed bloodflow and thus heart health.

The participants were 66 patients with proven coronary artery disease. The researchers examined both short-term consumption (drinking either 450 milliliters, or almost 2 cups, of black tea or water, followed 2 hours later by a series of tests) and long-term (drinking 900 milliliters, or about 4 cups, of

tea or water daily for 4 weeks, then tested). The water drinkers had no measurable effects one way or the other. However, with both short-term and long-term tea drinking, endothelial dysfunction was reversed.

TEA RECIPE

- Green Tea–Oatmeal Pancakes (page 80)

HEART HEALTH BENEFITS

- Lowers "bad" LDL cholesterol
- Lowers triglycerides
- Raises "good" HDL cholesterol
- Lowers blood pressure
- Lowers homocysteine levels

- Inhibits blood clot formation
- Reduces plaque buildup
- Improves bloodflow
- Lowers blood sugar
- Improves glycemic control

Summertime vine-ripened heirloom tomatoes are a palate-pleasing, juicy, culinary delight! And heart health–wise, regularly incorporating tomatoes into your diet is one of the best choices you can make.

Tomatoes are loaded with the superpotent, red pigment–causing carotenoid called lycopene—on top of being rich in vitamins C and A. All of these antioxidants help lower bad cholesterol and, ultimately, the risk of heart disease. Tomatoes are also rich in potassium and folate, both of which help lower blood pressure. They are also a fine source of niacin (vitamin B$_3$), which studies have shown helps lower cholesterol levels, stabilize blood sugar levels, and metabolize fat. They're also a good source of fiber, and they have a nice amount of magnesium, which can significantly reduce your risk for heart disease. Plus, their phytosterols help block cholesterol from getting absorbed in your intestines. Bottom line: Any way you slice it, the tomato is an incredibly heart healthy food.

LYCOPENE: GOOD, BETTER, BEST

Lycopene is even more bioavailable (absorbed more efficiently into the body) after heating. Here are some examples of the different lycopene contents in tomatoes, measured in micrograms per gram of tomato product (wet weight).

Fresh tomatoes	8.8 to 42
Cooked tomatoes	37
Tomato sauce	62
Tomato soup (condensed)	80
Tomato juice	50 to 116
Pizza sauce	127
Ketchup	99 to 134
Tomato paste	54 to 1,500

TOMATO JUICE, BLOOD CLOTS, AND TYPE 2 DIABETES

People with type 2 diabetes are particularly vulnerable to developing blood clots and are at increased risk of atherosclerosis and heart disease. A study investigated whether drinking tomato juice could inhibit platelet aggregation (clumping together of blood cells) in people with type 2 diabetes. The study participants were 14 men and 6 women, ranging in age from 43 to 82, all with type 2 diabetes but no history of thrombosis (previous blood clots).

Half of the participants drank about 1 cup of tomato juice every day. The others drank a liquid that looked and tasted like tomato juice but in fact (and unbeknownst to them) was a placebo. After just 3 short weeks, those who drank the real thing showed significantly less clumping. The placebo did nothing. (When buying tomato juice, be sure to choose the low-sodium variety.)

TOMATOES AND HEART DISEASE

A study investigated what role carotenoid-rich vegetables might play in reducing LDL cholesterol levels in men. The study followed 23 healthy men, with

BEYOND RED, YELLOW, AND ROUND

Tomatoes (which, by the way, are fruits, not vegetables) come in practically every color of the rainbow, including red, pink, orange, yellow, green (even when fully ripe), purple, black, white, and even multicolor stripes! The yellow ones tend to be sweetest and the red ones most acidic. They grow in a lot more shapes than round, too, including heart-shaped, ruffled, oblong, and flat with ribs.

no history of heart disease, over the course of four 2-week periods. The first 2 weeks were a washout period, during which no carotenoid-rich foods were eaten. The second 2 weeks, the men consumed 330 milliliters, or about 1¾ cups, of tomato juice (with 40 milligrams lycopene). The third 2 weeks, they had the same amount of carrot juice. And the final 2 weeks, they had 10 grams of spinach powder.

The results? Tomato juice was the only carotenoid-rich food to reduce bad cholesterol levels. However, men, it seems, aren't the only ones to benefit from the humble tomato.

A large-scale study investigated what role dietary lycopene might play in relation to heart disease in women. The study participants were 39,876 female health care professionals, ranging in age from 46 to 61, all free of heart disease at the start. The 7.2-year follow-up found that there were 719 total coronary events, including 201 heart attacks and 247 strokes.

The results: The women who ate seven to 10 servings of lycopene-rich tomato foods a week had a 29 percent lower risk of heart disease. Further, those who ate two or more servings of tomato-based foods a week prepared with oil (such as tomato sauce and pizza) had a 34 percent lower risk. The major contributors of lycopene eaten by the participants were tomato sauce (40.5 percent), tomatoes (39.8 percent), tomato juice (12.3 percent), and pizza (4.7 percent).

Cooking tomatoes increases the bioavailability of lycopene, particularly when you use olive oil, as suggested in the above study. In fact, there may be a synergistic component to cooking tomatoes with olive oil. For example, a study compared cooking tomatoes with and without olive oil. While both methods increase lycopene bioavailability, the tomatoes cooked in olive oil resulted in an increase of 82 percent lycopene plasma concentrations in the study participants.

THE INFAMOUS "WOLF PEACH"

What's in a name? You decide: The scientific name for tomato is *Lycopersicon esculentum* from the Greek words *lykos* ("wolf") and *persicon* ("peach"). Why such a perilous sounding name? Because people used to believe that tomatoes were deadly. Boy, were they wrong.

TOMATO RECIPES

- Arugula Tabbouleh (page 153)
- Baked Pasta and Spinach (page 171)
- Barley Edamame Salad (page 119)
- Basic Tomato Sauce (page 266)
- Better-for-You Black Bean Chili (page 163)
- Chicken and Eggplant Pasta Salad (page 130)
- Chicken Ragout (page 205)
- Chicken-Zucchini Pasta Toss (page 212)
- Corn Salsa (page 265)
- Curry Chicken and Rice Salad (page 127)
- Eggplant Lasagna (page 167)
- Escarole and Bean Soup (page 100)
- Greek-Inspired Pasta (page 177)
- Healthy Chef's Salad (page 126)
- Mediterranean Pasta with Shrimp (page 184)
- Paella (page 189)
- Quick Arugula and Shrimp Salad (page 126)
- Rich Tomato Soup (page 98)
- Scallops Fra Diavolo (page 190)
- Slow-Cooked Chili Con Carne (page 280)
- Souped-Up Sloppy Joes (page 225)
- Soy Delicious Guacamole (page 265)
- Spaghetti with Puttanesca Sauce (page 179)
- Spiced Salmon Tacos (page 192)
- Spicy Fajitas (page 222)
- Spinach Linguine with Fresh Tomatoes and Pork (page 185)
- Tomato-Basil Vinaigrette (page 260)
- Tortellini Salad (page 118)
- Turkey Cutlets with Avocado Salsa (page 214)
- Turkey Picadillo (page 217)
- Zesty Clam Chowder (page 103)

HEART HEALTH BENEFITS

- Lowers "bad" LDL cholesterol
- Lowers triglycerides
- Raises "good" HDL cholesterol
- Lowers blood pressure
- Lowers homocysteine levels
- Inhibits blood clot formation
- Reduces plaque buildup
- Improves bloodflow
- Lowers blood sugar
- Improves glycemic control

TROPICAL FRUITS

Once so exotic and rare that they could only be found in gourmet and specialty stores, tropical fruits are now readily available in markets all across the country. From the delectably sweet and juicy, silken-fleshed mango to the luscious, sweet-tart, buttery papaya to the sweet, musky guava and the exceedingly juicy pineapple, tropical fruits offer a world of heart healthy benefits!

Mangos, papayas, guavas, and pineapples are all jam-packed with powerful antioxidants, such as vitamins A and C, as well as beta-carotene and lycopene, super carotenoids that can appreciably reduce the risk for heart disease and heart attack. Tropical fruits also provide healthy doses of fiber (both soluble and insoluble), potassium, and the important B vitamins folate and pyridoxine. Bromelain, an enzyme found only in pineapple, can inhibit the clumping of blood cells and thrombosis (blood clots).

LOADED WITH C!

So just how much vitamin C do you get when you dig into juicy tropical fruits? A lot! For every cup of chopped fruit, you get:

- Mango: 45.7 milligrams
- Papaya: 86.5 milligrams
- Pineapple: 87.4 milligrams
- Guava: a whopping 377 milligrams

TROPICAL FRUITS PACK A HEART HEALTHY PUNCH

Regarding the benefits lycopene confers, a large-scale, long-term, case-controlled study involving 10 European countries investigated various antioxidants and the risk of sudden heart attack. The results revealed that regularly eating lycopene-rich foods does indeed help protect against heart attacks.

TROPICAL FRUIT RECIPES

- Grilled Shrimp with Mango Salsa (page 195)
- Tropical Phyllo Cups (page 253)
- Tropical Fruit Pops (page 240)

HEART HEALTH BENEFITS

- Lowers "bad" LDL cholesterol
- Lowers triglycerides
- Raises "good" HDL cholesterol
- Lowers blood pressure
- Lowers homocysteine levels
- Inhibits blood clot formation
- Reduces plaque buildup
- Improves bloodflow
- Lowers blood sugar
- Improves glycemic control

WHOLE GRAINS

Four of the most perfectly wonderful "comfort foods" on the planet are wheat, barley, brown rice, and buckwheat. While they're all called whole grains in the culinary world, as well as by the government, technically speaking, the latter two aren't grains at all. Brown rice is actually a grass, and buckwheat is a fruit seed that's related to rhubarb. Nevertheless, their heart healthy benefits are incredible.

Studies have shown that eating a diet rich in whole grains can appreciably help lower blood pressure; lower LDL and increase HDL cholesterol levels; improve glycemic control, insulin sensitivity, and homocysteine levels; and significantly reduce your risk of developing atherosclerosis, having a heart attack, and dying from heart disease.

THE WHOLE TRUTH . . .

The Dietary Guidelines for Americans, published jointly every 5 years (by law) since 1980 by the USDA and the Department of Health and Human Services, provides "science-based advice to promote health and reduce risk for major chronic diseases through diet and physical activity." Now, for the first time, they've made the following specific recommendations concerning whole grains and health: "Consume 3 or more ounce-equivalents of whole-grain products per day, with the rest of the recommended grains coming from enriched or whole-grain products. In general, at least half the grains should come from whole grains." Of note, it is also required that "foods that bear the whole-grain health claim [must] 1) contain 51% or more whole grain ingredients by weight and 2) be low in fat."

But buyer beware! A lot of wheat and grain products out there aren't what they say they are.

1. The words *whole* or *whole grain* on a food label do not necessarily indicate how much whole grain is in the product. Sometimes the amount is so tiny, it's unconscionable. So how can you be sure you're getting what you think you are? Check if the "whole grain" touted on the label is the very first listed ingredient. If it's not, choose something else.
2. Just because a label says "100 percent wheat" or "multigrain" or "stoneground" does not mean it came from whole grains. *Caveat emptor*—buyer beware.

Why do these labels matter for people with heart disease? According to the FDA, clinical studies have shown that you can reduce your cholesterol levels an incredible 0.5 percent to 2 percent for every gram of soluble fiber eaten per day. Wheat, barley, brown

---

FIBER COUNTS

The fiber from whole grains quickly adds up. For every 1 cup cooked, you get:

Barley	6 grams
Wheat (farina)	5.3 grams
Buckwheat	4.5 grams
Brown rice	3.5 grams

If you're sensitive to gluten, know that buckwheat is gluten free (despite the word *wheat* in its name). Unroasted buckwheat has a lovely soft flavor and texture, while roasted buckwheat (often called kasha) has a nutty, earthy flavor. And, of course, brown rice is gluten free, too.

rice, and buckwheat are all terrific sources of both soluble and insoluble fiber.

As you'll recall, soluble fiber soaks up artery-clogging LDL cholesterol and does a great job of helping you maintain steadier blood sugar levels. Insoluble fiber paves the way to regular and easy elimination.

These labels could also matter if you're concerned about diabetes because whole grains provide magnesium. A large-scale study with a 30-year follow-up investigated calcium, magnesium, and major food sources and the risk of type 2 diabetes in US black women. The 41,186 participants ranged in age from 21 to 69 and had no history of heart attack, heart disease, diabetes, stroke, or cancer at the beginning. Over the course of the study, 1,964 new cases of diabetes were documented. A diet high in magnesium-rich foods, particularly whole grains, was associated with a 31 percent lower risk of developing type 2 diabetes.

And if you're wondering which grain is best, it may interest you to know about a study that examined whether grains with a greater percentage of insoluble fiber (brown rice and whole wheat) or soluble fiber (barley) would confer better cardiovascular benefits, such as lower blood pressure. The study participants were 18 men ages 28 to 62 with moderately elevated total plasma cholesterol levels (hypercholesterolemia).

The men ate different combinations of the three grains for 5 weeks each, with evaluative tests taken throughout. The participants' blood pressure was "significantly reduced by whole grain diets whether the fiber source was predominantly soluble (barley) or insoluble (brown rice and whole wheat)," according to the authors. In other words, all three grains did a terrific job of lowering blood pressure.

FDA RULING OF 2006: BARLEY MAKES THE GRADE!

Authorized health claims on food product labels by the FDA are few and far between. The scientific evidence has to be superb. Barley received its official heart healthy authorization ruling in 2006. According to the FDA: Whole grain barley and dry-milled barley products such as flakes, grits, flour, and pearled barley that contain at least 0.75 gram soluble fiber per ½-cup serving as part of a diet low in saturated fat and cholesterol may reduce the risk of heart disease.

WHOLE GRAIN RECIPES

- Barley Edamame Salad (page 119)
- Beef and Asparagus Stir-Fry (page 224)
- Best Burgers (page 273)
- Black Beans and Rice (page 155)
- Broccoli and Cheese Strata (page 77)
- Broccoli-Barley Pilaf (page 154)
- Brown Rice with Greens and Feta (page 151)
- Chicken and Eggplant Pasta Salad (page 130)
- Chicken Zucchini Pasta Toss (page 212)
- Chocolate Almond Scones (page 84)
- Curried Couscous (page 149)
- Curry Chicken and Rice Salad (page 127)
- Edamame Pilaf (page 150)
- French Toast with Orange Cream (page 82)
- Fruit and Bran Muffins (page 87)
- Fruit 'n' Nut Coffee Cake (page 249)
- Gingered Carrot Loaf (page 92)
- Greek-Inspired Pasta (page 177)
- Happy Heart Primavera (page 175)
- Harvest Cookies (page 236)
- Herbed Bread Dressing (page 276)
- Orange-Ginger Pork Chops (page 227)
- Peach-Blueberry Shortcakes (page 224)
- Peanut Noodle Salad (page 116)
- Penne with Alfredo Sauce (page 181)
- Penne with Roasted Autumn Vegetables (page 174)
- Peppered Couscous (page 149)
- Quick and Easy Rice Pudding (page 243)
- Quick Chicken Noodle Soup (page 104)
- Raspberry Buckle (page 248)
- Salmon Cakes (page 199)
- Soba Noodle Salad (page 117)
- Souped-Up Sloppy Joes (page 225)
- Spicy Fajitas (page 222)
- Sweet-and-Sour Shrimp Soup (page 102)
- Tuna Tetrazzini (page 197)
- Turkey Burgers (page 216)

HEART HEALTH BENEFITS

- Lowers "bad" LDL cholesterol
- Raises "good" HDL cholesterol
- Lowers blood pressure
- Lowers homocysteine levels
- Inhibits blood clot formation
- Reduces plaque buildup
- Improves bloodflow
- Improves glycemic control
- Improves insulin sensitivity

WINE, RED

As you gracefully pour the fruit of the vine into a glass, you marvel at the lovely claret color. Then, as you gently swirl the wine to appreciate its sumptuous body, the first notes of fruit, oak, and perhaps a hint of chocolate fill your nose with anticipation. Finally, you take that first sip. . . . Ahhh, you truly understand that "wine that maketh glad the heart of man." (Ps. 104:15)

How marvelous to know that wine, in moderation, can actually be good for your heart.

Studies have found that people who drink one to two glasses of wine a day (and particularly those people who drink it with a meal) have a lower incidence of heart disease. Wine consumption has been shown to inhibit the formation of blood clots, lower blood pressure, lower LDL cholesterol (and help prevent the artery damage it causes), and elevate HDL cholesterol.

One popular catchphrase associated with this is the French paradox, first noted in 1819 in scholarly papers by Irish physician Samuel Black. He observed that the French had a relatively low incidence of heart disease, despite a diet high in saturated fats. This unexpected finding was brought to light again in the early 1990s, and nutritionists and heart experts have been studying it ever since. Indeed, they found that, compared with the typical American diet, the French eat almost three times more pork, four times more butter, and 60 percent more cheese (according to the Food and Agriculture Organization of the United Nations). But surprisingly, the rate of death from heart disease for the French was 83 per 100,000, compared with 230 per 100,000 in the United States. The high red wine intake of the French is believed to be a major factor behind neutralizing the deleterious effects of a diet rich in animal sources.

ANOTHER PARADOX

Studies show that women may experience heart healthy benefits by drinking one glass of wine a day (two for men). But studies also show that drinking more than that can actually increase blood pressure, increase "bad" cholesterol levels, and even cause heart failure.

So go ahead and enjoy a glass or two of nice wine with dinner—and then cork the bottle.

What Constitutes One Glass or Drink?

- 5 ounces of wine
- 12 ounces of beer
- 1½ ounces of 80-proof distilled spirits

WINE AND HEART DISEASE

It's thought that much of the heart health association of red wine and coronary heart disease has to do with wine's high phytochemical content, particularly the protective flavonoids quercetin and resveratrol.

A study investigated the effects of resveratrol and red wine on blood clot formation in healthy men and rabbits with high cholesterol. Given to both man and rabbit in concentrated forms, resveratrol consumption was significantly associated with reduced clotting. The authors suggest that resveratrol could be one of the "mechanisms" by which the red wine exerts its cardio-protective effects.

More research from a large-scale study, with a 10- to 12-year follow-up, investigated the association between different types of alcoholic drinks and mortality. The participants included 6,051 men and 7,234 women, ranging in age from 30 to 70. Over the course of the study, 765 men and 354 women died of cardiovascular or cerebrovascular disease.

The authors reported that those participants who drank a light or moderate amount of wine experienced a "significantly lower all-cause mortality than the subjects who drank no wine"—which means that during the study, wine drinkers experienced fewer deaths in general. Thus, the light/moderate wine drinkers were also significantly less likely to die from cardiovascular or cerebrovascular disease. Of note, this study found that drinking spirits *increased* the risk of all-cause mortality, and beer had no effect one way or the other.

However, it is important to remember that no one single food or beverage is a cure-all. Rather, it's your food choices and lifestyle changes that hold the real magic to heart health. For example, a huge study involving 48,763 Danish men and women found that people who drink a glass or two of wine on a daily

IF WINE ISN'T YOUR THING

Scientific studies have documented that grapes and grape juice are just as cardio-protective as red wine. A recent study comparing the cardio-protective abilities of the flesh versus the skin concluded that "the flesh of grapes [is] equally cardio-protective as skin, and antioxidant potential of skin and flesh of grapes are comparable with each other despite the fact that flesh does not possess any anthocyanin activities."

basis are also more likely to have a higher intake of "fruit, fish, cooked vegetables, salad [and to use] olive oil for cooking." While that certainly doesn't negate the specific heart health benefits of wine, keep in mind that many factors influence heart health, and neither wine, beer, nor spirits should in any way be considered a treatment for heart disease.

Of particular note, a published report of the AHA discusses research suggesting that a moderate intake of one to two alcoholic beverages per day "is associated with a reduced risk of CHD [coronary heart disease] in populations." However, in the same report, the AHA also cautions against considering alcohol (specifically wine) as a "cardio-protective strategy" and recommends that "alcohol use should be an item of discussion between physician and patient."

RED WINE RECIPES

- Balsamic-Rosemary Pork Kebabs (page 230)
- Basic Tomato Sauce (page 266)
- Beef and Vegetable Stroganoff (page 223)
- Beef Tenderloin with Cranberry Port Sauce (page 221)
- Chicken Ragout (page 205)
- Flourless Chocolate Cake (page 251)
- Frozen Yogurt with Fruit Wine Sauce (page 274)
- Makeover Veal Marsala (page 226)
- Sautéed Mushrooms and Spinach (page 138)
- Scallops Fra Diavolo (page 190)
- Spaghetti with Puttanesca Sauce (page 179)
- Summer Fruit Compote (page 257)

HEART HEALTH BENEFITS

- Lowers "bad" LDL cholesterol
- Raises "good" HDL cholesterol
- Lowers blood pressure
- Inhibits blood clot formation
- Reduces plaque buildup
- Reduces all-cause mortality

YOGURT

From the Turkish word *yoghurmak* (which means "to thicken"), yogurt is one of the best "feels like you're being bad" good-for-you foods! With its rich, thick, creamy texture and variety of fabulous flavors like chocolate, strawberry-kiwi, banana, and apple cinnamon (not to undermine the tart, refreshing zing of plain yogurt), it's amazing that it's also super heart healthy. No wonder the ancient people of Assyria called yogurt *lebeny,* which is the Assyrian word for "life."

In just 1 cup (8 ounces) of low-fat plain yogurt, you get 16 percent of the DV of potassium, which helps lower blood pressure, reduces the formation of blood clots and artery-clogging plaque, and lowers the risk of aneurysms. Yogurt also has a decent amount of folate, which helps control high blood pressure, ease bloodflow, relax blood vessels, and lower homocysteine levels. Plus, there are trace amounts of vitamins A and C and omega-3 and omega-6 essential fatty acids (hey, every little bit helps)—and, of course, a ton of calcium.

That's all well and good, but what makes yogurt a standout is . . . well, scientists aren't exactly sure what specific components are responsible for the exceptional health benefits of yogurt. It appears, however, to have a lot to do with the live active cultures—

notably, *Lactobacillus acidophilus* (*L. acidophilus*). What we do know for sure is that evidence-based scientific studies prove that yogurt is incredibly heart healthy.

YOGURT REDUCES RISK FOR HEART DISEASE

A study investigated whether a daily serving of yogurt with *L. acidophilus* would reduce serum lipids (cholesterol levels). The study included 27 men and 42 women with high cholesterol, ranging in age from 51 to 58. Conducted in two 4-week phases, the study participants ate 200 grams (just under 1 cup) of yogurt a day, either with or without the live cultures.

The participants who ate the *L. acidophilus* yogurt had a 2 to 3 percent reduction in their serum cholesterol levels! As discussed by the study authors, these results are clinically meaningful because every "1 percent reduction in serum cholesterol concentrations leads to a 2 to 3 percent reduction in estimated risk for coronary heart disease." Thus, regularly eating yogurt with *L. acidophilus* "could decrease estimated risk for coronary heart disease by 4 to 9 percent."

THE "TOTALLY WOW" YOGURT AND WEIGHT LOSS STUDY

First, some background: A large body of scientific evidence strongly suggests that not just body fat but, more important, body fat *location* plays a significant role in the development and severity of several types of heart disease, including atherosclerosis and myocardial hypertrophy (an enlarged overworked heart). Technically called intra-abdominal fat and referred to as waist circumference or WHR (waist-hip ratio), belly fat is the crux of the problem. Additionally, being overweight or obese increases the risk for heart disease as well as diabetes (which is also a risk for heart disease).

Now onto the study, which looked at how yogurt might affect fat loss in obese people: For 12 weeks,

CULTURE CLUB

Be sure the yogurt you buy contains live (sometimes called live active) cultures. Much of the scientific literature indicates that the heart health benefits (as well as other benefits, such as fortifying your immune response and improving bone density) only make a significant impact when the yogurt has active cultures.

Fortunately, the FDA labeling requirements are very specific. Here's what the different statements actually mean.

1. "Heat-treated after culturing." Some manufacturers heat cultured yogurt to increase shelf life. However, this process also kills living cultures. Steer clear.

2. "Made with active cultures." All yogurts are made with active cultures. Only those that are not heat treated, however, retain them on the grocery shelves. So this doesn't give you any meaningful information.

3. "Contains active yogurt cultures." This yogurt has not been heat treated after culturing and therefore contains live yogurt cultures. This is the one to buy!

34 obese men and women followed a balanced-deficit diet (everyone ate 500 fewer calories a day than they normally would), with 18 participants including three servings of yogurt every day.

The yogurt eaters lost a whopping 61 percent more fat and maintained 31 percent more lean muscle mass than those on yogurt-free diets. Plus, those on the yogurt plan lost 81 percent more abdominal fat and had a greater reduction in waist circumference.

And, it seems, yogurt may have a positive effect on HDL cholesterol, too, according to results of a 6-month study. Participants included 14 women with high cholesterol and 15 with normal levels; both groups were free of CHD and diabetes. For the duration of the study, the women ate 300 grams (about 1¼ cups) a day of one of two types of yogurt, both made with live active cultures (*Streptococcus thermophilus, L. lactis,* and *L. acidophilus*). One was probiotic and the other wasn't.

Regardless of whether they had high cholesterol or not and regardless of which type of yogurt they ate, all the women had significant increases in HDL levels, "which lead to the desired improvement of the LDL/HDL ratio," according to the authors.

YOGURT RECIPES

- Berry Smoothie (page 94)
- Cherry Corn Muffins (page 90)
- Chocolate Angel Food Cake (page 252)
- Chocolate Berry Crepes (page 256)
- Coleslaw with Lemon Dressing (page 106)
- Cran-Raspberry Ice (page 256)
- Creamy Garlic Dressing (page 259)
- Creamy Potato Salad (page 274)
- Curried Chicken Salad (page 213)
- Flavorful Fruit Tart (page 254)
- Frozen Berry Pops (page 240)
- Frozen Yogurt with Fruit Wine Sauce (page 274)
- Fruit 'n' Nut Coffee Cake (page 249)
- Fruit with Creamy Chocolate Dip (page 234)
- Garlic Smashed Potatoes (page 144)
- Garlicky Hummus (page 266)
- Gingered Fruit Salad (page 93)
- Lemon Blueberry Muffins (page 89)
- Peach-Blueberry Shortcakes (page 244)
- Tandoori Chicken (page 202)

HEART HEALTH BENEFITS

- Lowers total cholesterol
- Raises "good" HDL cholesterol
- Lowers blood pressure
- Inhibits blood clot formation
- Reduces plaque buildup
- Enhances weight loss

175

Family-Pleasing,

Heart-Protecting

Recipes

CHAPTER 1

Good Mornings

Broccoli and Cheese Strata

A strata, an eggy breakfast casserole, is great for entertaining. Prepare it the night before, keep it covered and chilled, then simply pop it into the oven for breakfast or brunch. You may vary this recipe by changing the vegetables and type of cheese.

8 egg whites

4 eggs

1½ cups reduced-fat milk

¼ teaspoon salt

♥ ¼ teaspoon ground red pepper

♥ 6 slices whole grain bread

♥ 1 package (10 ounces) frozen chopped broccoli, thawed, drained, and squeezed dry

1½ cups (6 ounces) shredded low-fat sharp Cheddar cheese

1. Preheat the oven to 425°F. Coat a 13" × 9" × 2" baking dish with cooking spray.

2. In a large bowl, whisk together the egg whites, eggs, milk, salt, and pepper. Place the bread and broccoli in the prepared dish. Pour the egg mixture over the bread. Sprinkle with the cheese. Cover with foil. Let sit for 10 minutes. (If preparing ahead of time, refrigerate for up to 10 hours and remove from the refrigerator 30 minutes before baking.)

3. Bake for 10 minutes. Uncover and bake 15 minutes longer, or until the eggs are set and the top is lightly browned. Let stand 10 minutes before serving.

Serves 8

♥ **Heart healthy ingredients: 3**

Per serving: 168 calories, 49 calories from fat, 5 g total fat, 2 g saturated fat, 2 g monounsaturated fat, 1 g polyunsaturated fat, 1 mg cholesterol, 382 mg sodium, 15 g carbohydrates, 5 g fiber, 4 g sugar, 16 g protein

Asparagus Frittata

Lower-fat Canadian bacon is a great way to add some smoky meat flavor to this open-faced omelet—without all the fat and cholesterol of bacon or ham.

- ♥ 2 tablespoons extra-virgin olive oil
- ♥ 2 shallots, finely chopped
- 2 ounces Canadian bacon, cut into thin strips
- ♥ 1 pound asparagus, trimmed and cut into 1" pieces
- ♥ 1 clove garlic, minced
- ¼ teaspoon salt
- ¼ teaspoon ground black pepper
- 1½ cups egg substitute
- 1 cup shredded low-fat Jarlsberg cheese

1. Preheat the broiler.

2. Heat the oil in a large nonstick skillet over medium-high heat. Add the shallots, bacon, and asparagus and cook, stirring occasionally, for 10 minutes, or until the asparagus is tender-crisp. Add the garlic, salt, and pepper and cook for another minute. Stir in the egg substitute and ¾ cup of the cheese. Cook, without stirring, for 5 minutes longer, or until the bottom is lightly browned.

3. If your skillet is not heatproof, wrap the handle with foil. Sprinkle the remaining ¼ cup cheese over the frittata. Broil 6" from the heat for 5 minutes, or until the cheese melts and the frittata is set.

Serves 6

♥ **Heart healthy ingredients: 4**

Per serving: 161 calories, 71 calories from fat, 8 g total fat, 2 g saturated fat, 4 g monounsaturated fat, 2 g polyunsaturated fat, 10 mg cholesterol, 347 mg sodium, 7 g carbohydrates, 2 g fiber, 3 g sugar, 16 g protein

GETTING INTO THE THICK OF IT

If pencil-thin asparagus isn't available or you prefer it thick, go ahead and buy the larger spears (they're delicious grilled). Just snap off the woody ends and use a potato peeler to remove the tough outer layer and reveal the tender insides. (Not to worry; nearly all of the heart healthy benefits are stored inside.)

Green Tea–Oatmeal Pancakes

This makes a big batch of pancakes, which may be more than you'll need. But prepare the whole recipe anyway and freeze leftovers for a delicious breakfast in a hurry. Simply remove from the freezer and pop into the toaster. Top with fresh fruit and yogurt, and in minutes you've got a healthful way to start the day.

♥ 1½ cups vanilla soy milk

♥ 2 flavored green tea bags, such as pomegranate or acai berry

♥ 2 cups old-fashioned rolled oats

1 cup buttermilk

♥ 1 tablespoon light olive oil

2 eggs

♥ ½ cup whole wheat pastry flour

1 teaspoon baking powder

1 teaspoon baking soda

¼ teaspoon salt

1. Bring the milk to a simmer in a small saucepan over medium heat. Remove from the heat, add the tea bags, and steep for 3 minutes. Discard the tea bags. Cool the milk to room temperature. Stir in the oats and let stand for 15 minutes.

2. In a large bowl, whisk together the buttermilk, oil, and eggs until well blended. Stir in the milk mixture. Add the flour, baking powder, baking soda, and salt. Stir until well blended.

3. Coat a large nonstick griddle or nonstick skillet with cooking spray and place over medium-high heat. Drop the batter by scant ¼ cups onto the griddle and cook for 3 minutes, or until bubbles appear on the top. Turn and cook for 3 minutes longer, or until lightly browned.

Serves 6
♥ **Heart healthy ingredients: 5**

Per serving: 250 calories, 66 calories from fat, 7 g total fat, 2 g saturated fat, 3 g monounsaturated fat, 1 g polyunsaturated fat, 74 mg cholesterol, 478 mg sodium, 34 g carbohydrates, 4 g fiber, 7 g sugar, 11 g protein

French Toast with Orange Cream

Here's a great twist to ordinary French toast: a citrusy cream cheese topping. Use whole grain bread for the best flavor and most fiber. Fiber not only lowers "bad" LDL cholesterol, it also keeps blood sugar levels from spiking, which helps manage or prevent diabetes.

3 ounces reduced-fat cream cheese, softened

1 tablespoon confectioners' sugar

1 teaspoon grated orange peel

1½ teaspoons orange juice

1 egg

1 egg white

♥ ½ teaspoon ground nutmeg

♥ 6 slices whole grain bread

♥ 1 cup blueberries

1. In a medium bowl, whisk together the cream cheese, sugar, orange peel, and orange juice. Set aside.

2. Coat a large nonstick griddle or nonstick skillet with cooking spray. Heat the griddle to 375°F or the skillet over medium-high heat.

3. In a shallow dish or pie plate, whisk together the egg, egg white, and nutmeg. Dip the bread into the egg mixture, turning to coat. Place on the hot griddle or skillet, in batches if necessary, and cook, turning once, for 8 minutes, or until golden brown.

4. To serve, top each slice with some of the cream cheese mixture and sprinkle with some of the blueberries.

Serves 6

♥ **Heart healthy ingredients: 3**

Per serving: 128 calories, 36 calories from fat, 4 g total fat, 2 g saturated fat, 1 g monounsaturated fat, 0 g polyunsaturated fat, 43 mg cholesterol, 143 mg sodium, 20 g carbohydrates, 6 g fiber, 5 g sugar, 5 g protein

Fruited Granola

Many store-bought granolas are loaded with fat and sugar. This recipe is loaded instead with antioxidant-rich and fiber-packed fruit, whole grains, nuts, and seeds—a deliciously healthy way to start the day.

½ cup packed brown sugar

¼ cup orange juice concentrate

1 teaspoon ground cinnamon

2 cups old-fashioned rolled oats

⅓ cup sliced natural almonds

⅓ cup sunflower seeds

⅓ cup pepitas (green pumpkin seeds)

¼ cup ground flaxseed

1 cup dried fruit such as cranberries, blueberries, and/or cherries

1. Preheat the oven to 325°F. Coat a baking sheet with sides (jelly-roll pan) with cooking spray.

2. In a large bowl, stir together the sugar, orange juice concentrate, and cinnamon. Stir in the oats, almonds, sunflower seeds, pepitas, and flaxseed. Spread onto the prepared pan. Bake, turning occasionally, for 20 minutes, or until lightly browned.

3. Remove from the oven and cool completely. Place in an airtight container and stir in the dried fruit. Store at room temperature for up to 1 week or freeze for up to 2 months.

Makes about 4 cups (8 servings)

Heart healthy ingredients: 8

Per serving: 313 calories, 89 calories from fat, 10 g total fat, 1 g saturated fat, 3 g monounsaturated fat, 5 g polyunsaturated fat, 0 mg cholesterol, 10 mg sodium, 48 g carbohydrates, 7 g fiber, 25 g sugar, 9 g protein

MAKEOVER MAGIC

Although considered a "health food," granola is often tossed in oil before cooking, making it a high-fat, high-calorie choice. Tossed with fruit juice concentrate instead of oil, this granola is certainly a healthy breakfast.

	Traditional Granola	Fruited Granola
Calories	565	313
Fat (g)	34	10
Percent calories from fat	54	29

Chocolate Almond Scones

How lovely that chocolate is good for us! To really enjoy the health benefits of its flavonoids—which lower "bad" LDL cholesterol and raise "good" HDL cholesterol—go for chocolate with at least 60 percent cocoa.

♥ 2 cups whole wheat pastry flour

½ cup + 1 tablespoon sugar

2 teaspoons baking powder

½ teaspoon baking soda

¼ teaspoon salt

⅔ cup reduced-fat sour cream

♥ 3 tablespoons light olive oil

1 teaspoon pure vanilla extract

2 egg whites, divided

♥ 4 ounces bittersweet chocolate (60% cocoa or more), finely chopped

♥ ¼ cup toasted chopped almonds

1 teaspoon water

1. Preheat the oven to 325°F. Coat a large baking sheet with cooking spray.

2. In a large bowl, whisk together the flour, ½ cup of the sugar, the baking powder, baking soda, and salt. In a small bowl, whisk together the sour cream, oil, vanilla extract, and 1 of the egg whites. Add to the dry ingredients, stirring just until blended. Stir in the chocolate and almonds.

3. Turn the dough onto a lightly floured surface. With floured hands, knead lightly 8 times. The dough will be crumbly. Divide the dough in half and place each half on the prepared baking sheet. Pat each half into a 6" circle. Score each circle into 6 equal wedges.

4. Beat the remaining egg white with the water. Brush over the scones and sprinkle with the remaining 1 tablespoon sugar. Bake for 25 minutes, or until lightly browned and a wooden pick inserted in the centers comes out clean.

Makes 12

♥ **Heart healthy ingredients: 4**

Per serving: 204 calories, 92 calories from fat, 10 g total fat, 4 g saturated fat, 4 g monounsaturated fat, 1 g polyunsaturated fat, 5 mg cholesterol, 207 mg sodium, 27 g carbohydrates, 2 g fiber, 13 g sugar, 4 g protein

MAKEOVER MAGIC

Go ahead—enjoy these decadent breakfast treats. Eliminating the butter and switching to reduced-fat sour cream slashes the fat by almost 60 percent!

	Traditional Scone	Chocolate Almond Scone
Calories	282	204
Fat (g)	17	10
Percent calories from fat	54	44

Baked Oatmeal Pudding

"I attend cardiac rehab maintenance classes 3 days a week at our local hospital. One day my cardiac rehab nurse brought in this yummy oatmeal pudding to celebrate one of our classmates' 500th visit. We were all given the recipe to take home and add to our heart healthy collections. I revised it to make it even more heart healthy!"

LINDA O., SOLDOTNA, ALASKA

1 cup fat-free milk

2 eggs

2 tablespoons light olive oil

⅓ cup packed brown sugar

1 teaspoon ground cinnamon

1½ cups old-fashioned rolled oats

1¼ teaspoons baking powder

¼ teaspoon salt

¼ cup chopped nuts

¼ cup dried cranberries, cherries, or strawberries

1 firm ripe apple or pear, chopped

½ cup fresh or frozen blueberries

1. Preheat the oven to 325°F. Coat an 8" square baking pan with cooking spray.

2. In a large bowl, whisk together the milk, eggs, oil, sugar, and cinnamon. Stir in the oats, baking powder, salt, nuts, dried fruit, and apple or pear. Stir just until well blended.

3. Pour into the prepared pan. Bake for 25 minutes, or until the liquid is absorbed and the top is light golden brown. Spoon into bowls and top with the blueberries.

Serves 6

Heart healthy ingredients: 7

Per serving: 278 calories, 96 calories from fat, 11 g total fat, 2 g saturated fat, 4 g monounsaturated fat, 3 g polyunsaturated fat, 71 mg cholesterol, 257 mg sodium, 39 g carbohydrates, 4 g fiber, 22 g sugar, 8 g protein

Fruit and Bran Muffins

"I was tired of the same old bran muffins, so I decided to add fruit and nuts—and what better fruits than blueberries and cranberries, two of the top heart healthy super foods!"

ANN H., MACON, GEORGIA

♥ 1½ cups shredded bran cereal

♥ 1½ cups vanilla soy milk

½ cup packed brown sugar

♥ ¼ cup light olive oil

1 egg, beaten

♥ 1½ cups whole wheat flour

1 tablespoon baking powder

♥ ½ cup dried cranberries

♥ ½ cup dried blueberries

♥ ¼ cup almonds, toasted and chopped

¼ cup confectioners' sugar

1 teaspoon lemon juice

1. Preheat the oven to 400°F. Line 18 muffin pan cups with paper liners.

2. Place the cereal and milk in a large bowl and stir to combine. Stir in the brown sugar, oil, and egg. Add the flour and baking powder and stir just until blended. Stir in the cranberries, blueberries, and almonds.

3. Evenly divide the batter among the muffin cups. Bake for 18 minutes, or until a wooden pick inserted in the centers comes out clean. Remove to a rack and cool for 10 minutes.

4. In a small bowl, whisk together the confectioners' sugar and lemon juice. Drizzle on top of the muffins on the rack. Let cool completely.

Makes 18

♥ **Heart healthy ingredients: 7**

Per serving: 167 calories, 41 calories from fat, 5 g total fat, 1 g saturated fat, 3 g monounsaturated fat, 1 g polyunsaturated fat, 12 mg cholesterol, 137 mg sodium, 29 g carbohydrates, 4 g fiber, 15 g sugar, 3 g protein

BRAN NEW START

If you've written off bran-filled foods because they don't "agree" with you, try experimenting with other forms of bran. For example, many people find that rice bran is gentler on the system.

Bran is one of those foods that you really want to eat on a regular basis (unless you've been otherwise advised by your doctor). Just be sure you only introduce one new type of bran into your diet at a time, and keep a food log so that you can better determine which foods work best for you.

Lemon Blueberry Muffins

Muffins provide a great way to sneak some whole grain goodness into your meals. Here, wheat bran is tossed with the flour—but ground flaxseed would work just as well. Both add fiber and nutrients without altering the flavor of the muffins.

1¼ cups all-purpose flour

♥ 1 cup old-fashioned rolled or quick-cooking oats

½ cup packed brown sugar

♥ 2 tablespoons wheat bran

½ teaspoon baking soda

¼ teaspoon salt

♥ 1½ cups low-fat lemon yogurt

♥ 3 tablespoons light olive oil

1 egg

1 teaspoon grated lemon peel (optional)

♥ 1 cup fresh or frozen blueberries

1. Preheat the oven to 425°F. Coat a 12-cup muffin pan with cooking spray or fill with paper muffin liners.

2. In a large bowl, whisk together the flour, oats, sugar, bran, baking soda, and salt. Make a well in the center and add the yogurt, oil, egg, and lemon peel, if using. Stir just until blended. Stir in the blueberries. Evenly divide the batter among the muffin cups.

3. Bake for 18 minutes, or until a wooden pick inserted in the centers comes out clean. Cool in the pan for 10 minutes. Remove to a rack and cool completely.

Makes 12

♥ **Heart healthy ingredients: 5**

Per serving: 161 calories, 41 calories from fat, 5 g total fat, 1 g saturated fat, 3 g monounsaturated fat, 1 g polyunsaturated fat, 19 mg cholesterol, 129 mg sodium, 26 g carbohydrates, 1 g fiber, 12 g sugar, 5 g protein

Cherry Corn Muffins

Perfect for a grab-and-go breakfast, these muffins use yogurt to virtually eliminate fat while pumping up the protein. For a change of pace, substitute dried blueberries or cranberries for the cherries.

1 cup yellow cornmeal

1 cup all-purpose flour

♥ 2 tablespoons ground flaxseed

⅓ cup sugar

1 teaspoon baking powder

½ teaspoon baking soda

½ teaspoon salt

1 egg, lightly beaten

♥ 1 container (8 ounces) low-fat vanilla yogurt

♥ ½ cup vanilla or plain soy milk

♥ ½ cup dried cherries

1. Preheat the oven to 425°F. Coat a 12-cup muffin pan with cooking spray.

2. In a large bowl, whisk together the cornmeal, flour, flaxseed, sugar, baking powder, baking soda, and salt. Make a well in the center and add the egg, yogurt, milk, and cherries. Stir just until blended. Evenly divide the batter among the muffin cups.

3. Bake for 18 minutes, or until a wooden pick inserted in the centers comes out clean. Cool in the pan for 10 minutes. Remove to a rack and cool completely.

Makes 12

♥ **Heart healthy ingredients: 4**

Per serving: 146 calories, 12 calories from fat, 1 g total fat, 0 g saturated fat, 0 g monounsaturated fat, 0 g polyunsaturated fat, 19 mg cholesterol, 221 mg sodium, 30 g carbohydrates, 2 g fiber, 12 g sugar, 4 g protein

Cinnamon-Raisin Quick Bread

When adding whole wheat flour to bread recipes, it's often best to use half whole wheat and half all-purpose. This increases your heart healthy ingredients while keeping the bread from being too dense.

¾ cup buttermilk

½ cup packed brown sugar

🌱 2 tablespoons light olive oil

2 eggs

¾ cup all-purpose flour

🌱 ¾ cup whole wheat flour

1½ teaspoons baking soda

🌱 1 teaspoon ground cinnamon

¼ teaspoon salt

¾ cup raisins

🌱 ½ cup chopped walnuts

1. Preheat the oven to 350°F. Coat an 8" × 4" baking pan.

2. In a large measuring cup or small bowl, whisk together the buttermilk, sugar, oil, and eggs. In a large bowl, whisk together the all-purpose flour, whole wheat flour, baking soda, cinnamon, salt, raisins, and walnuts. Make a well in the center and add the buttermilk mixture, stirring just until blended.

3. Pour the batter into the prepared pan. Bake for 40 minutes, or until a wooden pick inserted in the center comes out clean. Cool in the pan for 10 minutes. Remove to a rack and cool completely.

Serves 12

🌱 **Heart healthy ingredients: 4**

Per serving: 192 calories, 61 calories from fat, 7 g total fat, 1 g saturated fat, 3 g monounsaturated fat, 3 g polyunsaturated fat, 36 mg cholesterol, 237 mg sodium, 29 g carbohydrates, 2 g fiber, 17 g sugar, 4 g protein

Gingered Carrot Loaf

Reminiscent of carrot cake, this quick bread is delicious as is—or try a slice toasted and spread with low-fat cream cheese or apricot preserves. The carrot alone is a rich source of beta-carotene and potassium, both of which can lower blood pressure.

- 1¾ cups whole wheat pastry flour
- ½ cup pecans, toasted and chopped
- 1 tablespoon crystallized ginger
- 1 teaspoon baking soda
- ¼ teaspoon baking powder
- ¼ teaspoon salt
- 1 cup shredded carrots
- ⅔ cup packed brown sugar
- ½ cup vanilla soy milk
- 3 tablespoons light olive oil
- 1 large egg

1. Preheat the oven to 350°F. Coat an 8" × 4" baking pan with cooking spray.

2. In a large bowl, whisk together the flour, pecans, ginger, baking soda, baking powder, and salt. In a large measuring cup or small bowl, combine the carrots, sugar, milk, oil, and egg. Make a well in the center of the flour mixture and add the milk mixture, stirring just until blended.

3. Pour the batter into the prepared pan. Bake for 1 hour, or until a wooden pick inserted in the center comes out clean. Cool in the pan for 10 minutes. Remove to a rack and cool completely.

Serves 12

Heart healthy ingredients: 6

Per serving: 192 calories, 70 calories from fat, 8 g total fat, 1 g saturated fat, 5 g monounsaturated fat, 2 g polyunsaturated fat, 18 mg cholesterol, 185 mg sodium, 28 g carbohydrates, 3 g fiber, 13 g sugar, 3 g protein

Gingered Fruit Salad

Crystallized ginger is also known as candied ginger, as that's just what it is: spicy fresh ginger cooked in a sugary syrup and then dried. Look for it in the spice section of your supermarket or in specialty or Asian markets.

½ honeydew melon, cut into 1" cubes

♥ 1 mango, halved, pitted, peeled, and chopped

♥ 2 kiwifruits, peeled and chopped

♥ 1 cup strawberries, stemmed and halved

♥ ½ cup orange juice

¼ cup chopped fresh mint

♥ 1½ teaspoons minced crystallized ginger

♥ 2 cups low-fat vanilla yogurt

1. In a large bowl, combine the melon, mango, kiwifruits, strawberries, orange juice, mint, and ginger. Toss to coat well.

2. Evenly divide the salad among 4 bowls and top each serving with ½ cup of the yogurt.

Serves 4

♥ **Heart healthy ingredients: 6**

Per serving: 235 calories, 21 calories from fat, 2 g total fat, 1 g saturated fat, 1 g monounsaturated fat, 0 g polyunsaturated fat, 6 mg cholesterol, 106 mg sodium, 50 g carbohydrates, 4 g fiber, 41 g sugar, 8 g protein

Berry Smoothie

This refreshing breakfast shake is bursting with berries, which are packed with antioxidants and fiber to help lower blood pressure and total cholesterol. In fact, a cup of blueberries a day may actually prevent heart disease. Frozen berries are just as nutritious as fresh, as long as they are dry packed and not bathed in sugary syrup.

♥ ½ cup frozen blueberries

♥ ½ cup frozen whole strawberries

♥ 1 small ripe banana, quartered

♥ 1 cup low-fat plain yogurt

2 tablespoons frozen lemonade concentrate

In a blender, combine the blueberries, strawberries, banana, yogurt, and lemonade concentrate. Blend until smooth.

Serves 2

♥ **Heart healthy ingredients: 4**

Per serving: 184 calories, 21 calories from fat, 2 g total fat, 1 g saturated fat, 1 g monounsaturated fat, 0 g polyunsaturated fat, 7 mg cholesterol, 87 mg sodium, 36 g carbohydrates, 3 g fiber, 28 g sugar, 8 g protein

Peach Melba Smoothie

Custardlike silken tofu blends perfectly in smoothies, especially this peachy one! Rich in isoflavonoids and protein, tofu also makes a great substitute for sour cream or yogurt in baking.

♥ ¾ cup frozen raspberries (not in syrup)

½ cup frozen peaches (not in syrup)

♥ 3 ounces reduced-fat silken soft tofu, drained

♥ ½ cup orange juice

2 tablespoons honey

In a blender, combine the raspberries, peaches, tofu, orange juice, and honey. Blend until smooth.

Serves 2

♥ **Heart healthy ingredients: 3**

Per serving: 149 calories, 8 calories from fat, 1 g total fat, 0 g saturated fat, 0 g monounsaturated fat, 0 g polyunsaturated fat, 0 mg cholesterol, 43 mg sodium, 34 g carbohydrates, 3 g fiber, 24 g sugar, 4 g protein

CHAPTER 2

Super Soups

Creamy Carrot Soup

The "cream" of this beta-carotene–rich soup comes from soy milk, a heart health powerhouse. Curry powder, a staple in Indian cooking, gives the soup a bit of an exotic flavor; the powder is a blend of spices, herbs, and seeds including turmeric, which gives the powder its yellow color. Turmeric is rich in antioxidants and may help lower cholesterol and prevent blood clots.

- 6 carrots, sliced
- 1 onion, chopped
- 1 clove garlic, minced
- 1 teaspoon curry powder
- ½ teaspoon ground ginger
- 2 cups fat-free, reduced-sodium vegetable or chicken broth
- 1½ cups low-fat plain soy milk

1. Coat a large saucepan with cooking spray. Add the carrots and onion and cook, stirring occasionally, for 5 minutes, or until tender. Add the garlic, curry powder, and ginger and cook, stirring frequently, for 1 minute longer.

2. Add the broth and bring to a boil. Reduce the heat to low, cover, and simmer for 20 minutes, or until the carrots are very tender. Remove from the heat and cool for 5 minutes. Pour into a food processor or blender and purée until very smooth.

3. Pour the soup back into the saucepan and add the milk. Heat over low heat for 3 minutes, or just until heated through.

Serves 4

♥ Heart healthy ingredients: 6

Per serving: 109 calories, 6 calories from fat, 1 g total fat, 0 g saturated fat, 0 g monounsaturated fat, 0 g polyunsaturated fat, 0 mg cholesterol, 321 mg sodium, 22 g carbohydrates, 5 g fiber, 12 g sugar, 4 g protein

CARROTS AND SUGAR: MYTH BUSTER

It's critically important to bust a widely held myth about carrots. Yes, their sugar content is rivaled only by that in beets. But eating carrots does not (repeat, does *not*) flood your bloodstream with a sudden sugar rush. On the contrary, the high fiber content actually prevents that unhealthy spike. So enjoy those wonderful carrots.

Rich Tomato Soup

Silken tofu gives this antioxidant-packed soup richness and body. Tofu is available in two basic types, regular and silken. Silken works best when you want a smooth, creamy texture, like with this soup. Use regular tofu when you want it to keep its shape, as in stir-frying. Each type is available in soft, firm, or extra-firm.

- 1 tablespoon extra-virgin olive oil
- 2 shallots, minced
- 4 large tomatoes, peeled, seeded, and chopped
- 1 clove garlic, minced
- 1 can (8 ounces) no-salt-added tomato sauce
- 1 package (12 ounces) light firm silken tofu, drained

1. Heat the oil in a medium saucepan over medium heat. Add the shallots and cook, stirring occasionally, for 3 minutes, or until lightly browned. Add the tomatoes and garlic and cook, stirring occasionally, for 4 minutes longer, or until softened. Stir in the tomato sauce and cook, stirring occasionally, for another 10 minutes, or until the vegetables are very tender. Remove from the heat.

2. Place the tofu in the food processor and pulse until smooth. Gradually add the tomato mixture and pulse until well blended. Return the soup to the pot to heat through over medium heat.

Serves 4

♥ Heart healthy ingredients: 6

Per serving: 148 calories, 44 calories from fat, 5 g total fat, 1 g saturated fat, 3 g monounsaturated fat, 1 g polyunsaturated fat, 0 mg cholesterol, 86 mg sodium, 19 g carbohydrates, 2 g fiber, 9 g sugar, 8 g protein

Spicy Red Lentil Soup

Packed with the antioxidants, protein, fiber, vitamins, and minerals of nine heart healthy foods, this rich, hearty soup becomes a meal when served with salad and dense 12-grain bread. It's a great defense against high cholesterol and blood pressure, diabetes, and heart disease.

❧ 1 tablespoon extra-virgin olive oil

❧ 2 carrots, chopped

❧ 1 onion, chopped

❧ 1 red bell pepper, chopped

1 rib celery, chopped

❧ 1 clove garlic, minced

❧ 1 cup dried red lentils

❧ 2 tablespoons reduced-sodium tomato paste

❧ ½ teaspoon ground cumin

❧ ¼ teaspoon ground red pepper

3 cups fat-free, reduced-sodium vegetable broth

2 cups water

1. Heat the oil in large saucepan over medium-high heat. Add the carrots, onion, bell pepper, celery, and garlic and cook, stirring frequently, for 3 minutes, or until lightly browned.

2. Stir in the lentils, tomato paste, cumin, ground red pepper, broth, and water. Bring to a boil over high heat. Reduce the heat to medium-low and simmer, stirring occasionally, for 30 minutes, or until the lentils are soft and the soup is thick.

3. Remove 1½ cups of the soup to a food processor or blender and purée until smooth. Return to the pot with the soup and stir well.

Serves 6

❧ **Heart healthy ingredients: 9**

Per serving: 189 calories, 33 calories from fat, 4 g total fat, 1 g saturated fat, 2 g monounsaturated fat, 0 g polyunsaturated fat, 0 mg cholesterol, 66 mg sodium, 28 g carbohydrates, 7 g fiber, 5 g sugar, 12 g protein

---

CHOICES, CHOICES, AND MORE CHOICES!

More and more grocery stores are carrying a nice variety of lentils beyond the traditional and nutritious plain brown lentil and the French green (Puy) lentil. If you're lucky enough to live near an Indian market, your selection will be even better. And all of the following lentils are available online.

- Channa dal: yellow, with a sweet, nutty, robust flavor and soft texture
- Masoor dal: orange, with a deep, earthy flavor and very soft texture
- Matki: greenish-brown, with a deep, rich, nutty taste and chewy texture
- Urad dal or black beluga: black, with a strong, rich, earthy flavor and soft texture
- Tuvar dal: yellow, with a sweet flavor and very soft texture; the most popular lentil in India, often described as having a gelatinous, meaty consistency

Escarole and Bean Soup

Beans and greens are a match made in heaven. If you forget to soak the beans overnight, here's a quick-soak method: Place the beans in a pot and cover with 2" water. Boil for 2 minutes, then remove from the heat, cover, and let stand for 1 hour. Drain and rinse before using.

♥ 2 tablespoons extra-virgin olive oil

♥ 2 large onions, chopped

2 ribs celery, chopped

♥ 4 cloves garlic, minced

♥ 2 cups dried white beans, soaked overnight, drained, and rinsed (or quick-soaked as described above)

6 cups water

♥ 2 cans (28 ounces each) crushed tomatoes in tomato puree

♥ ¼ cup tomato paste

¾ teaspoon ground black pepper

½ teaspoon salt

♥ 1 large bunch escarole (about 1½ pounds), trimmed and coarsely chopped

1. Heat the oil in a large saucepan over medium-high heat. Add the onions, celery, and garlic and cook, stirring frequently, for 5 minutes, or until lightly browned.

2. Add the beans and water and bring to a boil over high heat. Reduce the heat to medium-low, cover, and simmer, stirring occasionally, for 1½ hours, or until the beans are just tender.

3. Add the tomatoes, tomato paste, pepper, and salt. Bring to a boil over high heat. Reduce the heat to medium-low, cover, and simmer for 15 minutes. Add the escarole and cook, stirring occasionally, for 15 minutes, or until the escarole and beans are tender.

Serves 6

♥ **Heart healthy ingredients: 7**

Per serving: 348 calories, 51 calories from fat, 6 g total fat, 1 g saturated fat, 3 g monounsaturated fat, 1 g polyunsaturated fat, 0 mg cholesterol, 431 mg sodium, 59 g carbohydrates, 17 g fiber, 3 g sugar, 21 g protein

Broccoli Rabe and Chickpea Soup

Also known as broccoli raab or rapini, broccoli rabe is a classic Italian vegetable with a bold, peppery flavor and a touch of bitterness. When cooked in liquid, as in this soup, the bitterness dissipates.

- 1 small bunch broccoli rabe (about 1 pound)
- 2 tablespoons extra-virgin olive oil
- 2 large carrots, chopped
- 1 large onion, chopped
- 2 cloves garlic, minced
- ¼ teaspoon red-pepper flakes
- 5 cups fat-free, reduced-sodium vegetable broth
- 1 can (15 ounces) reduced-sodium garbanzo beans (chickpeas), rinsed and drained
- 4 tablespoons (1 ounce) grated Parmesan cheese

1. Remove and discard the tough ends from the broccoli rabe stems. Coarsely chop the broccoli rabe.

2. Heat the oil in a large saucepan over medium heat. Add the carrots and onion and cook for 5 minutes, stirring frequently. Add the broccoli rabe, garlic, and pepper and cook for another minute, stirring constantly. Add the broth and bring to a boil over medium-high heat. Reduce the heat to low, cover, and simmer for 15 minutes longer. Stir in the beans and cook for another 5 minutes, or until heated through.

3. To serve, evenly divide the soup among 4 bowls. Sprinkle each serving with 1 tablespoon of the cheese.

Serves 4

Heart healthy ingredients: 7

Per serving: 285 calories, 102 calories from fat, 12 g total fat, 2 g saturated fat, 7 g monounsaturated fat, 2 g polyunsaturated fat, 4 mg cholesterol, 318 mg sodium, 32 g carbohydrates, 6 g fiber, 10 g sugar, 18 g protein

ONION STORAGE TIPS

- Never store onions alongside potatoes. The onions will draw out the moisture from the potatoes, causing the onions to rot and the potatoes to dry out.

- Always store onions at room temperature and away from sunlight.

- Always store shallots in a cool, dry, well-ventilated place.

- Always store scallions in an unsealed plastic bag in the refrigerator.

Sweet-and-Sour Shrimp Soup

This substantial soup features heart healthy shiitake mushrooms and soba noodles. Soba is made from buckwheat, which gives the pasta a brown-specked color. These Japanese noodles can be 100 percent buckwheat or a blend of buckwheat and wheat or wild yam flour. If you can't find them, substitute whole wheat thin spaghetti.

- 1 package (8 ounces) soba (buckwheat) noodles, broken in half
- 2 tablespoons extra-virgin olive oil
- 6 scallions, sliced into 1" pieces
- 3 carrots, diagonally sliced
- 4 ounces shiitake mushrooms, stemmed and sliced
- 2 cloves garlic, minced
- 2 tablespoons minced fresh ginger
- 2 teaspoons ground coriander
- 1 teaspoon sugar
- 2 cups fat-free, reduced-sodium vegetable broth
- 1 tablespoon rice wine or white wine vinegar
- ½ pound medium peeled and deveined shrimp
- 1 bag (5 ounces) baby spinach

1. In a large saucepan, cook the noodles according to package directions. Drain, reserving 2 cups of the water. Wipe the pan dry.

2. Heat the oil in the same saucepan over medium heat. Add the scallions, carrots, and mushrooms and cook, stirring occasionally, for 5 minutes, or until lightly browned. Stir in the garlic, ginger, coriander, and sugar. Cook for 1 minute longer.

3. Add the broth, vinegar, and reserved noodle water. Bring to a boil. Add the shrimp, spinach, and noodles and cook for 2 minutes, or until the shrimp are opaque.

Serves 4

Heart healthy ingredients: 8

Per serving: 427 calories, 92 calories from fat, 11 g total fat, 1 g saturated fat, 5 g monounsaturated fat, 2 g polyunsaturated fat, 86 mg cholesterol, 281 mg sodium, 59 g carbohydrates, 6 g fiber, 10 g sugar, 25 g protein

Zesty Clam Chowder

Don't peel the potatoes for this chowder—or any dish. The most vitamin C in potatoes is found just under the skin, so it's discarded when they're peeled. Be sure to scrub them well to remove any grit.

- 2 tablespoons extra-virgin olive oil
- 2 large carrots, chopped
- 1 large onion, chopped
- 1 orange bell pepper, chopped
- 2 cloves garlic, minced
- 1 teaspoon dried thyme, crushed
- 2 cans (14½ ounces each) no-salt-added whole tomatoes, undrained
- 1 bottle (8 ounces) clam juice
- 1 cup water
- 2 medium russet potatoes, scrubbed and chopped
- 2 cans (6½ ounces each) whole clams, undrained

1. Heat the oil in a large saucepan over medium-high heat. Add the carrots, onion, and pepper and cook, stirring occasionally, for 5 minutes, or until lightly browned. Add the garlic and thyme and cook for 1 minute longer.

2. Add the tomatoes, clam juice, water, and potatoes, breaking up the tomatoes with a spoon. Bring to a boil. Reduce the heat to medium, cover, and simmer for 15 minutes, or until the potatoes are tender. Stir in the clams and cook for 2 minutes longer, or until heated through.

Serves 6

Heart healthy ingredients: 7

Per serving: 183 calories, 49 calories from fat, 6 g total fat, 1 g saturated fat, 3 g monounsaturated fat, 1 g polyunsaturated fat, 25 mg cholesterol, 375 mg sodium, 27 g carbohydrates, 3 g fiber, 8 g sugar, 9 g protein

Quick Chicken Noodle Soup

No need to open a can loaded with sodium when this delicious soup comes together in just 20 minutes. Serve with Apple and Jicama Slaw (page 108) and crusty whole grain bread for a satisfying meal in no time.

- ♥ 1 tablespoon extra-virgin olive oil

- 1 pound boneless, skinless chicken breasts, cut into 1" pieces

- ½ teaspoon Italian seasoning, crushed

- 3 cups fat-free, reduced-sodium chicken broth

- 3 cups water

- ♥ 1 cup whole grain rotini or corkscrew pasta

- ♥ 1 bag (16 ounces) frozen vegetable medley such as broccoli, onions, mushrooms, and peppers

1. Heat the oil in a large nonstick saucepan over medium-high heat. Add the chicken and seasoning and cook, stirring occasionally, for 5 minutes, or until browned. Add the broth and water and bring to a boil.

2. Add the pasta and vegetables and return to a simmer. Cook, stirring occasionally, for 9 minutes, or until the pasta and vegetables are tender.

Serves 4

♥ **Heart healthy ingredients: 3**

Per serving: 246 calories, 46 calories from fat, 5 g total fat, 1 g saturated fat, 3 g monounsaturated fat, 1 g polyunsaturated fat, 66 mg cholesterol, 455 mg sodium, 16 g carbohydrates, 4 g fiber, 3 g sugar, 31 g protein

CHAPTER 3

A Salad a Day

Zesty Succotash Salad

At the peak of the summer, use fresh corn kernels cut right off the ear. Of course, since fresh basil is usually available in most grocery stores throughout the year, this salad, which relies on many other frozen and canned ingredients, is also a great way to enjoy a taste of summer even in the dead of winter.

- 1 cup frozen edamame (green soybeans)

  1½ cups frozen corn kernels (or kernels cut from 2 fresh ears)

- 1 cup frozen baby lima beans
- 1 tablespoon extra-virgin olive oil
- 1 tablespoon flaxseed oil

  3 tablespoons red wine vinegar
- 1 clove garlic, minced

  ¼ cup chopped fresh basil
- 1 can (15 ounces) kidney beans, rinsed and drained
- 1 red onion, chopped

1. Place the edamame in a medium saucepan and cover with 2" water. Bring to a boil over medium-high heat. Cook for 2 minutes. Add the corn and lima beans and cook for 3 minutes longer, or until tender. Drain, rinse under cold water, and drain completely.

2. In a large serving bowl, whisk together the olive oil, flaxseed oil, vinegar, garlic, and basil. Stir in the drained vegetables, kidney beans, and onion.

Serves 4

Heart healthy ingredients: 7

Per serving: 197 calories, 56 calories from fat, 7 g total fat, 1 g saturated fat, 2 g monounsaturated fat, 2 g polyunsaturated fat, 0 mg cholesterol, 143 mg sodium, 27 g carbohydrates, 7 g fiber, 3 g sugar, 9 g protein

Coleslaw with Lemon Dressing

This salad comes together in minutes, thanks to preshredded coleslaw mix. Adding fresh chives and lemon enlivens the dish.

- ½ cup low-fat plain yogurt

  ½ teaspoon grated lemon peel

- 2 tablespoons fresh lemon juice

- 1 clove garlic, minced

  1 teaspoon sugar

- 1 bag (16 ounces) coleslaw mix

- 10 chives, cut into 1" pieces

In a large bowl, whisk together the yogurt, lemon peel, lemon juice, garlic, and sugar. Add the coleslaw mix and chives and toss to coat well.

Serves 4

Heart healthy ingredients: 5

Per serving: 58 calories, 7 calories from fat, 1 g total fat, 0 g saturated fat, 0 g monounsaturated fat, 0 g polyunsaturated fat, 2 mg cholesterol, 42 mg sodium, 11 g carbohydrates, 3 g fiber, 4 g sugar, 3 g protein

Apple and Jicama Slaw

Underused jicama is a large round root vegetable with a thin brown skin. Its white, crunchy flesh is refreshing in salads, adding a mild, sweet, nutty flavor. Got leftover jicama? Cut it into sticks for a great low-fat snack.

- 2 tablespoons extra-virgin olive oil

- 2 tablespoons lime juice

- ¼ teaspoon ground red pepper

  1 medium jicama (about 1½ pounds), peeled and julienned

- 1 apple, cored and julienned

- ½ medium onion, cut into thin strips

  ¼ cup chopped cilantro

In a large bowl, whisk together the oil, lime juice, and pepper. Add the jicama, apple, onion, and cilantro and toss to coat well.

Serves 4

Heart healthy ingredients: 5

Per serving: 162 calories, 62 calories from fat, 7 g total fat, 1 g saturated fat, 5 g monounsaturated fat, 1 g polyunsaturated fat, 0 mg cholesterol, 9 mg sodium, 25 g carbohydrates, 10 g fiber, 9 g sugar, 2 g protein

Grape and Fennel Salad

Peppery arugula forms a bed for a crunchy, colorful salad of red grapes and white fennel bulb. Fennel, sometimes referred to as sweet anise, is a pale green vegetable with a white bulbous base, long celery-like stalks, and feathery green fronds.

½ cup reduced-fat sour cream

🌱 1 tablespoon lemon juice

1 medium head fennel, trimmed, quartered, cored, and chopped

🌱 3 cups red grapes, halved

🌱 5 fresh chives, chopped

¼ teaspoon ground black pepper

🌱 1 bag (5 ounces) baby arugula

🌱 ¼ cup natural almonds, toasted and chopped

In a large bowl, combine the sour cream and lemon juice. Stir in the fennel, grapes, chives, and pepper. Arrange the arugula on a serving platter. Top with the fennel mixture and sprinkle with the almonds.

Serves 4

🌱 **Heart healthy ingredients: 5**

Per serving: 187 calories, 65 calories from fat, 7 g total fat, 3 g saturated fat, 3 g monounsaturated fat, 1 g polyunsaturated fat, 12 mg cholesterol, 55 mg sodium, 30 g carbohydrates, 4 g fiber, 20 g sugar, 5 g protein

---

Warm Kale Salad

Kale is a green, leafy vegetable related to broccoli and cauliflower. It's a nutritional powerhouse, giving you plenty of vitamins A, C, and K. For the most tender leaves, select smaller bunches with crisp, dark green leaves.

🌱 2 tablespoons extra-virgin olive oil

🌱 1 red onion, cut into wedges

🌱 3 cloves garlic, minced

🌱 1 pound kale, coarsely chopped and rinsed

🌱 3 tablespoons fresh lemon juice

🌱 1 apple, cut into thin strips

¼ cup raisins

Heat the oil in a large skillet over medium heat. Add the onion and cook, stirring occasionally, for 5 minutes, or until lightly browned. Add the garlic and kale and cook, turning often with tongs, until the kale wilts. Add the lemon juice and cook, stirring occasionally, for 2 minutes longer. Transfer to a serving bowl and top with the apple and raisins.

Serves 6

🌱 **Heart healthy ingredients: 6**

Per serving: 129 calories, 45 calories from fat, 5 g total fat, 1 g saturated fat, 3 g monounsaturated fat, 0 g polyunsaturated fat, 0 mg cholesterol, 36 mg sodium, 20 g carbohydrates, 3 g fiber, 9 g sugar, 3 g protein

Greens with Strawberries and Kiwifruit

Sometimes called Chinese gooseberries, kiwifruits are grown in New Zealand and California, allowing them to be available year-round. Their sweet-tart flavor is a cross between a pineapple and a strawberry.

- 2 tablespoons flaxseed oil
- 2 tablespoons lemon juice
- ¼ teaspoon salt
- ¼ teaspoon ground black pepper
- 1 bag (5 ounces) mixed baby greens
- 1 cup strawberries, hulled and halved
- 1 kiwifruit, peeled, quartered, and sliced
- ¼ cup crumbled feta cheese

In a large bowl, whisk together the oil, lemon juice, salt, and pepper. Add the greens, strawberries, kiwifruit, and cheese and gently toss to coat well.

Serves 4

Heart healthy ingredients: 5

Per serving: 117 calories, 81 calories from fat, 9 g total fat, 2 g saturated fat, 2 g monounsaturated fat, 5 g polyunsaturated fat, 8 mg cholesterol, 259 mg sodium, 8 g carbohydrates, 2 g fiber, 4 g sugar, 2 g protein

CHINESE, NOT AUSSIE

Contrary to popular belief, kiwifruits are not native to Australia; they're actually from China, where they're known as *yang tao*. Here's what happened: Missionaries brought the fruits to Australia, where they were renamed Chinese gooseberries. Then, in the early 1960s, Americans "discovered" this wonderful little fruit and thought that it would be well suited for the American palate. The problem was that name—the Cold War was in full swing. So they were renamed once again, now as kiwifruits, ostensibly as a tip of the hat to the native Australian bird, the kiwi, which also has a fuzzy little brown coat.

Asparagus Salad with Goat Cheese

Soft, creamy goat cheese gives a lovely tart flavor to dishes and is a natural partner to the woodsy flavor of asparagus. Goat cheese is sold in cylinders in the specialty cheese section of your market. It is often labeled "chèvre," which is French for "goat."

- 1 pound asparagus, trimmed
- 4 large roasted red bell peppers, cut into thin strips
- ¼ cup Citrus Vinaigrette (page 260)
- 2 shallots, minced
- ¼ cup pecans, toasted and chopped

  3 ounces reduced-fat goat cheese, crumbled

1. Place 1" water in the bottom of a deep skillet. Add a steamer basket and place the asparagus in the basket. Bring to a boil over high heat. Reduce the heat to medium and steam for 5 minutes, or until crisp-tender. Drain and rinse under cold water.

2. Arrange the asparagus and red peppers on a serving platter. Drizzle with the vinaigrette and top with the shallots, pecans, and cheese.

Serves 4

Heart healthy ingredients: 5

Per serving: 176 calories, 54 calories from fat, 9 g total fat, 2 g saturated fat, 4 g monounsaturated fat, 2 g polyunsaturated fat, 8 mg cholesterol, 195 mg sodium, 20 g carbohydrates, 5 g fiber, 8 g sugar, 9 g protein

Spinach Salad with Warm Onion Dressing

Canadian bacon subs for regular bacon, and we add toasted walnuts for flavor and richness in this heart healthy take on the bistro classic. Toasting nuts and seeds brings out their rich, natural sweetness and imparts a golden-brown color.

4 ounces Canadian bacon

🌱 1 tablespoon extra-virgin olive oil

🌱 1 large sweet onion, such as Vidalia, chopped

🌱 6 scallions, chopped

3 tablespoons red wine vinegar

1 tablespoon frozen apple juice concentrate

1 tablespoon Dijon mustard

🌱 1 tablespoon fresh chopped thyme leaves or 1 teaspoon dried

🌱 1 package (10 ounces) spinach

8 ounces white mushrooms, sliced

🌱 ¼ cup walnuts, toasted and chopped

1. Heat a nonstick skillet coated with cooking spray over medium heat. Add the bacon and cook, turning once, for 5 minutes, or until browned. Remove to a cutting board. When cooled, cut into strips.

2. Add the oil to the skillet and cook the onion and scallions, stirring occasionally, for 8 minutes, or until very tender. Add the vinegar, apple juice concentrate, mustard, and thyme. Cook, stirring occasionally, for 2 minutes longer, or until heated through.

3. Place the spinach and mushrooms in a large serving bowl. Pour over the onion mixture and toss to coat well. Sprinkle with the bacon strips and walnuts.

Note: To toast nuts, place in a dry skillet over medium heat, stirring frequently until lightly browned and fragrant.

Serves 4

🌱 **Heart healthy ingredients: 6**

Per serving: 189 calories, 89 calories from fat, 10 g total fat, 2 g saturated fat, 4 g monounsaturated fat, 4 g polyunsaturated fat, 14 mg cholesterol, 471 mg sodium, 18 g carbohydrates, 4 g fiber, 6 g sugar, 10 g protein

MAKEOVER MAGIC

You'll get the same smoky flavor from Canadian bacon as ordinary bacon but without all the fat. We left out the eggs found in a traditional spinach salad but added nuts for a healthy crunch and rich flavor.

	Traditional Spinach Salad	Spinach Salad with Warm Onion Dressing
Calories	329	189
Fat (g)	31	10
Percent calories from fat	85	48

175 Family-Pleasing, Heart-Protecting Recipes

Tofu Citrus Salad

This sprightly main-dish salad features baked tofu. Available in a variety of flavors, it has a firmer texture and consistency than even the firmest tofu. It's delicious tossed in salads, pastas, or soups.

- 1 large orange
- 1 teaspoon Dijon mustard
- ¼ teaspoon salt
- ¼ teaspoon ground black pepper
- 2 tablespoons extra-virgin olive oil
- 4 cups mesclun or spring mix
- 12 ounces baked tofu (Caribbean flavored or smoked), cubed
- ½ small red onion, cut into thin strips
- ¼ cup kalamata olives, pitted and chopped

1. With a small paring knife, cut off the top and bottom of the orange. Place cut side down on a cutting board and cut down around the orange to remove the skin, white pith, and outer membrane. Over a large serving bowl, cut between the membranes to release the sections, placing the sections in another bowl and allowing the juices to drip into the serving bowl. Squeeze the membranes over the serving bowl to release the juices.

2. Whisk the mustard, salt, and pepper into the juice in the serving bowl. Whisk in the oil. Add the orange sections, mesclun, tofu, onion, and olives. Toss to coat well.

Serves 4

Heart healthy ingredients: 6

Per serving: 186 calories, 114 calories from fat, 13 g total fat, 2 g saturated fat, 0 g monounsaturated fat, 2 g polyunsaturated fat, 0 mg cholesterol, 456 mg sodium, 12 g carbohydrates, 4 g fiber, 6 g sugar, 9 g protein

Creamy "Egg" Salad

Give this a try before writing it off as "too far out there." It's delicious—and so similar to egg salad that many folks never notice the difference. The salad makes a terrific sandwich, using whole grain bread and crispy lettuce.

- ♥ 1 package (14 ounces) extra-firm reduced-fat tofu, drained well and chopped

- ♥ 2 carrots, finely chopped

- 2 ribs celery, finely chopped

- ♥ 3 tablespoons low-fat plain yogurt

- 3 tablespoons reduced-fat mayonnaise

- 2 tablespoons sweet relish

- 1 tablespoon Dijon or brown mustard

- ¼ teaspoon salt

- ⅛ teaspoon ground black pepper

Place the tofu, carrots, celery, yogurt, mayonnaise, relish, mustard, salt, and pepper in a medium bowl and toss to coat well.

Serves 4

♥ **Heart healthy ingredients: 3**

Per serving: 96 calories, 22 calories from fat, 2 g total fat, 0 g saturated fat, 0 g monounsaturated fat, 0 g polyunsaturated fat, 0 mg cholesterol, 466 mg sodium, 12 g carbohydrates, 2 g fiber, 6 g sugar, 8 g protein

Peanut Noodle Salad

Whole wheat pasta stands up well to a robust peanut sauce. Rice wine vinegar is readily available in supermarkets, either with the vinegars or Asian sauces. It is made from fermented rice and has a mild, slightly sweet flavor. Seasoned rice wine vinegar is sweeter than plain due to added sugar.

- 8 ounces whole grain thin spaghetti
- ¼ cup creamy peanut butter
- 2 tablespoons reduced-sodium soy sauce
- 1 tablespoon rice wine vinegar
- 2 teaspoons toasted sesame oil
- 1 clove garlic, minced
- ½ teaspoon ground ginger
- ¼ teaspoon red-pepper flakes (optional)
- 1 small red bell pepper, cut into thin strips
- 1 cucumber, peeled, halved, seeded, and cut into thin 3" strips

1. Prepare the spaghetti according to package directions. Drain, reserving ½ cup of the cooking water.

2. Meanwhile, in a serving bowl, whisk together the peanut butter, soy sauce, vinegar, oil, garlic, ginger, and pepper flakes, if using (mixture may look separated). Gradually add ¼ cup of the pasta water, whisking until the mixture is creamy.

3. Add the hot pasta to the dressing and toss to coat well, adding more pasta water if necessary. Stir in the bell pepper and cucumber.

Serves 4

Heart healthy ingredients: 5

Per serving: 340 calories, 100 calories from fat, 11 g total fat, 2 g saturated fat, 5 g monounsaturated fat, 3 g polyunsaturated fat, 0 mg cholesterol, 345 mg sodium, 52 g carbohydrates, 10 g fiber, 6 g sugar, 14 g protein

Soba Noodle Salad

The buckwheat noodles in this Asian-inspired salad are good for your heart. One study showed that eating six servings of whole grains, like buckwheat, each week was especially helpful in postmenopausal women with high blood pressure and high cholesterol.

- 8 ounces soba (buckwheat) noodles

- 4 ounces snow peas (about 1 cup), julienned

- ¼ cup rice vinegar

- ¼ cup reduced-sodium soy sauce

- 1 tablespoon toasted sesame oil

- 2 tablespoons sugar

- 2 teaspoons grated peeled fresh ginger

- ½ cup mini peeled carrots (about 3 ounces), julienned

- 4 scallions, chopped

- 4 cups shredded romaine lettuce

1. Prepare the noodles according to package directions, adding the snow peas during the last 3 minutes of cooking. Drain.

2. Meanwhile, in a large serving bowl, whisk together the vinegar, soy sauce, oil, sugar, and ginger. Add the noodles and snow peas, along with the carrots, scallions, and lettuce. Toss to coat well.

Serves 6

Heart healthy ingredients: 5

Per serving: 210 calories, 34 calories from fat, 4 g total fat, 0 g saturated fat, 1 g monounsaturated fat, 1 g polyunsaturated fat, 0 mg cholesterol, 416 mg sodium, 35 g carbohydrates, 3 g fiber, 8 g sugar, 7 g protein

Tortellini Salad

Flaxseed oil, a great source of omega-3 fatty acids, should not be cooked, as heat can damage those good fats—so cold salads are the perfect place to add the heart healthy oil. To retain the great flavor of olive oil, use half flaxseed and half olive oil.

1 pound frozen cheese tortellini

♥ 1 tablespoon extra-virgin olive oil

♥ 1 tablespoon flaxseed oil

3 tablespoons white balsamic or white wine vinegar

♥ 1 clove garlic, minced

½ teaspoon coarsely ground black pepper

♥ ½ cup sun-dried tomatoes, thinly sliced

♥ 2 bags (5 ounces each) baby arugula

1. Prepare the tortellini according to package directions. Drain, rinse under cold water, and drain again.

2. In a large bowl, whisk together the olive oil, flaxseed oil, vinegar, garlic, and pepper. Stir in the tortellini, tomatoes, and arugula.

Serves 6

♥ **Heart healthy ingredients: 5**

Per serving: 288 calories, 97 calories from fat, 11 g total fat, 3 g saturated fat, 3 g monounsaturated fat, 2 g polyunsaturated fat, 12 mg cholesterol, 234 mg sodium, 26 g carbohydrates, 2 g fiber, 2 g sugar, 9 g protein

Barley Edamame Salad

Edamame are fresh soybeans picked when green instead of dried, like the white soybeans that are canned or used to make tofu, soy milk, and other processed soy products. Look for fresh edamame, either in the pod or shelled, in the produce section from late spring to fall or in the frozen vegetable section year-round.

1½ cups water

🌱 ½ cup pearl barley

¼ teaspoon salt

🌱 1 cup frozen shelled edamame (green soybeans), thawed

🌱 3 tablespoons extra-virgin olive oil

🌱 2 tablespoons lemon juice

1 teaspoon Dijon mustard

🌱 4 scallions, chopped

🌱 1 cup grape tomatoes, halved

¼ cup fresh chopped basil

1. Bring the water to a boil in a small saucepan. Stir in the barley and salt. Reduce the heat to low, cover, and simmer for 30 minutes. Add the edamame and simmer for 10 minutes longer, or until the edamame are tender and the liquid is absorbed. Remove from the heat and allow to cool to room temperature, if desired, for about 20 minutes.

2. In a large bowl, whisk together the oil, lemon juice, and mustard. Add the barley mixture, scallions, tomatoes, and basil. Toss to coat well.

Serves 6

🌱 **Heart healthy ingredients: 6**

Per serving: 159 calories, 71 calories from fat, 8 g total fat, 1 g saturated fat, 5 g monounsaturated fat, 1 g polyunsaturated fat, 0 mg cholesterol, 198 mg sodium, 18 g carbohydrates, 4 g fiber, 1 g sugar, 5 g protein

Black Bean Salad

"This recipe was given to me by a friend from Cuba and has become a family recipe that I am requested to bring to all of our potluck dinners, including Thanksgiving. This fresh, healthy, and colorful salad has a spicy kick and goes along with any menu."

SUSAN Y., MIAMI, FLORIDA

- ¼ cup extra-virgin olive oil
- 1–2 tablespoons red wine vinegar
- 1 teaspoon ground cumin
- 1 teaspoon ground black pepper
- ¼ teaspoon ground red pepper
- 2 cans (15 ounces each) black turtle beans, rinsed and drained
- 2 ribs celery, chopped
- 1 green, red, or yellow bell pepper, chopped
- 1 red onion, cut into thin wedges
- 1 clove garlic, minced
- 1 cup chopped cilantro

In a large bowl, whisk together the oil, vinegar, cumin, black pepper, and red pepper. Add the beans, celery, bell pepper, onion, garlic, and cilantro. Toss to coat well.

Serves 6

Heart healthy ingredients: 6

Per serving: 208 calories, 89 calories from fat, 10 g total fat, 1 g saturated fat, 7 g monounsaturated fat, 2 g polyunsaturated fat, 0 mg cholesterol, 209 mg sodium, 22 g carbohydrates, 8 g fiber, 2 g sugar, 7 g protein

Italian Three Bean Salad

This delicious salad comes together in minutes, but it really tastes best the next day. So if time permits, make it a day ahead and refrigerate until serving.

- 2 tablespoons fresh lemon juice
- 1 tablespoon red wine vinegar
- 1 teaspoon Italian seasoning, crushed
- 2 tablespoons extra-virgin olive oil
- 1 red onion, chopped
- 1 green bell pepper, chopped
- 1 can (15 ounces) cannellini beans, rinsed and drained
- 1 can (15 ounces) kidney beans, rinsed and drained
- 1 can (15 ounces) garbanzo beans (chickpeas), rinsed and drained
- 1 package (9 ounces) frozen artichoke hearts, thawed

In a large serving bowl, whisk together the lemon juice, vinegar, and seasoning. Whisk in the oil until well blended. Add the onion, pepper, cannellini beans, kidney beans, garbanzo beans, and artichoke hearts. Toss to mix and coat well with the dressing.

Serves 6

Heart healthy ingredients: 7

Per serving: 212 calories, 50 calories from fat, 6 g total fat, 1 g saturated fat, 4 g monounsaturated fat, 1 g polyunsaturated fat, 0 mg cholesterol, 212 mg sodium, 31 g carbohydrates, 9 g fiber, 5 g sugar, 11 g protein

GREEN MEANS STOP; RED MEANS GO

If you allow green peppers to mature for up to 10 days at room temperature, that will increase their ascorbic acid content (vitamin C). In fact, if left alone, green peppers can reach almost as high a content as red peppers. However, allowing red peppers to continue to "mature" results in a vitamin C *loss* of around 25 percent. So after buying green peppers, don't eat them right away. *Stop* and put them on the counter (away from direct sunlight) for a few days. When you buy red peppers, *go* ahead and eat *toute de suite!*

Asian Slaw with Chicken

Hiziki *(or hijiki) is just one of the many sea vegetables available in health food stores today. The salty-flavored delicacy contributes a subtle smokiness to this crunchy salad. It has an abundance of folic acid, which breaks down homocysteine, a risk factor for plaque-filled arteries and diabetes.*

♥ 2 tablespoons dried hiziki seaweed

♥ ¼ cup orange juice concentrate

2 tablespoons rice wine vinegar

♥ 1 tablespoon flaxseed oil

1 tablespoon toasted sesame oil

1 tablespoon reduced-sodium soy sauce

♥ 1 teaspoon freshly grated ginger

♥ 1 bag (16 ounces) coleslaw mix

1 pound cooked chicken breasts, shredded (about 3 cups)

1. Place the hiziki in a small saucepan and cover with cold water. Bring to a boil over high heat. Reduce the heat to low, cover, and simmer for 10 minutes. Place in a fine sieve, rinse with cold water, and drain.

2. In a large bowl, whisk together the orange juice concentrate, vinegar, flaxseed oil, sesame oil, soy sauce, and ginger. Add the hiziki and coleslaw mix and toss to coat well. Stir in the chicken.

Serves 6

♥ **Heart healthy ingredients: 5**

Per serving: 201 calories, 69 calories from fat, 8 g total fat, 1 g saturated fat, 3 g monounsaturated fat, 3 g polyunsaturated fat, 60 mg cholesterol, 164 mg sodium, 9 g carbohydrates, 2 g fiber, 6 g sugar, 23 g protein

Chopped Niçoise Salad

This hearty salad makes a wonderful healthy lunch or lighter dinner. The antioxidant-rich mesclun and onion help lower "bad" LDL cholesterol and triglycerides, as well as raise "good" HDL cholesterol, while the folate and potassium lower blood pressure.

1 pound small red potatoes, halved

½ pound green beans, diagonally sliced into 2" pieces

💜 ½ cup Herb-Dijon Vinaigrette (page 262)

💜 1 bag (7 ounces) mesclun or spring mix

💜 2 cans (6 ounces each) solid white tuna packed in water, drained

💜 1 small red onion, cut into rings

1. Place the potatoes in a large saucepan and cover with 2" water. Bring to a boil over medium-high heat. Reduce the heat to low, cover, and simmer for 15 minutes, or until almost tender. Add the beans and cook for 4 minutes longer, or until the potatoes are tender and the beans are tender-crisp. Drain and place in a medium bowl. Toss with ¼ cup of the vinaigrette.

2. Arrange the salad greens, tuna, potatoes, beans, and onion on a large serving plate. Drizzle with the remaining ¼ cup vinaigrette.

Serves 6

💜 **Heart healthy ingredients: 4**

Per serving: 221 calories, 63 calories from fat, 7 g total fat, 2 g saturated fat, 3 g monounsaturated fat, 1 g polyunsaturated fat, 24 mg cholesterol, 325 mg sodium, 25 g carbohydrates, 3 g fiber, 8 g sugar, 16 g protein

THE MORE PUNGENT, THE BETTER

As a general rule, the more pungent the onion, the greater its antioxidant value. For example, shallots have six times the antioxidants of sweet Vidalia onions. And the classic yellow onion has 11 times more than the milder white onion. So the next time chopping onions, scallions, or shallots makes you weepy, think to yourself, "That means these are extra good for me!"

Quick Arugula and Shrimp Salad

Arugula, sometimes called rocket or rugula, is a bitter green rich in iron and vitamins A and C. It adds a peppery flavor to dishes and is at home in salads but also delicious in sautés.

- ¼ cup fresh lemon juice
- ¼ cup chopped fresh herbs such as basil, cilantro, or parsley
- 2 teaspoons Dijon mustard
- 1 teaspoon sugar
- 1 tablespoon extra-virgin olive oil
- 2 tablespoons flaxseed oil
- 1 bag (5 ounces) baby arugula
- 1 cup grape tomatoes, halved
- 8 ounces cooked, peeled, and deveined large shrimp

In a large bowl, whisk together the lemon juice, herbs, mustard, and sugar. Whisk in the olive oil and flaxseed oil until emulsified. Add the arugula, tomatoes, and shrimp and toss to coat.

Serves 6

♥ **Heart healthy ingredients: 5**

Per serving: 116 calories, 68 calories from fat, 8 g total fat, 1 g saturated fat, 3 g monounsaturated fat, 4 g polyunsaturated fat, 57 mg cholesterol, 85 mg sodium, 4 g carbohydrates, 1 g fiber, 2 g sugar, 9 g protein

Healthy Chef's Salad

Using meat from the deli counter is a quick and easy solution to meal preparation, but even low-sodium varieties have more sodium than homemade products. So use deli meats sparingly, or substitute home-baked turkey for the meats here.

- 8 cups shredded romaine lettuce
- 3 ounces low-sodium, fat-free deli-style turkey breast
- 3 ounces low-sodium, fat-free deli-style ham
- 1 cup grape tomatoes, halved
- 1 apple, cored and chopped
- 2 ounces crumbled reduced-fat feta cheese
- ½ cup fat-free Thousand Island dressing

Arrange the lettuce on a serving plate. Slice the turkey and ham into thin strips and arrange over the lettuce with the tomatoes, apple, and cheese. Drizzle with the dressing.

Serves 6

♥ **Heart healthy ingredients: 3**

Per serving: 102 calories, 18 calories from fat, 2 g total fat, 1 g saturated fat, 0 g monounsaturated fat, 0 g polyunsaturated fat, 16 mg cholesterol, 466 mg sodium, 14 g carbohydrates, 3 g fiber, 8 g sugar, 8 g protein

Curry Chicken and Rice Salad

When preparing rice, pasta, or potatoes (baked or mashed), always double the amount. This way you will have some ready to go in the fridge for later in the week. With prepared rice on hand, this salad comes together in minutes.

¼ cup light coconut milk

♥ ¼ cup lime juice

1 teaspoon honey

1 teaspoon reduced-sodium soy sauce

♥ ¾ teaspoon green curry paste

1½ cups chopped cooked chicken breast (8 ounces)

♥ 1 cup cooked brown rice

1 cucumber, peeled, halved, seeded, and chopped

♥ 2 tomatoes, seeded and chopped

¼ cup chopped cilantro

In a large serving bowl, whisk together the coconut milk, lime juice, honey, soy sauce, and curry paste. Stir in the chicken, rice, cucumber, tomatoes, and cilantro and toss to coat well.

Serves 4

♥ **Heart healthy ingredients: 4**

Per serving: 202 calories, 39 calories from fat, 4 g total fat, 2 g saturated fat, 1 g monounsaturated fat, 1 g polyunsaturated fat, 48 mg cholesterol, 97 mg sodium, 20 g carbohydrates, 2 g fiber, 5 g sugar, 20 g protein

Warm Steak and Orange Salad

Fresh orange juice, sherry vinegar, and olive oil make a fantastic vinaigrette for a salad of greens, sweet orange pieces, and thin slices of grilled flank steak. A sprinkling of olives adds a piquant touch. If you've only eaten olives from a can, give some fresh ones a try. Delicious kalamata (or calamata) olives, which hail from Greece, contain monounsaturated fats that increase "good" HDL cholesterol and reduce plaque buildup in the arteries.

1 flank steak, about 8 ounces

½ teaspoon cracked black pepper

¼ teaspoon salt

♥ 2 oranges

2 tablespoons sherry vinegar

2 teaspoons Dijon mustard

♥ 1 tablespoon extra-virgin olive oil

♥ 1 bag (5 ounces) mixed greens

♥ 1 medium red onion, cut into slices and separated into rings

♥ 10 kalamata olives, pitted and quartered

1. Coat the grill rack or broiler pan with cooking spray. Preheat the grill or broiler. Season the steak with the pepper and salt.

2. Grill or broil the steak, turning once, for 8 minutes, or until a thermometer inserted in the center registers 145°F for medium-rare. Cook for 2 to 4 minutes longer, if desired, for medium (160°F) or well-done (165°F). Let stand for 10 minutes before slicing.

3. Meanwhile, with a small paring knife, cut off the top and bottom of each orange. Place cut side down on a cutting board and cut down around each orange to remove the skin, white pith, and outer membrane. Over a large bowl, cut between the membranes to release the sections, placing the sections in a small bowl and allowing the juices to drip into the large bowl. Squeeze the membranes over the large bowl to release the juice and discard.

4. Add the vinegar and mustard to the juice in the bowl. Gradually whisk in the oil until emulsified. Add the greens and onion and toss to coat well. Evenly divide among 4 plates. Top each with one-fourth of the sliced steak, orange sections, and olives.

Serves 4

♥ **Heart healthy ingredients: 5**

Per serving: 168 calories, 44 calories from fat, 5 g total fat, 1 g saturated fat, 2 g monounsaturated fat, 1 g polyunsaturated fat, 19 mg cholesterol, 421 mg sodium, 17 g carbohydrates, 5 g fiber, 9 g sugar, 14 g protein

Chicken and Eggplant Pasta Salad

Eggplant has a lot to offer beyond the traditional eggplant Parmesan. Here it combines with tomatoes and grilled chicken for a rich-tasting pasta salad that's delicious served warm or at room temperature.

- 8 ounces whole wheat rotini
- 1 medium eggplant, peeled and cut into thick slices
- 1 pound boneless, skinless chicken breasts
- ¼ cup Tomato-Basil Vinaigrette (page 260)
- 2 large tomatoes, seeded and chopped

1. Coat a grill rack or broiler pan with cooking spray. Preheat the grill or broiler. Prepare the pasta according to package directions. Drain.

2. Coat the eggplant with cooking spray. Grill or broil the chicken and eggplant, turning once, for 6 minutes, or until the eggplant is lightly browned. Transfer the eggplant to a cutting board. Continue cooking the chicken for 9 minutes longer, or until a thermometer inserted in the thickest portion registers 160°F and the juices run clear. Transfer to the cutting board. Loosely cover and let stand for 5 minutes before cutting the eggplant and chicken into bite-size pieces.

3. Place the vinaigrette in a large serving bowl. Add the pasta, eggplant, chicken, and tomatoes and toss to coat well.

Serves 6

Heart healthy ingredients: 3

Per serving: 274 calories, 30 calories from fat, 3 g total fat, 1 g saturated fat, 1 g monounsaturated fat, 1 g polyunsaturated fat, 44 mg cholesterol, 80 mg sodium, 37 g carbohydrates, 6 g fiber, 5 g sugar, 23 g protein

CHAPTER 4

Fruit and Vegetables at Every Meal

Apricot Asparagus and Carrots

A glaze of apricot marmalade and fresh ginger enlivens crisp steamed veggies. If you haven't used fresh ginger before, it's the rootlike knobs found in the produce section near the herbs. For the freshest ginger, make sure each piece is firm with smooth skin. The easiest way to peel it is to use the bowl of a spoon and simply scrape away the skin.

♥ 1 pound asparagus, trimmed and halved crosswise

♥ 2 carrots, julienned

½ cup all-fruit apricot marmalade

♥ 1 teaspoon freshly grated ginger or ½ teaspoon ground

½ teaspoon salt

Place 1" water in the bottom of a deep skillet. Insert a steamer basket and add the asparagus and carrots. Cover and bring the water to a boil over high heat. Reduce the heat to medium and steam for 5 minutes, or until the vegetables are crisp-tender. Transfer to a serving platter. Add the marmalade, ginger, and salt and toss to coat well.

Serves 4

♥ **Heart healthy ingredients: 3**

Per serving: 122 calories, 0 calories from fat, 0 g total fat, 0 g saturated fat, 0 g monounsaturated fat, 0 g polyunsaturated fat, 0 mg cholesterol, 311 mg sodium, 29 g carbohydrates, 3 g fiber, 21 g sugar, 3 g protein

CHOOSING AND STORING ASPARAGUS

Look for asparagus with tips that are tightly compact, bright green, and tinged with a lovely purple-blue hue. The spears themselves should be straight and firm (not droopy!), look fresh and crisp, and, of course, be a lovely, blemish-free green.

Asparagus doesn't have much of a shelf life, so proper storage is essential. In a perfect world, you'd buy asparagus and serve it the same day. Real life usually requires storage. One method is to wrap the bottom ends (not the tips) in a moistened paper towel. Then place the asparagus in an unsealed plastic bag (sealing will cut off the oxygen supply, and the asparagus will quickly deteriorate), and store it for no more than 2 days in the refrigerator. The second method is to place the asparagus, standing up, in a wide-mouthed glass jar (Mason jars work great), and add a few inches of cold water. Loosely cover the asparagus with a clean plastic bag (again, don't seal) and store in the fridge. Either way, enjoy the spears as soon as possible.

Sautéed Bitter Greens

Apple and raisins contribute a sweet touch to this powerhouse side dish starring escarole and frisée. These dark leafy greens are among nature's most nutritious vegetables, with large amounts of potassium and vitamins A and C. The greens lower cholesterol and blood pressure by neutralizing the damage caused by oxidative stress on the arteries.

- 1 tablespoon extra-virgin olive oil

- 1 red onion, cut into thin wedges

- 1 apple, cored and cut into thin wedges

- 3 cloves garlic, minced

  ½ cup fat-free, reduced-sodium vegetable or chicken broth

- 2 pounds bitter greens such as escarole or frisée (curly endive)

  ¼ teaspoon salt

  ⅓ cup raisins

1. Heat the oil in a large skillet over medium-high heat. Add the onion and cook, stirring occasionally, for 5 minutes, or until soft. Add the apple and garlic and cook for 1 minute longer.

2. Stir in the broth and bring to a simmer. Add the greens and salt and cook, stirring occasionally, for 3 minutes, or until wilted. Stir in the raisins.

Serves 4

Heart healthy ingredients: 5

Per serving: 143 calories, 34 calories from fat, 4 g total fat, 1 g saturated fat, 2 g monounsaturated fat, 1 g polyunsaturated fat, 0 mg cholesterol, 401 mg sodium, 26 g carbohydrates, 9 g fiber, 15 g sugar, 4 g protein

Orange-Glazed Broccoli

Large sections of orange and a sprightly citrus glaze turn everyday broccoli into an enticing side dish; grated nutmeg adds a bit of warmth. Go for freshly grated nutmeg over the already ground for the most delicious results. Actually a seed, whole nutmeg is about an inch long and sold in jars in supermarkets. If you don't have a nutmeg grinder, use the fine rasp side of your grater.

- ♥ 2 oranges

- ♥ 1 large bunch broccoli, cut into florets

- ♥ 10 fresh chives, coarsely chopped

- ¼ teaspoon freshly grated nutmeg

- ¼ teaspoon salt

1. With a small paring knife, cut off the top and bottom of each orange. Place cut side down on a cutting board and cut down around the orange to remove the peel, white pith, and outer membrane of the orange. Over a small bowl, cut between the membranes to release the sections, placing the sections in another bowl and allowing the juices to drip into the small bowl. Squeeze the membranes over the small bowl to release the juice. Reserve ½ cup of the juice and the sections.

2. Bring 2" water to a boil in a large saucepan over high heat. Place a steamer basket in the pan and add the broccoli. Cover and steam over medium heat for 10 minutes, or until crisp-tender.

3. Meanwhile, in a small saucepan, combine the reserved orange juice, the chives, nutmeg, and salt. Bring to a simmer over medium heat. Cook, uncovered, for 10 minutes, or until syrupy and reduced to about ¼ cup.

4. Place the broccoli in a serving bowl. Top with the orange sections and drizzle with the orange syrup.

Serves 4

♥ Heart healthy ingredients: 3

Per serving: 94 calories, 6 calories from fat, 1 g total fat, 0 g saturated fat, 0 g monounsaturated fat, 0 g polyunsaturated fat, 0 mg cholesterol, 196 mg sodium, 21 g carbohydrates, 8 g fiber, 10 g sugar, 5 g protein

Brussels Sprouts Amandine

The buttery flavor of almonds is a nice contrast to Brussels sprouts' slightly bitter taste. Nuts contain a bit of healthful monounsaturated fat, making them a good choice in a healthy diet. Because they do contain fat, however, they can get rancid. To prevent this, store them in a sealed container in the freezer for up to 6 months.

- 1½ pounds Brussels sprouts, trimmed and halved
- 2 tablespoons extra-virgin olive oil
- 3 shallots, minced
- 1 clove garlic, minced
- 1 tablespoon lemon juice
- ½ teaspoon salt
- ¼ cup sliced almonds, toasted

1. Bring 2" of water to a boil in a large saucepan over high heat. Place a steamer basket in the pan and add the Brussels sprouts. Cover and steam over medium heat for 10 minutes, or until crisp-tender. Transfer the sprouts to a bowl and set aside. Empty the pan and wipe clean.

2. Heat the oil in the same pan over medium heat. Add the shallots and garlic and cook, stirring occasionally, for 3 minutes. Add the lemon juice and cook for 1 minute longer. Stir in the reserved Brussels sprouts and salt and cook for another 2 minutes, or until heated through. Transfer to a serving bowl and top with the almonds.

Serves 6

 Heart healthy ingredients: 6

Per serving: 122 calories, 62 calories from fat, 7 g total fat, 1 g saturated fat, 4 g monounsaturated fat, 1 g polyunsaturated fat, 0 mg cholesterol, 206 mg sodium, 13 g carbohydrates, 5 g fiber, 1 g sugar, 6 g protein

Sautéed Mushrooms and Spinach

Spinach, the premier dark leafy vegetable, is a nutrient powerhouse that can lower blood pressure and fight plaque buildup in your arteries. You'll get even more nutrients from cooked spinach because cooking shrinks and condenses it.

- ♥ 2 tablespoons extra-virgin olive oil
- ♥ 1 sweet onion, chopped
- ♥ 1 pound shiitake mushrooms, stemmed and sliced
- ♥ 1 clove garlic, minced

  ¼ teaspoon salt

  1 tablespoon fresh chopped sage or 1 teaspoon dried
- ♥ ¼ cup red wine
- ♥ 1 bag (10 ounces) baby spinach

1. Heat the oil in a large skillet over medium-high heat. Add the onion and cook, stirring occasionally, for 5 minutes, or until lightly browned. Add the mushrooms, garlic, and salt and cook for 1 minute longer. Cover and cook for another 5 minutes, or until the mushrooms release their liquid.

2. Uncover and increase the heat to high. Cook, stirring occasionally, for 5 minutes, or until the liquid has evaporated and the mushrooms are browned.

3. Add the sage and wine and cook, stirring occasionally, for 1 minute. Stir in the spinach and cook for 1 minute longer, or until wilted.

Serves 4

♥ **Heart healthy ingredients: 6**

Per serving: 161 calories, 63 calories from fat, 7 g total fat, 1 g saturated fat, 5 g monounsaturated fat, 1 g polyunsaturated fat, 0 mg cholesterol, 209 mg sodium, 23 g carbohydrates, 4 g fiber, 6 g sugar, 3 g protein

Sugar Snap Peas with Shiitakes

Shiitake mushrooms are a great addition to any dish, thanks to their delicious smoky flavor and immune-boosting qualities. They also carry eritadenine, a compound that lowers cholesterol, and ergothioneine, a potent antioxidant that reduces blood pressure—even when the mushrooms are cooked.

1 pound sugar snap or snow peas, trimmed

♥ 2 tablespoons extra-virgin olive oil

♥ 8 ounces shiitake mushrooms, stemmed and sliced

♥ 1 clove garlic, minced

♥ 1 tomato, seeded and chopped

1 tablespoon reduced-sodium soy sauce

1. Bring 2" water to a boil in a large saucepan over high heat. Place a steamer basket in the pan and add the peas. Cover and steam over medium heat for 4 minutes, or until crisp-tender. Drain.

2. Meanwhile, heat the oil in a large skillet over medium-high heat. Add the mushrooms and cook, stirring occasionally, for 8 minutes, or until browned. Add the garlic, tomato, and soy sauce and cook, stirring occasionally, for 3 minutes longer, or until the mixture forms a sauce. Add the peas and cook for another minute to heat through.

Serves 4

♥ **Heart healthy ingredients: 4**

Per serving: 152 calories, 62 calories from fat, 7 g total fat, 1 g saturated fat, 5 g monounsaturated fat, 1 g polyunsaturated fat, 0 mg cholesterol, 137 mg sodium, 19 g carbohydrates, 4 g fiber, 7 g sugar, 4 g protein

A MUSHROOM BY ANY OTHER NAME

The shiitake mushroom goes by a lot of different names, including: *hua gu,* oak mushroom, golden oak mushroom, Oriental black mushroom, Chinese black mushroom, glossagyne, and Chinese shiitake mushroom. But no matter what you call them, they're just as healthy!

Carrot and Sweet Potato Puree

Typically, heavy cream is added to vegetable purees, making them rich and creamy. Here, reduced-fat cream cheese takes its place, lowering the fat and cholesterol while keeping the richness.

- ♥ 1 pound carrots, chopped
- ♥ 1 pound sweet potatoes, peeled and chopped
- ♥ 1 apple, peeled, cored, and chopped
- 2 ounces reduced-fat cream cheese
- ♥ ¼ cup orange juice
- ♥ 1 teaspoon ground ginger

1. In a large saucepan, place the carrots, potatoes, and apple and cover with water. Bring to a boil over high heat. Reduce the heat to low, cover, and simmer for 25 minutes, or until tender. Drain.

2. Transfer to a food processor and add the cream cheese, orange juice, and ginger. Puree until smooth.

Serves 4

♥ **Heart healthy ingredients: 5**

Per serving: 204 calories, 24 calories from fat, 3 g total fat, 2 g saturated fat, 1 g monounsaturated fat, 0 g polyunsaturated fat, 8 mg cholesterol, 163 mg sodium, 41 g carbohydrates, 7 g fiber, 15 g sugar, 5 g protein

Curry-Roasted Cauliflower

Roasting cauliflower gives the florets a mild flavor and creamy texture. For a completely different take on this dish, use 1 teaspoon Italian seasoning in place of the curry powder.

- 1 medium head cauliflower, cut into florets
- 1 red bell pepper, cut into 1" pieces
- 2 tablespoons extra-virgin olive oil
- 1 clove garlic, minced
- 1 teaspoon curry powder
- ¼ teaspoon salt

Preheat the oven to 400°F. In a large roasting pan, combine the cauliflower, pepper, oil, garlic, curry powder, and salt and toss to coat well. Roast, turning occasionally, for 30 minutes, or until tender and browned.

Serves 4

Heart healthy ingredients: 5

Per serving: 108 calories, 62 calories from fat, 7 g total fat, 1 g saturated fat, 5 g monounsaturated fat, 1 g polyunsaturated fat, 0 mg cholesterol, 189 mg sodium, 10 g carbohydrates, 4 g fiber, 4 g sugar, 3 g protein

Roasted Winter Vegetables

If the butternut skin is too hard to cut through, cook the squash in the microwave on high for 2 minutes. This will soften the skin just enough to easily slice.

- 1 butternut squash, peeled, seeded, and cut into 1" pieces
- 1 pound parsnips, peeled and cut into 1" pieces
- 1 red onion, cut into wedges
- 2 tablespoons extra-virgin olive oil
- 1 tablespoon freshly grated ginger
- ½ teaspoon cinnamon
- ½ teaspoon salt

Preheat the oven to 400°F. In a large roasting pan, combine the squash, parsnips, onion, oil, ginger, cinnamon, and salt and toss to coat well. Roast, turning occasionally, for 40 minutes, or until tender and browned.

Serves 6

Heart healthy ingredients: 5

Per serving: 157 calories, 37 calories from fat, 5 g total fat, 1 g saturated fat, 3 g monounsaturated fat, 1 g polyunsaturated fat, 0 mg cholesterol, 206 mg sodium, 29 g carbohydrates, 6 g fiber, 7 g sugar, 2 g protein

Garlic-Roasted Sweet Potatoes with Arugula

The sweetness of roasted garlic and sweet potatoes sometimes needs a contrasting flavor—slightly bitter arugula does the trick. There are many varieties of sweet potatoes (often erroneously called yams), from pale yellow to almost red. Go for those with the most color, as they have the most antioxidants.

♥ 2 pounds sweet potatoes, peeled and cut into 2" pieces

♥ 4 cloves garlic, sliced

♥ 2 tablespoons extra-virgin olive oil

½ teaspoon salt

½ teaspoon ground black pepper

2 Bartlett pears, cored and cut into 2" pieces

♥ 1 package (5 ounces) arugula

½ teaspoon grated lemon peel

1. Preheat the oven to 425°F. In a large roasting pan, combine the potatoes, garlic, oil, salt, and pepper and toss to coat well.

2. Roast for 40 minutes, tossing occasionally, until tender and browned, adding the pears during the last 10 minutes of cooking.

3. Place the arugula in a large bowl. Add the cooked potato mixture and toss until the arugula wilts. Sprinkle with the lemon peel.

Serves 6

♥ **Heart healthy ingredients: 4**

Per serving: 218 calories, 45 calories from fat, 5 g total fat, 1 g saturated fat, 3 g monounsaturated fat, 1 g polyunsaturated fat, 0 mg cholesterol, 291 mg sodium, 41 g carbohydrates, 7 g fiber, 13 g sugar, 4 g protein

NOPE, NOT POTATOES—OR YAMS

Contrary to popular belief, sweet potatoes aren't potatoes. They're not a type of yam, either. Sweet potatoes are roots, members of the morning glory family, and superrich in beta-carotene. Potatoes are tubers, members of the nightshade family, and have zero beta-carotene. Yams are tubers, members of the lily family, and have much less beta-carotene than a sweet potato. Just to complicate matters a bit more, Garnet and Jewel yams aren't yams, they're sweet potatoes. And those candied yams that come in a can? Yup, sweet potatoes.

Garlic Smashed Potatoes

"Smashed" potatoes are made with unpeeled potatoes, while "mashed" potatoes use peeled spuds. Since most of the vitamins are located just under the skin, smashed is the healthier option.

1½ pounds Yukon gold potatoes, scrubbed and quartered

♥ 4 cloves garlic, halved

♥ 1¼ cups low-fat plain yogurt

¼ teaspoon salt

¼ teaspoon ground black pepper

♥ 4 scallions, sliced

1. In a medium saucepan, combine the potatoes and garlic and cover with water. Bring to a boil over high heat. Reduce the heat to low and simmer for 15 minutes, or until the potatoes are very tender. Drain and return to the pan.

2. Add the yogurt, salt, and pepper and mash or whip the potatoes until they reach the desired consistency. Stir in the scallions.

Serves 4

♥ **Heart healthy ingredients: 3**

Per serving: 109 calories, 11 calories from fat, 1 g total fat, 1 g saturated fat, 0 g monounsaturated fat, 0 g polyunsaturated fat, 5 mg cholesterol, 213 mg sodium, 17 g carbohydrates, 5 g fiber, 8 g sugar, 8 g protein

MAKEOVER MAGIC

Your family will love these potatoes for their taste—you'll love how healthy they are. Starting with golden-fleshed potatoes means a natural buttery flavor. By adding yogurt instead of butter and milk, the fat is slashed to just 1 gram and the calories to only 109 per serving!

	Traditional Mashed Potatoes	Garlic Smashed Potatoes
Calories	328	109
Fat (g)	24	1
Percent calories from fat	66	8

CHAPTER 5

The Great Grains

Vegetable Quinoa

Quinoa is often billed as a supergrain, as it contains more protein than any other grain and all eight essential amino acids. It's also lower in carbs and higher in unsaturated fats than other grains.

♥ 1 cup quinoa

♥ 1 tablespoon extra-virgin olive oil

♥ 3 scallions, chopped

♥ 1 carrot, chopped

♥ 1 red bell pepper, chopped

♥ 4 ounces small shiitake mushrooms, stemmed and chopped

2 cups fat-free, reduced-sodium vegetable or chicken broth

♥ ½ teaspoon dried thyme, crushed

1. Place the quinoa in a fine-mesh sieve and rinse under cold running water until the water runs clear.

2. Heat the oil in a medium saucepan over medium heat. Add the scallions, carrot, pepper, and mushrooms and cook, stirring occasionally, for 5 minutes, or until lightly browned. Add the quinoa, broth, and thyme. Bring to a boil. Reduce the heat to low, cover, and simmer for 20 minutes, or until all the liquid is absorbed. Fluff with a fork.

Serves 6

♥ **Heart healthy ingredients: 7**

Per serving: 150 calories, 35 calories from fat, 4 g total fat, 1 g saturated fat, 2 g monounsaturated fat, 1 g polyunsaturated fat, 0 mg cholesterol, 164 mg sodium, 25 g carbohydrates, 3 g fiber, 2 g sugar, 5 g protein

Quinoa Florentine

Although quinoa is technically a seed, it's cooked and served like a grain—and an amazing, heart healthy grain, at that! Always rinse quinoa under cold running water until the water runs clear. This will remove the saponin, a naturally occurring coating on the grain that has a very bitter flavor.

♥ 1 cup quinoa

2½ cups fat-free, reduced-sodium vegetable broth

♥ 1 tablespoon extra-virgin olive oil

♥ 1 red onion, chopped

♥ 3 cloves garlic, minced

♥ 1 bag (5 ounces) spinach

♥ 1 can (14½ ounces) garbanzo beans (chickpeas), rinsed and drained

¼ cup chopped fresh basil

1. Place the quinoa in a fine-mesh sieve and rinse under cold running water until the water runs clear. Bring 2 cups of the broth to a boil in a medium saucepan over high heat. Add the quinoa and return to a boil. Reduce the heat to low, cover, and simmer for 20 minutes, or until all the liquid is absorbed.

2. Meanwhile, heat the oil in a large nonstick skillet over medium heat. Add the onion and cook, stirring occasionally, for 5 minutes, or until tender. Add the garlic and spinach and cook for 1 minute longer. Stir in the beans and the remaining ½ cup broth and cook for another 2 minutes.

3. Fluff the quinoa with a fork and stir in the basil. Place in a serving bowl and top with the bean mixture.

Serves 4

♥ **Heart healthy ingredients: 6**

Per serving: 297 calories, 65 calories from fat, 7 g total fat, 1 g saturated fat, 3 g monounsaturated fat, 2 g polyunsaturated fat, 0 mg cholesterol, 440 mg sodium, 49 g carbohydrates, 8 g fiber, 8 g sugar, 12 g protein

Peppered Couscous

Couscous is made from semolina, coarsely ground durum wheat that is high in fiber and magnesium, both of which help reduce the risk of type 2 diabetes and weight gain. Busy cooks value its quick cooking time.

- 1 tablespoon extra-virgin olive oil
- 1 red bell pepper, finely chopped
- 1 yellow bell pepper, finely chopped
- 6 scallions, sliced
- 2 cloves garlic, minced
- 1 cup fat-free, reduced-sodium vegetable or chicken broth
- 1 cup whole wheat couscous

Heat the oil in a medium saucepan over medium-high heat. Add the red and yellow peppers and cook, stirring occasionally, for 4 minutes, or until slightly tender. Add the scallions and garlic and cook for 2 minutes longer. Add the broth and bring to a boil. Stir in the couscous. Remove from the heat, cover, and let stand for 10 minutes, or until all the broth is absorbed. Fluff and toss with a fork.

Serves 4

Heart healthy ingredients: 6

Per serving: 199 calories, 37 calories from fat, 4 g total fat, 1 g saturated fat, 2 g monounsaturated fat, 1 g polyunsaturated fat, 0 mg cholesterol, 118 mg sodium, 38 g carbohydrates, 7 g fiber, 2 g sugar, 6 g protein

Curried Couscous

The walnuts in this Indian-inspired couscous add nutty flavor as well as omega-3 essential fatty acids, which lower blood pressure, reduce the possibility of blood clots and heart attacks, and improve the ratio of "good" HDL to "bad" LDL cholesterol.

- 1 cup fat-free, reduced-sodium chicken broth
- 1 tablespoon curry powder
- 1 cup whole wheat couscous
- ½ cup frozen peas, thawed
- 2 tablespoons chopped walnuts

In a medium saucepan, combine the broth, curry powder, and couscous over medium heat. Bring to a boil. Remove from the heat, cover, and let stand for 10 minutes, or until all the liquid is absorbed. Stir in the peas and walnuts and fluff with a fork.

Serves 4

Heart healthy ingredients: 3

Per serving: 226 calories, 45 calories from fat, 5 g total fat, 1 g saturated fat, 1 g monounsaturated fat, 2 g polyunsaturated fat, 0 mg cholesterol, 154 mg sodium, 43 g carbohydrates, 11 g fiber, 2 g sugar, 9 g protein

Fruited Rice Pilaf

Dried fruit is an easy way to add a bit of sweetness to rice. Hailing from Thailand, aromatic jasmine rice has a slight flowery flavor and fragrance. If you wish, you can use basmati or long-grain white instead.

- 1 tablespoon extra-virgin olive oil
- 1 onion, minced

  1 cup jasmine rice
- 1 tablespoon grated fresh ginger

  2 cups fat-free, reduced-sodium vegetable or chicken broth

  ½ teaspoon allspice
- ½ cup dried cranberries or raisins
- ½ cup whole almonds, chopped

Heat the oil in a medium saucepan over medium heat. Add the onion and cook, stirring occasionally, for 5 minutes, or until tender. Add the rice and ginger and cook for 3 minutes longer, or until the rice is golden. Stir in the broth and allspice and bring to a boil. Reduce the heat to low, cover, and simmer for 15 minutes, or until all of the liquid is absorbed. Stir in the cranberries or raisins and almonds.

Serves 4

Heart healthy ingredients: 5

Per serving: 287 calories, 111 calories from fat, 13 g total fat, 1 g saturated fat, 8 g monounsaturated fat, 3 g polyunsaturated fat, 0 mg cholesterol, 227 mg sodium, 39 g carbohydrates, 4 g fiber, 14 g sugar, 6 g protein

Edamame Pilaf

Besides being a good source of protein without the saturated fat and cholesterol found in meat, edamame lowers blood pressure and cholesterol, reduces the risk of blood clots, and controls blood sugar levels in people with type 2 diabetes.

- 1 tablespoon extra-virgin olive oil
- 1 red onion, chopped
- 2 carrots, chopped
- 1 cup brown rice

  3 cups fat-free, reduced-sodium vegetable or chicken broth
- 1 cup shelled edamame (green soybeans), fresh or frozen

Heat the oil in a medium saucepan over medium heat. Add the onion and carrots and cook, stirring occasionally, for 5 minutes, or until lightly browned. Add the rice and cook, stirring constantly, for 3 minutes longer. Add the broth and bring to a boil. Reduce the heat to low, cover, and simmer for 35 minutes. Stir in the edamame and cook for 10 minutes longer, or until the liquid is absorbed.

Serves 8

Heart healthy ingredients: 5

Per serving: 140 calories, 28 calories from fat, 3 g total fat, 0 g saturated fat, 2 g monounsaturated fat, 1 g polyunsaturated fat, 0 mg cholesterol, 246 mg sodium, 23 g carbohydrates, 2 g fiber, 2 g sugar, 5 g protein

Brown Rice with Greens and Feta

Nutrient-rich brown rice offers antioxidant protection, lowers cholesterol and blood pressure, slows the buildup of plaque in the arteries, reduces the risk of type 2 diabetes, and may even help you lose weight.

♥ 1 tablespoon extra-virgin olive oil

♥ 1 cup brown rice

2½ cups fat-free, reduced-sodium vegetable or chicken broth

♥ 2 tablespoons finely chopped sun-dried tomato

♥ 2 cloves garlic, minced

♥ 1 bag (5 ounces) baby field greens

½ cup crumbled reduced-fat feta cheese

Heat the oil in a medium saucepan over medium heat. Add the rice and cook for 3 minutes, or until golden. Stir in the broth, tomato, and garlic and bring to a boil. Reduce the heat to low, cover, and simmer for 40 minutes, or until all of the liquid is absorbed and the rice is tender. Remove from the heat and stir in the greens. Cover and let stand for 5 minutes. Place in a serving bowl and sprinkle with the cheese.

Serves 4

♥ **Heart healthy ingredients: 5**

Per serving: 289 calories, 71 calories from fat, 8 g total fat, 3 g saturated fat, 3 g monounsaturated fat, 1 g polyunsaturated fat, 10 mg cholesterol, 487 mg sodium, 45 g carbohydrates, 4 g fiber, 0 g sugar, 12 g protein

Wild Rice with Almonds and Currants

Wild rice is not rice at all but the seed of a grass native to the Great Lakes region. It has a nutty flavor and chewier texture than brown rice but can be used in any rice dish. If you have a half-full box of wild rice in the pantry, use half brown and half wild rice in your favorite rice dishes for a nice change of pace.

♥ 1 tablespoon extra-virgin olive oil

♥ 2 shallots, chopped

♥ ½ cup wild rice

♥ 1 cup orange juice

½ cup water

¼ teaspoon salt

♥ ¼ cup chopped toasted almonds

¼ cup currants

Heat the oil in a medium saucepan over medium heat. Add the shallots and cook, stirring occasionally, for 2 minutes. Add the wild rice and cook, stirring occasionally, for 3 minutes longer. Add the orange juice, water, and salt. Bring to a boil and reduce the heat to low. Cover and simmer for 45 minutes, or until all the liquid is absorbed. Stir in the almonds and currants.

Serves 4

♥ **Heart healthy ingredients: 5**

Per serving: 217 calories, 76 calories from fat, 9 g total fat, 1 g saturated fat, 6 g monounsaturated fat, 2 g polyunsaturated fat, 0 mg cholesterol, 148 mg sodium, 32 g carbohydrates, 3 g fiber, 7 g sugar, 6 g protein

Arugula Tabbouleh

Tabbouleh is a traditional Lebanese dish chock-full of heart healthy foods like bulgur wheat, tomatoes, lemon juice, and olives. Even higher in nutrients than couscous or rice, bulgur wheat (aka cracked wheat) also has little fat and plenty of fiber and folate. It helps to lower cholesterol and blood pressure while its nutty flavor enhances soups and pilafs.

♥ 1 cup bulgur wheat

¼ teaspoon salt

2 cups boiling water

♥ ¼ cup freshly squeezed lemon juice (from 2 lemons)

♥ 3 tablespoons extra-virgin olive oil

♥ 1 clove garlic, minced

♥ 1 bag (5 ounces) baby arugula or spinach, coarsely chopped

♥ 1 large tomato, seeded and chopped

1 large cucumber, peeled, halved, seeded, and chopped

♥ 2 tablespoons chopped kalamata olives

1. In a medium bowl, combine the bulgur, salt, and boiling water. Cover and let stand for 30 minutes, or until the bulgur is tender (it will still be a bit chewy). Drain through a fine-mesh sieve. Wipe the bowl dry.

2. To the bowl, add the lemon juice, oil, and garlic. Whisk to blend well. Stir in the bulgur, arugula or spinach, tomato, cucumber, and olives.

Serves 6

♥ **Heart healthy ingredients: 7**

Per serving: 174 calories, 68 calories from fat, 8 g total fat, 1 g saturated fat, 5 g monounsaturated fat, 1 g polyunsaturated fat, 0 mg cholesterol, 133 mg sodium, 24 g carbohydrates, 6 g fiber, 3 g sugar, 5 g protein

Broccoli-Barley Pilaf

Serve this hearty side dish with broiled or grilled pork chops and Coleslaw with Lemon Dressing (page 108) for a speedy weeknight supper.

- 1 tablespoon extra-virgin olive oil
- 1 red onion, chopped
- 1 cup quick-cooking barley
- 1 clove garlic, minced
- 2 cups fat-free, reduced-sodium vegetable or chicken broth
- 1 package (10 ounces) frozen chopped broccoli, thawed and drained
- 1/3 cup (1 1/3 ounces) grated Parmesan cheese

1. Heat the oil in a medium saucepan over medium heat. Add the onion and cook, stirring occasionally, for 5 minutes, or until lightly browned. Add the barley and garlic and cook, stirring occasionally, for 2 minutes longer.

2. Add the broth and bring to a boil. Reduce the heat to low, cover, and simmer for 10 minutes. Stir in the broccoli and cook for 2 minutes longer, or until the liquid is absorbed and the broccoli is heated through. Place in a bowl and sprinkle with the cheese.

Serves 6

Heart healthy ingredients: 5

Per serving: 177 calories, 36 calories from fat, 4 g total fat, 1 g saturated fat, 2 g monounsaturated fat, 1 g polyunsaturated fat, 4 mg cholesterol, 234 mg sodium, 30 g carbohydrates, 7 g fiber, 2 g sugar, 7 g protein

Black Beans and Rice

Look for short-grain brown rice as an alternative to the more common long-grain. Brown rice is filled with flavor because only the inedible outer husk is removed.

- ♥ 1 cup brown rice

- ♥ 1 tablespoon extra-virgin olive oil

- ♥ 1 small onion, chopped

- ♥ 1 small red bell pepper, chopped

- ♥ 2 cloves garlic, minced

- ♥ 1 can (15 ounces) black beans, rinsed and drained

  ¼ cup fat-free, reduced-sodium vegetable or chicken broth

  2 teaspoons red wine vinegar

- ♥ ⅛ teaspoon hot-pepper sauce

  ¼ cup chopped cilantro

1. Prepare the rice according to package directions.

2. Fifteen minutes before the rice is cooked, heat the oil in a nonstick skillet over medium-high heat. Add the onion and bell pepper and cook, stirring occasionally, for 5 minutes, or until lightly browned. Add the garlic and cook for 1 minute longer. Stir in the beans, broth, vinegar, and hot-pepper sauce. Cook for 5 minutes, or until heated through.

3. Stir the cilantro into the rice and place in a serving bowl. Top with the bean mixture.

Serves 4

♥ **Heart healthy ingredients: 7**

Per serving: 302 calories, 48 calories from fat, 6 g total fat, 1 g saturated fat, 3 g monounsaturated fat, 2 g polyunsaturated fat, 0 mg cholesterol, 300 mg sodium, 54 g carbohydrates, 8 g fiber, 4 g sugar, 9 g protein

CHAPTER 6

Bean Cuisine and Meatless Mains

Vegetarian Gumbo

Filé powder, made from the leaves of the sassafras tree, is essential in authentic Cajun cooking. Not only does it add flavor, it also helps to thicken gumbo.

1 cup long-grain rice

♥ 2 tablespoons extra-virgin olive oil

2 ribs celery, chopped

♥ 1 red bell pepper, chopped

♥ 1 orange bell pepper, chopped

♥ 1 large onion, chopped

♥ 4 cloves garlic, minced

2 tablespoons all-purpose flour

3 cups fat-free, reduced-sodium vegetable broth

♥ 1 can (15 ounces) reduced-sodium kidney beans, rinsed and drained

2 teaspoons filé powder or Cajun seasoning

♥ 1 teaspoon dried thyme, crushed

♥ ¼ teaspoon ground red pepper

1 package (10 ounces) frozen sliced okra, thawed

1. Prepare the rice according to package directions.

2. Meanwhile, heat 1 tablespoon of the oil in a large saucepan over medium-high heat. Add the celery, red and orange bell peppers, and onion and cook for 5 minutes, stirring frequently. Add the garlic and cook for 1 minute longer. Using a slotted spoon, remove the vegetables to a bowl.

3. Add the remaining 1 tablespoon oil to the pan and heat over medium heat. Whisk in the flour and cook, stirring constantly, for 8 minutes, or until golden brown. Gradually whisk in the broth. Return the vegetables and any accumulated juices to the pan along with the beans, filé or seasoning, thyme, and ground red pepper. Bring to a simmer, then reduce the heat to low and simmer for 10 minutes. Add the okra and cook for 5 minutes longer, or until heated through.

4. To serve, evenly divide the rice and mound in 4 bowls. Spoon one-fourth of the gumbo around each rice mound.

Serves 4

♥ **Heart healthy ingredients: 8**

Per serving: 409 calories, 75 calories from fat, 9 g total fat, 1 g saturated fat, 6 g monounsaturated fat, 1 g polyunsaturated fat, 0 mg cholesterol, 402 mg sodium, 70 g carbohydrates, 8 g fiber, 9 g sugar, 15 g protein

MAKEOVER MAGIC

Traditional gumbo with sausage and chicken can have almost as many calories and fat grams as a person should have in a day! Making a vegetarian version cuts the fat, along with a roux (flour cooked in butter, oil, or lard) made with just 1 tablespoon olive oil—but you still get tasty results.

	Traditional Gumbo	Vegetarian Gumbo
Calories	1,304	409
Fat (g)	68	9
Percent calories from fat	47	20

Tex-Mex Beans and Rice

The pinto has more fiber than any other bean, making it a great choice for lowering cholesterol and controlling insulin levels. Serve this flavorful dish alongside grilled chicken or beef. It serves 2 as a vegetarian meal with salad and corn bread.

½ cup long-grain rice

1 tablespoon extra-virgin olive oil

1 red bell pepper, finely chopped

4 scallions, chopped

3 cloves garlic, minced

1 teaspoon chili powder

½ teaspoon ground cumin

1 can (15 ounces) reduced-sodium pinto beans, rinsed and drained

½ cup water

½ cup chopped cilantro

4 tablespoons (1 ounce) shredded reduced-fat pepper-Jack cheese

1. Prepare the rice according to package directions.

2. Meanwhile, heat the oil in a medium saucepan over medium heat. Add the pepper and scallions and cook, stirring occasionally, for 5 minutes, or until tender. Add the garlic, chili powder, and cumin and cook for 1 minute longer. Add the beans and water and bring to a boil over high heat. Reduce the heat to low, cover, and simmer for 10 minutes, or until heated through and well seasoned. Stir in the cilantro.

3. Evenly divide the rice among 4 plates. Top each serving with one-fourth of the bean mixture and sprinkle with 1 tablespoon of the cheese.

Serves 4

Heart healthy ingredients: 6

Per serving: 202 calories, 51 calories from fat, 6 g total fat, 1 g saturated fat, 3 g monounsaturated fat, 1 g polyunsaturated fat, 4 mg cholesterol, 153 mg sodium, 29 g carbohydrates, 6 g fiber, 3 g sugar, 8 g protein

BEAN MATH

- 1 pound dry beans = 2 cups dry
- 2 cups dry beans = 6 cups cooked
- 15-ounce can of beans, drained = 1½ cups

Braised Lentils with Spinach

Lentils are a wonder food that can lower blood pressure and cholesterol and reduce the risk of dying from a heart attack. For a lovely dish, spoon this tasty lentil/veggie combo into soup plates or shallow bowls and top with grilled salmon.

🌱 2 tablespoons extra-virgin olive oil

🌱 2 carrots, chopped

🌱 1 onion, chopped

1 rib celery, chopped

🌱 3 cloves garlic, minced

1 tablespoon chopped fresh rosemary or 1 teaspoon crushed dried

¼ teaspoon ground black pepper

🌱 1½ cups petite green lentils

2 cups fat-free, reduced-sodium vegetable or chicken broth

1½ cups water

🌱 1 bag (5 ounces) baby spinach

1. Heat the oil in a medium saucepan over medium heat. Add the carrots, onion, and celery and cook, stirring occasionally, for 5 minutes, or until tender. Add the garlic, rosemary, and pepper and cook for 1 minute.

2. Stir in the lentils, broth, and water. Bring to a boil over high heat. Reduce the heat to low, cover, and simmer for 30 minutes, or until the lentils are tender.

3. Remove from the heat, stir in the spinach, and cook, stirring, until wilted.

Serves 6

🌱 **Heart healthy ingredients: 6**

Per serving: 243 calories, 54 calories from fat, 6 g total fat, 1 g saturated fat, 4 g monounsaturated fat, 1 g polyunsaturated fat, 0 mg cholesterol, 90 mg sodium, 37 g carbohydrates, 10 g fiber, 4 g sugar, 13 g protein

TAKE YOUR PICK

Whether you prefer to purchase your fresh spinach in bunches or prepackaged bags, there are four types from which to choose.

Savoy: deep green with curly, crinkly leaves

Semi-savoy: deep green but with slightly less crinkly (easier-to-clean) leaves

Baby spinach: emerald green with soft, delicate, flat, rounded leaves, often included in mesclun green salad mixes

Flat, smooth leaf: emerald green, often sold as loose leaves and commonly used in processed foods such as soups and baby food

Spinach and Cannellini Beans

"This recipe is great with roasted chicken or grilled salmon. My daughter and I had a version of it with arugula at an Italian restaurant and everyone loved it, but I like things with a little more color, so I used spinach and added the red pepper and red onion."

CINDI R., BIG ROCK, ILLINOIS

- ♥ 2 tablespoons extra-virgin olive oil
- ♥ 1 small red bell pepper, thinly sliced
- ♥ 1 small red onion, thinly sliced
- ♥ 1 bag (9 ounces) spinach
- ♥ 1 can (15 ounces) cannellini beans, rinsed and drained
- ♥ 2 cloves garlic, sliced

  ¼ teaspoon salt

  ¼ teaspoon ground black pepper

Heat the oil in a medium saucepan over medium heat. Add the bell pepper and onion and cook, stirring occasionally, for 5 minutes, or until lightly browned. Stir in the spinach, beans, garlic, salt, and pepper and cook, stirring occasionally, for 5 minutes longer, or until the spinach wilts.

Serves 4

♥ Heart healthy ingredients: 6

Per serving: 162 calories, 68 calories from fat, 8 g total fat, 1 g saturated fat, 5 g monounsaturated fat, 1 g polyunsaturated fat, 0 mg cholesterol, 224 mg sodium, 18 g carbohydrates, 6 g fiber, 2 g sugar, 7 g protein

Curried Vegetables with Beans

Broccoli, carrots, and black beans are brightened with fresh ginger and curry powder in this easy veggie curry. Coconut milk is a common ingredient in Indian and Asian curries. Always go for the light version to save calories and fat. Store unused portions in a glass jar in the refrigerator for up to 1 week.

- 1 large head broccoli, cut into florets
- 2 large carrots, chopped
- 2 tablespoons extra-virgin olive oil
- 1 medium onion, chopped
- 2 cloves garlic, minced
- 1 tablespoon minced fresh ginger
- 1 tablespoon all-purpose flour
- 2 teaspoons curry powder
- ⅔ cup fat-free, reduced-sodium chicken or vegetable broth
- ½ cup light coconut milk
- ⅛ teaspoon green curry paste (optional)
- 1 can (15½ ounces) black beans or garbanzo beans (chickpeas), rinsed and drained
- 1 tomato, seeded and chopped

1. Bring 2" water to a boil in a large saucepan over high heat. Place a steamer basket in the pan and add the broccoli and carrots. Cover, reduce the heat to medium, and steam for 10 minutes, or until tender. Place in a serving bowl and set aside. Rinse and dry the saucepan.

2. Heat the oil in the same saucepan over medium heat. Add the onion, garlic, and ginger and cook, stirring frequently, for 3 minutes, or until soft. Stir in the flour and curry powder and cook, stirring, for 1 minute longer. Gradually stir in the broth, coconut milk, and curry paste, if using. Bring to a simmer. Reduce the heat to low and simmer, stirring frequently, for 5 minutes, or until the sauce is slightly thickened.

3. Add the reserved vegetables, beans, and tomato. Cook, stirring, for 3 minutes, or until heated through.

Serves 6

Heart healthy ingredients: 10

Per serving: 244 calories, 135 calories from fat, 15 g total fat, 7 g saturated fat, 5 g monounsaturated fat, 2 g polyunsaturated fat, 1 mg cholesterol, 385 mg sodium, 22 g carbohydrates, 7 g fiber, 7 g sugar, 7 g protein

Better-for-You Black Bean Chili

Bingo! Almost every single ingredient in this quick, satisfying chili is a heart healthy food. Take the time to thoroughly rinse canned beans before draining and reduce the sodium content by up to 30 percent.

🌿 2 tablespoons extra-virgin olive oil

🌿 1 large onion, chopped

🌿 1 green bell pepper, chopped

🌿 1 large sweet potato, peeled and cut into ½" pieces

🌿 4 cloves garlic, minced

🌿 2 tablespoons chili powder

½ teaspoon ground cumin

🌿 2 cans (15 ounces each) black beans, rinsed and drained

🌿 2 cans (14½ ounces each) no-salt-added whole tomatoes with juice, chopped

🌿 1 can (4½ ounces) chopped green chile peppers, drained

🌿 1 ripe avocado, halved, seeded, peeled, and chopped

Heat the oil in a large saucepan over medium-high heat. Add the onion, bell pepper, and potato and cook for 5 minutes, stirring frequently. Add the garlic, chili powder, and cumin and cook for 1 minute longer. Stir in the beans, tomatoes, and chile peppers. Bring to a boil. Reduce the heat to medium-low and simmer for 15 minutes, or until the potato is tender. Spoon the chili into bowls and top each serving with some of the avocado.

Serves 6

🌿 **Heart healthy ingredients: 10**

Per serving: 234 calories, 94 calories from fat, 11 g total fat, 1 g saturated fat, 7 g monounsaturated fat, 2 g polyunsaturated fat, 0 mg cholesterol, 300 mg sodium, 31 g carbohydrates, 10 g fiber, 7 g sugar, 7 g protein

Grandma's Baked Beans

These classic beans will be a hit at your next barbecue or family reunion. They freeze well, so make two batches and freeze some for a later date.

- 1 pound dried Great Northern beans, soaked overnight, rinsed, and drained

  1½ cups boiling water

  ⅓ cup barbecue sauce

  ⅓ cup molasses

- 2 onions, 1 chopped and 1 whole

- 2 cloves garlic, minced

  1 tablespoon Dijon mustard

  1 teaspoon salt

  4 slices turkey bacon, sliced (optional)

  ¼ cup packed brown sugar

1. Place the beans in a large saucepan and add 8 cups water. Bring to a boil. Reduce the heat to low, cover, and simmer for 2 hours, or until the beans are tender. Drain.

2. Preheat the oven to 250°F. In a Dutch oven or 3-quart casserole, whisk together the boiling water, barbecue sauce, molasses, chopped onion, garlic, mustard, and salt. Stir in the drained beans and bacon, if using. Place the whole onion in the center of the beans and sprinkle the brown sugar over the top. Cover and bake for 5 hours, or until the beans are tender.

Serves 8

Heart healthy ingredients: 3

Per serving: 266 calories, 6 calories from fat, 1 g total fat, 0 g saturated fat, 0 g monounsaturated fat, 0 g polyunsaturated fat, 0 mg cholesterol, 410 mg sodium, 54 g carbohydrates, 11 g fiber, 19 g sugar, 13 g protein

BEAN COOKING TIMES

- Black-eyed peas: ¾ to 1 hour
- Large lima beans: ¾ to 1 hour
- Baby lima beans: 1 hour
- Dark red kidney beans: 1 to 1½ hours
- Garbanzo beans (chickpeas): 1 to 1½ hours
- Light red kidney beans: 1 to 1½ hours
- Pink beans: 1 to 1½ hours
- Small white beans: 1 to 1½ hours

Sesame-Seared Tofu

Sesame seeds are rich in unsaturated fats, omega-3 fatty acids, and other nutrients that lower total cholesterol and blood pressure, ease bloodflow, and improve insulin sensitivity—all of which lower the risk for heart disease. Serve these crisp cutlets with wilted spinach and oven-baked sweet potato fries.

♥ ¼ cup orange juice

1 tablespoon reduced-sodium soy sauce

1 tablespoon toasted sesame oil

♥ 3 cloves garlic, minced

♥ 1 teaspoon ground ginger

♥ 1 package (14 ounces) extra-firm reduced-fat tofu, well drained

♥ 1 tablespoon sesame seeds

1. In a shallow glass dish, whisk together the orange juice, soy sauce, oil, garlic, and ginger. Cut the tofu crosswise into eight ½"-thick slices and place in the marinade. Cover and refrigerate, turning occasionally, for at least 30 minutes or up to 8 hours.

2. Remove the tofu from the marinade and pat dry. Spread the sesame seeds on a plate and gently press each tofu slice into the seeds, coating each side.

3. Heat a nonstick skillet coated with cooking spray over medium heat. Add half the tofu slices and cook, turning once, for 6 minutes, or until browned and heated through. Repeat with the remaining slices.

Serves 4

♥ **Heart healthy ingredients: 5**

Per serving: 100 calories, 49 calories from fat, 6 g total fat, 1 g saturated fat, 2 g monounsaturated fat, 2 g polyunsaturated fat, 0 mg cholesterol, 220 mg sodium, 6 g carbohydrates, 0 g fiber, 1 g sugar, 8 g protein

OPEN SESAME

Made famous by the movie *Arabian Nights*, the magical command "open sesame" was so coined because when sesame seed pods reach maturity, they burst open.

Tofu and Bok Choy Stir-Fry

The fiber, antioxidants, and other nutrients in bok choy, a vegetable in the cabbage family and popular in Asian cooking, make it a good choice for those who want to lower their cholesterol levels, blood pressure, or weight.

2 tablespoons reduced-sodium soy sauce

1 tablespoon rice wine vinegar

1 teaspoon toasted sesame oil

1 teaspoon cornstarch

♥ 1 tablespoon minced fresh ginger

♥ ⅛ teaspoon crushed red pepper

♥ 4 ounces shiitake mushrooms, stemmed and sliced

♥ 3 baby bok choy, quartered lengthwise

♥ 3 cloves garlic, minced

♥ 1 tablespoon extra-virgin olive oil

♥ 1 package (14 ounces) extra-firm reduced-fat tofu, drained well and cut into 1" cubes

1. In a small bowl, combine the soy sauce, vinegar, sesame oil, cornstarch, ginger, and pepper. Set aside.

2. Heat a large nonstick skillet coated with cooking spray over medium-high heat. Add the mushrooms and cook, stirring occasionally, for 5 minutes, or until they release their liquid and the liquid evaporates. Add the bok choy and garlic and cook, stirring occasionally, for 3 minutes longer. Remove to a serving plate.

3. Heat the olive oil in the same skillet over medium-high heat. Add the tofu and cook, turning, for 8 minutes, or until golden and crispy. Stir the reserved soy sauce mixture and add to the skillet. Cook, stirring occasionally, for 3 minutes longer, or until the sauce is thickened. Pour over the bok choy.

Serves 4

♥ **Heart healthy ingredients: 7**

Per serving: 178 calories, 102 calories from fat, 10 g total fat, 2 g saturated fat, 4 g monounsaturated fat, 4 g polyunsaturated fat, 0 mg cholesterol, 348 mg sodium, 8 g carbohydrates, 2 g fiber, 2 g sugar, 14 g protein

PLEASE DO DAMAGE

To enjoy the antioxidant benefits of allicin, you must first chop, crush, or otherwise "damage" the garlic clove. A natural chemical reaction between two compounds in garlic creates heart healthy, atherosclerosis-fighting allicin.

Eggplant Lasagna

This family favorite gets a new twist—there's no pasta!—and packs a heart healthy punch. Tomatoes and onions are both rich in vitamin C and antioxidants, which help lower cholesterol levels and blood pressure.

♥ 1 tablespoon extra-virgin olive oil

♥ 1 medium onion, cut into thick slices

♥ 1 clove garlic, minced

♥ 1½ cups canned crushed tomatoes

1½ teaspoons dried basil

♥ 1½ teaspoons dried oregano

1 medium eggplant, peeled and sliced very thin

♥ 2 large tomatoes, sliced very thin

1½ cups (6 ounces) shredded reduced-fat mozzarella cheese

1. Preheat the oven to 425°F. Coat an 8" square baking dish with cooking spray.

2. Heat the oil in a nonstick skillet over medium heat. Add the onion and cook, turning once, for 5 minutes, or until lightly browned. Place in the prepared pan. Add the garlic to the same skillet and cook for 1 minute. Add the crushed tomatoes, basil, and oregano. Reduce the heat to medium-low and simmer for 10 minutes.

3. Spread about one-third of the tomato mixture over the onion layer. Arrange one-third of the eggplant over the tomatoes and top with one-third of the sliced tomato. Top with one-third of the cheese. Repeat the layers two times. Cover with aluminum foil.

4. Bake for 25 minutes, or until the vegetables are tender. Uncover and bake for 10 to 15 minutes longer, or until the cheese is lightly browned.

Serves 4

♥ **Heart healthy ingredients: 6**

Per serving: 257 calories, 99 calories from fat, 11 g total fat, 5 g saturated fat, 3 g monounsaturated fat, 3 g polyunsaturated fat, 15 mg cholesterol, 433 mg sodium, 25 g carbohydrates, 8 g fiber, 8 g sugar, 17 g protein

175 Family-Pleasing, Heart-Protecting Recipes

Bulgur-Stuffed Roasted Peppers

Fiber-rich bulgur and omega 3–packed tofu are the foundations of a heart healthy stuffing for bell peppers. Spinach, raisins, and almonds contribute bite and flavor. And did you know that just a few almonds can go a long way toward reducing heart disease? These "nutty" foods can lower blood pressure and cholesterol, regulate blood sugar levels, reduce plaque buildup, and improve bloodflow.

♥ 4 large red, yellow, or green bell peppers, stemmed, seeded, and halved lengthwise

♥ 1 cup bulgur wheat

♥ ½ teaspoon curry powder

¼ teaspoon salt

2 tablespoons mango chutney

♥ 12 ounces baked smoked tofu, cubed

♥ 1 bag (5 ounces) baby spinach, coarsely chopped

¼ cup raisins

♥ 2 tablespoons chopped almonds

1. Preheat the oven to 425°F. Coat a baking sheet with sides (jelly-roll pan) with cooking spray. Place the peppers, cut side down, on the prepared sheet. Roast, turning once, for 30 minutes, or until just tender.

2. Meanwhile, in a medium saucepan over high heat, bring 2 cups of water to a boil. Add the bulgur, curry powder, and salt. Remove from the heat. Cover and let stand until the bulgur is tender, about 30 minutes. Drain well. Stir in the chutney, tofu, spinach, raisins, and almonds.

3. Place the roasted peppers on a serving plate and evenly divide the bulgur mixture among the peppers.

Serves 4

♥ **Heart healthy ingredients: 6**

Per serving: 323 calories, 63 calories from fat, 7 g total fat, 1 g saturated fat, 5 g monounsaturated fat, 1 g polyunsaturated fat, 0 mg cholesterol, 438 mg sodium, 55 g carbohydrates, 13 g fiber, 17 g sugar, 16 g protein

CHAPTER 7

Pasta and Noodles Galore

Baked Pasta and Spinach

When you use flavorful Parmesan or Romano, you don't need a lot for robust flavor. The two cheeses are very similar and can be used interchangeably in most recipes. The major difference is that true Romano is made from sheep's milk, while the slightly milder Parmesan is made from cow's milk.

12 ounces penne or shell pasta

🌱 2 tablespoons extra-virgin olive oil

🌱 1 onion, minced

🌱 1 clove garlic, minced

¼ cup all-purpose flour

2½ cups fat-free milk

¾ cup (3 ounces) preshredded Romano or Parmesan cheese

🌱 1 can (14½ ounces) diced no-salt-added tomatoes, drained

🌱 1 bag (5 ounces) baby spinach

¼ cup packed fresh basil leaves, cut into thin strips

🌱 2 tablespoons wheat germ

1. Preheat the oven to 350°F. Coat a 13" × 9" baking dish with non-stick cooking spray.

2. Prepare the pasta according to package directions. Drain.

3. Meanwhile, heat the oil in a large saucepan over medium-high heat. Add the onion and garlic and cook for 5 minutes, or until tender. Add the flour and cook, stirring constantly, for 30 seconds. Gradually add the milk and cook, stirring constantly, for 4 minutes longer, or until bubbly. Remove from the heat. Stir in ½ cup of the cheese.

4. Add the pasta, tomatoes, spinach, and basil to the cheese sauce and toss to coat well. Transfer to the prepared dish. Sprinkle the wheat germ and the remaining ¼ cup cheese over the top. Bake for 30 minutes, or until heated through.

Serves 6

🌱 **Heart healthy ingredients: 6**

Per serving: 281 calories, 86 calories from fat, 10 g total fat, 4 g saturated fat, 4 g monounsaturated fat, 1 g polyunsaturated fat, 16 mg cholesterol, 273 mg sodium, 35 g carbohydrates, 4 g fiber, 9 g sugar, 15 g protein

Quick Vegetable Mac 'n' Cheese

Your kids will never know this rich, creamy dish is good for them! You can use the cornstarch/fat-free milk combination as the base of any cheese sauce that typically starts with butter and flour.

8 ounces shells or elbow pasta

♥ 3 cups mixed vegetables such as broccoli and cauliflower florets, sliced carrots, and chopped bell pepper

1¼ cups fat-free milk

2 tablespoons cornstarch

♥ 2 tablespoons extra-virgin olive oil

♥ 1 medium onion, chopped

1 cup (4 ounces) shredded reduced-fat sharp Cheddar cheese

2 ounces reduced-fat cream cheese

1. Prepare the pasta according to package directions, adding the vegetables to the water during the last 5 minutes of cooking time. Drain and place in a serving bowl.

2. Meanwhile, in a measuring cup, whisk together the milk and cornstarch. Heat the oil in a medium saucepan over medium heat. Add the onion and cook, stirring frequently, for 5 minutes. Add the milk mixture and bring to a boil, stirring constantly. Reduce the heat to medium-low and add the Cheddar and cream cheese. Stir until melted. Pour over the pasta mixture and toss to coat well.

Serves 4

♥ **Heart healthy ingredients: 3**

Per serving: 427 calories, 107 calories from fat, 12 g total fat, 4 g saturated fat, 6 g monounsaturated fat, 1 g polyunsaturated fat, 14 mg cholesterol, 311 mg sodium, 60 g carbohydrates, 5 g fiber, 11 g sugar, 20 g protein

MAKEOVER MAGIC

This family-favorite dish becomes healthier simply by using lighter cheeses and milk. Instead of making a flour-and-butter roux to thicken the sauce, cornstarch and fat-free milk do the job without adding fat.

	Traditional Mac 'n' Cheese	Quick Vegetable Mac 'n' Cheese
Calories	670	427
Fat (g)	35	12
Percent calories from fat	47	25

Penne with Roasted Autumn Vegetables

Heart healthy winter squash's hard shell gives it a long storage life, making it easy to keep on hand for simple dinners. The orange flesh is especially high in beta-carotene, which may reduce plaque buildup in the arteries. Other nutrients may lower blood pressure and prevent heart attacks and strokes.

- 3 cups peeled, cubed (about 1") butternut squash
- 4 ounces shiitake mushrooms, stemmed and sliced
- 1 large red onion, cut into wedges

  ½ teaspoon ground black pepper
- 2 tablespoons extra-virgin olive oil
- 8 ounces whole wheat penne pasta

  1 tablespoon chopped fresh sage or 1 teaspoon dried rubbed

  4 ounces reduced-fat Jarlsberg cheese, cubed

1. Preheat the oven to 475°F. In a large baking pan, combine the squash, mushrooms, onion, and pepper. Drizzle with the oil and toss to coat well. Roast, stirring occasionally, for 20 minutes, or until tender.

2. Meanwhile, prepare the pasta according to package directions. Drain.

3. In a large serving bowl, combine the squash mixture, sage, and cheese. Add the pasta and toss well to mix.

Serves 4

Heart healthy ingredients: 5

Per serving: 437 calories, 89 calories from fat, 10 g total fat, 2 g saturated fat, 6 g monounsaturated fat, 1 g polyunsaturated fat, 10 mg cholesterol, 94 mg sodium, 73 g carbohydrates, 10 g fiber, 9 g sugar, 18 g protein

THE THREE SISTERS

The Native Americans were the original experts when it came to responsible farming. They figured out that planting squash, corn, and beans (which they called the three sisters) together was a brilliant thing to do. The sprawling squash vines provided ground cover to choke out weeds, the cornstalks supported the climbing beans, and the beans provided ideal amounts of nitrogen for each of them.

Happy Heart Pasta Primavera

"I wanted to put together an easy dish that was heart healthy and at the same time would be a favorite for the entire family. I started with a family choice of pasta, then added my favorite heart-wise foods. Everyone loves it!"

MARCI B., LAKE PLACID, FLORIDA

- 8 ounces whole wheat rotini pasta
- ¼ cup extra-virgin olive oil
- 1 medium onion, chopped
- 1 red bell pepper, thinly sliced
- 3 cloves garlic, minced
- 1 carrot, sliced

  1 small yellow squash, sliced
- 1 cup broccoli florets

  ½ teaspoon ground black pepper
- ¼–½ teaspoon crushed red pepper

  1½ cups small frozen cooked shrimp, thawed
- ½ cup grape tomatoes, halved

  ⅓ cup (1⅓ ounces) freshly grated Parmesan cheese

1. Prepare the pasta according to package directions. Drain and place in a large serving bowl.

2. Meanwhile, heat the oil in a large skillet over medium-high heat. Add the onion, bell pepper, and garlic and cook, stirring occasionally, for 3 minutes, or until lightly browned. Add the carrot, squash, broccoli, black pepper, and crushed red pepper. Cook, stirring constantly, for 5 minutes longer, or until crisp-tender.

4. Stir in the shrimp and tomatoes and cook for 3 minutes, or until heated through. Pour over the pasta and sprinkle with the cheese.

Serves 6

♥ Heart healthy ingredients: 9

Per serving: 296 calories, 103 calories from fat, 12 g total fat, 2 g saturated fat, 7 g monounsaturated fat, 2 g polyunsaturated fat, 36 mg cholesterol, 126 mg sodium, 37 g carbohydrates, 6 g fiber, 5 g sugar, 12 g protein

175 Family-Pleasing, Heart-Protecting Recipes

Greek-Inspired Pasta

"My love for spinach, tomatoes, and pasta was the basis for this recipe. It's quick and easy to prepare. And since your green vegetable is mixed into your pasta, you don't need to make a side salad if you are tired or crunched for time. Serve with whole wheat bread, Merlot, and fresh fruit for dessert."

MARIE V., KUTZTOWN, PENNSYLVANIA

♥ 12 ounces whole wheat bow-tie, ziti, or penne pasta

♥ 2 tablespoons extra-virgin olive oil

♥ 1 clove garlic, minced

♥ ½ cup sun-dried tomatoes, chopped, soaked in water, and drained

2 tablespoons chopped fresh parsley

1 tablespoon chopped fresh basil

♥ 2 bags (5 ounces each) baby spinach

4 ounces fat-free feta cheese, crumbled

♥ ½ cup kalamata olives, pitted

1. Prepare the pasta according to package directions; drain.

2. In the same pot, heat the oil over medium heat. Add the garlic and cook for 2 minutes. Add the tomatoes, parsley, and basil and cook, stirring occasionally, for 2 minutes longer. Add the pasta, spinach, cheese, and olives and toss to coat well.

Serves 6

♥ Heart healthy ingredients: 6

Per serving: 318 calories, 62 calories from fat, 7 g total fat, 1 g saturated fat, 4 g monounsaturated fat, 1 g polyunsaturated fat, 7 mg cholesterol, 525 mg sodium, 52 g carbohydrates, 8 g fiber, 4 g sugar, 13 g protein

Orzo Pilaf

Orange juice gives this veggie-specked side dish an intriguing flavor. The juice's high concentration of vitamin C neutralizes free radicals and prevents plaque buildup, while ginger reduces the formation of blood clots. The duo works to prevent heart attacks or strokes.

- 1 tablespoon extra-virgin olive oil
- 2 cloves garlic, minced
- ½ teaspoon ground ginger
- 1½ cups fat-free, reduced-sodium vegetable broth
- ½ cup orange juice
- 1 cup orzo pasta
- 2 scallions, chopped
- 1 carrot, shredded

1. Heat the oil in a medium saucepan over medium heat. Add the garlic and ginger and cook for 1 minute, or until fragrant. Stir in the broth, orange juice, and pasta and bring to a boil. Reduce the heat to low, cover, and simmer for 10 minutes, or until most of the liquid is absorbed.

2. Remove from the heat and stir in the scallions and carrot. Cover and let stand for 5 minutes, or until all of the liquid is absorbed. Fluff with a fork.

Serves 4

Heart healthy ingredients: 6

Per serving: 283 calories, 43 calories from fat, 5 g total fat, 1 g saturated fat, 3 g monounsaturated fat, 1 g polyunsaturated fat, 0 mg cholesterol, 41 mg sodium, 51 g carbohydrates, 3 g fiber, 4 g sugar, 10 g protein

OXYGEN AND ANTIOXIDANTS

The human body is made up of over a trillion cells, all of which need life-giving oxygen. When cells are deprived of oxygen, even for a very short period of time, they die. The seriousness of that death depends on the kind of cell, where it was, and for how long.

Oxygen reaches your cells via your blood, which in about 1 minute completely traverses all 65,000 miles of your body's transportation superhighway system (aka your arteries, veins, and capillaries), delivering oxygen and nutrients to every cell—meaning every muscle, tissue, and organ in your body. Simultaneously, your blood brings deoxygenated blood and waste back to your lungs for a fresh inhale of oxygen and an equally important exhale of carbon dioxide.

Nevertheless, oxygen is a double-edged sword. Just as your car needs an engine, your body needs oxygen to burn its fuel, but oxygen is a very reactive chemical that causes damage to your cells, much in the same way that it is responsible for rust. That's where antioxidants come in. Good sources of antioxidants include many foods from our Top 40:

- Bell peppers (red and green)
- Broccoli
- Blueberries
- Kiwifruit
- Mango
- Nuts
- Oils
- Spinach
- Strawberries
- Sweet potatoes
- Tomatoes

Spaghetti with Puttanesca Sauce

This piquant Italian pasta get its kick from black olives, capers, and crushed red pepper—and a touch of heart healthy red wine. When purchasing wine for cooking, avoid the cooking wines in the condiment section of your market. Not only are they of poor quality, but they also have added sodium. Instead, use a wine you enjoy drinking.

- 2 tablespoons extra-virgin olive oil
- 1 large onion, chopped
- 1 red bell pepper, chopped
- 4 cloves garlic, minced
- 2 teaspoons dried oregano, crushed
- 2 cans (14½ ounces each) no-salt-added whole tomatoes, drained, reserving ½ cup liquid, and chopped
- ½ cup dry red wine
- ¼ cup pitted kalamata olives, chopped
- 2 tablespoons capers, rinsed and drained
- ½ teaspoon red-pepper flakes
- 12 ounces spaghetti
- ¼ cup (1 ounce) grated Romano or Parmesan cheese

1. Heat the oil in a large saucepan over medium-high heat. Add the onion and bell pepper and cook, stirring occasionally, for 5 minutes, or until lightly browned. Add the garlic and oregano and cook for 1 minute longer.

2. Stir in the tomatoes with their reserved liquid, wine, olives, capers, and pepper flakes. Bring to a boil. Reduce the heat to medium and simmer, uncovered, for 15 minutes to blend flavors.

3. Meanwhile, prepare the pasta according to package directions. Drain and place in a serving bowl. Pour the sauce over the pasta and toss to coat. Sprinkle with the cheese.

Serves 6

Heart healthy ingredients: 9

Per serving: 334 calories, 68 calories from fat, 8 g total fat, 2 g saturated fat, 4 g monounsaturated fat, 1 g polyunsaturated fat, 5 mg cholesterol, 270 mg sodium, 52 g carbohydrates, 4 g fiber, 6 g sugar, 12 g protein

MAKEOVER MAGIC

Many Italian sauce recipes start with ½ cup of olive oil, but too much good fat can still be too much. We use just 2 tablespoons oil and let the tomatoes take center stage in the sauce.

	Traditional Pasta Puttanesca	Spaghetti with Puttanesca Sauce
Calories	531	334
Fat (g)	31	8
Percent calories from fat	53	22

Linguine with Walnut Pesto

Here's a great way to incorporate heart healthy walnuts into your dinner. Your family will get a healthy dose of vitamin E and reduce their cholesterol while enjoying this scrumptious fare.

12 ounces linguine

2 cups packed fresh basil leaves

½ cup grated Parmesan cheese

♥ ¼ cup walnut halves

♥ 2 cloves garlic

♥ 2 tablespoons lemon juice

♥ 2 tablespoons extra-virgin olive oil

1. Prepare the linguine according to package directions. Drain, reserving ½ cup of the pasta water. Place the drained pasta in a serving bowl.

2. Meanwhile, in a food processor or blender, combine the basil, cheese, walnuts, and garlic. Process or blend until minced. With the machine running, add the lemon juice and then the oil, pulsing until well blended.

3. Pour the pesto over the pasta and toss, adding ¼ to ½ cup of the reserved pasta water until the sauce reaches the desired consistency.

Serves 6

♥ **Heart healthy ingredients: 4**

Per serving: 312 calories, 90 calories from fat, 10 g total fat, 2 g saturated fat, 4 g monounsaturated fat, 3 g polyunsaturated fat, 6 mg cholesterol, 106 mg sodium, 45 g carbohydrates, 3 g fiber, 3 g sugar, 11 g protein

IN THE KITCHEN

Wash lemons and limes thoroughly before juicing or grating. And if you need both peel and juice, be sure to do the grating first—it's really hard to get the peel off a juiced lemon half! To get the most juice, either microwave briefly on high or roll the fruit on the countertop, pressing down with the palm of your hand.

Here are some suggestions for what to do with a bumper crop of lemons or limes.

- Fish and lemon or lime are natural companions. Try topping broiled fillets with thin slices or baking seafood on a bed of lemon slices.

- Here's a supereasy salad dressing: ¼ cup olive oil, 2 tablespoons lemon juice, salt, and pepper. Add a little minced garlic, if you like.

- Grilling kebabs? Skewer wedges of lemon or lime between large shrimp, chunks of fish, beef cubes, and/or vegetables.

- Stir a tablespoon or so of lemon juice into almost any sauce just before serving—it's virtually guaranteed to brighten the sauce and bring out its other flavors.

Penne with Alfredo Sauce

This rich, smooth sauce is made not from fat-laden heavy cream but from soft light silken tofu, which has a positive effect on cholesterol levels and blood pressure. Tofu's omega-3 fatty acids also reduce blood clots that can lead to a heart attack or stroke.

♥ 8 ounces whole wheat penne pasta

♥ 1 package (12 ounces) soft light silken tofu, drained

♥ 1 tablespoon extra-virgin olive oil

♥ ½ small onion, minced

♥ 2 cloves garlic, minced

1½ teaspoons dried basil, crushed

½ cup grated Romano cheese

1. Prepare the pasta according to package directions. Drain, reserving ½ cup pasta water.

2. Place the tofu in a food processor or blender and pulse until very creamy.

3. Heat the oil in a nonstick skillet over medium heat. Add the onion and cook, stirring occasionally, for 5 minutes, or until very tender. Add the garlic and basil and cook, stirring occasionally, for 2 minutes longer. Gradually add the tofu and cheese and cook, stirring constantly, for another 3 minutes, or until heated through.

4. Place the pasta in a serving bowl, add the sauce, and toss, adding some pasta water if needed to thin the sauce.

Serves 4

♥ **Heart healthy ingredients: 5**

Per serving: 350 calories, 91 calories from fat, 10 g total fat, 4 g saturated fat, 3 g monounsaturated fat, 1 g polyunsaturated fat, 15 mg cholesterol, 339 mg sodium, 47 g carbohydrates, 6 g fiber, 4 g sugar, 19 g protein

MAKEOVER MAGIC

Traditional Alfredo sauce comes together with a blend of heavy cream, butter, egg yolks, and cheese. Using tofu to create the same creamy texture cuts the calories in half and slashes the fat.

	Traditional Pasta Alfredo	Penne with Alfredo Sauce
Calories	739	350
Fat (g)	55	10
Percent calories from fat	67	26

Vegetable Noodle Bowl

Curry pastes are common in Southeast Asian cooking, often added to soups and stews. The color of the paste indicates the main ingredients, so green paste is often herb-based, while red paste is often spice-based.

4 ounces udon noodles (thick, round, fresh Japanese wheat noodles) or spaghetti

3 cups fat-free, reduced-sodium vegetable broth

1 can (13½ ounces) light coconut milk

♥ 1 tablespoon minced fresh ginger

♥ ¼ teaspoon red curry paste

♥ 1½ cups frozen shelled edamame (soybeans), thawed

♥ 2 cups prepared coleslaw mix

1 cup sugar snap peas

♥ 4 ounces shiitake mushrooms, stemmed and sliced

♥ 4 scallions, sliced

♥ 2 tablespoons fresh lime juice

2 tablespoons minced fresh cilantro

1. Prepare the noodles or spaghetti according to package directions. Drain, reserving 1 cup of the water.

2. Meanwhile, in a large saucepan over medium-high heat, bring the broth, coconut milk, ginger, and curry paste to a boil. Reduce the heat to medium and add the edamame, coleslaw, peas, mushrooms, and scallions and cook for 5 minutes longer.

3. Add the cooked noodles or spaghetti and reserved pasta water and cook until heated through. Remove from the heat and stir in the lime juice and cilantro.

Serves 6

♥ **Heart healthy ingredients: 7**

Per serving: 173 calories, 28 calories from fat, 3 g total fat, 0 g saturated fat, 0 g monounsaturated fat, 1 g polyunsaturated fat, 3 mg cholesterol, 393 mg sodium, 28 g carbohydrates, 5 g fiber, 3 g sugar, 9 g protein

Mediterranean Pasta with Shrimp

This quick, no-cook sauce offers plenty of flavor and heart healthy ingredients. Adding hot pasta to fresh vegetables slightly softens them without overcooking. The already-soft goat cheese melts to add a creamy texture to the dressing.

12 ounces rotelle or corkscrew pasta

♥ 2 tablespoons fresh lemon juice

♥ 4 cloves garlic, crushed

½ teaspoon ground black pepper

♥ 2 tablespoons extra-virgin olive oil

♥ 8 cups coarsely chopped arugula

♥ 1 large tomato, seeded and chopped

¾ pound cooked, peeled, and deveined medium shrimp

½ package (2½ ounces) reduced-fat goat cheese, crumbled

1. Prepare the pasta according to package directions. Drain.

2. Meanwhile, in a large serving bowl, whisk together the lemon juice, garlic, and pepper. Whisk in the oil until emulsified. Add the arugula, tomato, shrimp, and cheese.

3. Add the hot pasta to the vegetables and shrimp in the bowl and toss to coat well.

Serves 6

♥ **Heart healthy ingredients: 5**

Per serving: 393 calories, 81 calories from fat, 8 g total fat, 2 g saturated fat, 3 g monounsaturated fat, 2 g polyunsaturated fat, 117 mg cholesterol, 188 mg sodium, 55 g carbohydrates, 3 g fiber, 2 g sugar, 25 g protein

Spinach Linguine with Fresh Tomatoes and Pork

This colorful pasta dish is sure to become a family favorite. The red pigment in tomatoes, called lycopene, is an antioxidant that, along with vitamins A and C, prevents plaque buildup. Raw tomatoes are good for you, but cooking them in olive oil allows your body to absorb even more of the nutrient.

12 ounces spinach linguine

♥ 2 tablespoons extra-virgin olive oil

1 pork tenderloin (12 ounces), trimmed of any fat and cut into ¼" slices

♥ 2 cloves garlic, minced

♥ 1 large onion, finely chopped

1 teaspoon fennel seeds, crushed

♥ 8 large ripe tomatoes (about 3 pounds), seeded and chopped

1 cup packed fresh basil, cut into thin strips

½ teaspoon sugar

¼ teaspoon salt

1. Prepare the pasta according to package directions. Drain and place in a large serving bowl.

2. Meanwhile, heat the oil in a large skillet over medium-high heat. Add half of the pork and cook, stirring occasionally, for 3 minutes, or until no longer pink. Using a slotted spoon, remove to a bowl. Repeat with remaining pork.

3. Add the garlic, onion, and fennel to the skillet and cook, stirring, for 3 minutes, or until the onion is slightly tender. Add the tomatoes, basil, sugar, and salt and cook for 2 minutes longer. Return the pork and any accumulated juices to the skillet. Cook for another 2 minutes, or until heated through. Pour over the pasta and toss.

Serves 6

♥ **Heart healthy ingredients: 4**

Per serving: 396 calories, 73 calories from fat, 8 g total fat, 1 g saturated fat, 4 g monounsaturated fat, 2 g polyunsaturated fat, 37 mg cholesterol, 156 mg sodium, 58 g carbohydrates, 9 g fiber, 9 g sugar, 22 g protein

CHAPTER 8

Selections from the Sea

Coquilles St. Jacques

"I created this after watching my friend, a French-born woman, make a similar recipe with snails. Clams suited my taste a bit more, and the recipe is just as good! Serve with a salad of mixed greens tossed with extra-virgin olive oil, vinegar, and grated Parmesan cheese and whole wheat toast sticks."

FAE D., ELIZABETH CITY, NORTH CAROLINA

1 cup 2% milk

2 tablespoons cornstarch

♥ 3 shallots, minced

♥ 4 ounces shiitake mushrooms, stemmed and chopped

♥ 1 clove garlic, minced

⅛ teaspoon dried basil

½ teaspoon ground white or black pepper

2 cans (6½ ounces each) chopped clams, undrained

4 ounces (1 cup) shredded Swiss cheese or Gruyère cheese

Dash of paprika

1. Preheat the oven to 375°F. In a measuring cup or small bowl, whisk together the milk and cornstarch. Set aside.

2. Heat a skillet coated with cooking spray over medium heat. Add the shallots and cook, stirring occasionally, for 4 minutes, or until softened. Add the mushrooms and cook, stirring occasionally, for 5 minutes longer, or until softened. Add the garlic, basil, and pepper and cook for another minute. Stir the reserved milk mixture and then stir it into the skillet, along with the clams and their juice. Bring to a simmer. Add ½ cup of the cheese and stir to melt and combine well.

3. Pour the mixture into four 4-ounce (½-cup) ramekins or scallop shells. Top with the remaining ½ cup cheese and a sprinkle of the paprika. Bake for 15 minutes, or until lightly browned.

Serves 4

♥ **Heart healthy ingredients: 3**

Per serving: 210 calories, 83 calories from fat, 9 g total fat, 6 g saturated fat, 2.4 g monounsaturated fat, 0.5 g polyunsaturated fat, 48 mg cholesterol, 685 mg sodium, 16 g carbohydrates, 1 g fiber, 5 g sugar, 17 g protein

Paella

Although the ingredient list may seem long, this one-dish meal comes together in minutes. Use a paella pan if you have one; otherwise, a large (12") skillet will work best, as it allows the rice to cook evenly.

- ❤ 2 tablespoons extra-virgin olive oil

- ❤ 1 onion, chopped

- ❤ 2 red or green bell peppers, chopped

- ❤ 2 cloves garlic, minced

- ❤ ½ teaspoon ground turmeric

- ¾ cup long-grain rice

- 1½ cups fat-free, reduced-sodium chicken broth

- ¾ cup peas

- ❤ 2 tomatoes, seeded and chopped

- ½ pound sea scallops

- ½ pound large shrimp, peeled and deveined

- 16 littleneck clams, scrubbed

1. Heat the oil in a large skillet over medium-high heat. Add the onion and red and green peppers and cook, stirring occasionally, for 5 minutes, or until lightly browned. Add the garlic and turmeric and cook for 1 minute longer.

2. Stir in the rice, broth, peas, and tomatoes. Bring to a boil, reduce the heat to low, cover, and simmer for 10 minutes. Increase the heat to medium and stir in the scallops, shrimp, and clams. Cover and simmer for 10 minutes, or until the scallops and shrimp are opaque and the clams open. Discard any unopened clams.

Serves 6

❤ **Heart healthy ingredients: 6**

Per serving: 285 calories, 69 calories from fat, 8 g total fat, 1 g saturated fat, 4 g monounsaturated fat, 2 g polyunsaturated fat, 79 mg cholesterol, 279 mg sodium, 32 g carbohydrates, 3 g fiber, 5 g sugar, 21 g protein

Scallops Fra Diavolo

Red wine adds a robust flavor to this spicy tomato sauce full of antioxidant goodness. It's a delicious way to lower blood pressure and reduce the risk of heart attack and stroke.

- 2 tablespoons extra-virgin olive oil
- 1 large onion, chopped
- 1 red bell pepper, chopped
- 4 cloves garlic, minced
- ¼ cup red wine
- 2 cans (14½ ounces each) no-salt-added stewed tomatoes
- ¼ teaspoon crushed red pepper
- 1½ pounds sea scallops

1. Heat the oil in a large skillet over medium-high heat. Add the onion and bell pepper and cook, stirring occasionally, for 5 minutes, or until lightly browned. Add the garlic and cook for 1 minute longer. Add the wine and cook for another minute.

2. Stir in the tomatoes and crushed red pepper and bring to a boil. Reduce the heat to medium and simmer, uncovered, for 15 minutes, or until slightly thickened. Add the scallops and cook for 5 to 10 minutes longer, or until opaque.

Serves 4

🌱 **Heart healthy ingredients: 7**

Per serving: 324 calories, 72 calories from fat, 8 g total fat, 1 g saturated fat, 5 g monounsaturated fat, 1 g polyunsaturated fat, 56 mg cholesterol, 303 mg sodium, 26 g carbohydrates, 5 g fiber, 13 g sugar, 32 g protein

Simple Salmon with Almonds

Bursting with omega-3 fatty acids, all salmon is nutritionally beneficial. Wild salmon, however, has the highest amount of these essential fatty acids, so opt for it whenever possible.

- 4 salmon fillets (6 ounces each), skinned
- ¼ cup sliced almonds
- ⅓ cup dry sherry
- 1 tablespoon orange juice
- 1 tablespoon chopped fresh chives

1. Heat a nonstick skillet coated with cooking spray over medium heat. Add the salmon and cook, turning once, for 6 minutes, or until opaque. Remove to a serving plate.

2. Add the almonds to the skillet and cook for 3 minutes, or until lightly toasted. Stir in the sherry, orange juice, and chives. Cook for 2 minutes, or until heated through. Drizzle over the fish.

Serves 4

🌱 **Heart healthy ingredients: 4**

Per serving: 210 calories, 92 calories from fat, 10 g total fat, 1 g saturated fat, 4 g monounsaturated fat, 4 g polyunsaturated fat, 62 mg cholesterol, 52 mg sodium, 2 g carbohydrates, 1 g fiber, 0 g sugar, 24 g protein

Sesame Salmon with Spicy Cucumber Salad

"When my family and I first moved from Washington, DC, to Hilton Head Island in South Carolina, the owners of a prosperous local restaurant invited us to their Lowcountry home for dinner. True to the reputation of gracious Southern hospitality, our hostess modified her meal plan to serve a heart healthy dinner on my behalf. We sat down at a long table in their large dining room overlooking a spectacular sunset on the ocean's horizon. I hope you'll enjoy the recipe as much as we relished the meal and a budding friendship on that beautiful night! Serve with steamed asparagus, if desired."

KIM KACHMANN-GELTZ, HILTON HEAD ISLAND, SOUTH CAROLINA

Salad

3 hothouse cucumbers, peeled, quartered, and seeded

6 radishes, julienned

♥ 1 scallion, sliced

4 teaspoons rice wine vinegar

1 teaspoon sugar

♥ ⅛–¼ teaspoon red-pepper flakes

Salmon

♥ 4 salmon fillets (6 ounces each), skinned

2 tablespoons rice wine vinegar

2 tablespoons reduced-sodium soy sauce

½ teaspoon ground black pepper

♥ ¼ cup sesame seeds

1. Preheat the oven to 400°F. Coat a baking sheet with sides (jelly-roll pan) with cooking spray.

2. *To make the salad:* Slice the cucumbers at an angle into ½"-thick pieces. In a large bowl, toss together the cucumbers, radishes, scallion, vinegar, sugar, and pepper flakes. Cover and refrigerate until ready to use.

3. *To make the salmon:* Place the salmon on the prepared pan. In a small bowl, whisk together the vinegar and soy sauce. Brush the vinegar mixture on the salmon and sprinkle with the black pepper and sesame seeds, pressing the seeds onto the fillets. Roast for 8 minutes, or until the fish is opaque. Serve with the salad.

Serves 4

♥ Heart healthy ingredients: 4

Per serving: 200 calories, 92 calories from fat, 10 g total fat, 1 g saturated fat, 3 g monounsaturated fat, 4 g polyunsaturated fat, 47 mg cholesterol, 314 mg sodium, 7 g carbohydrates, 1 g fiber, 3 g sugar, 21 g protein

Spiced Salmon Tacos

These slightly messy tacos are bursting with heart healthy avocado. It's ironic that avocado, the fattiest of all vegetables, helps lower cholesterol levels: The phytochemical beta-sitosterol literally blocks the absorption of cholesterol from foods.

8 (6") corn tortillas

♥ 1 Hass avocado, halved and pitted

¼ cup cilantro, chopped

♥ 1 medium tomato, seeded and finely chopped

♥ 1 clove garlic, minced

½ teaspoon grated lime peel

♥ 1 tablespoon lime juice

½ teaspoon salt

1 teaspoon ground cumin

♥ 1 teaspoon chili powder

♥ ¼ teaspoon ground red pepper

♥ 1½ pounds salmon fillets, skinned

♥ 2 cups shredded romaine lettuce

1. Preheat the oven to 425°F. Coat a baking pan with cooking spray. Wrap the tortillas in foil.

2. Using a spoon, remove the avocado flesh from the shell. Place in a shallow bowl and mash with a fork. Add the cilantro, tomato, garlic, lime peel, lime juice, and ¼ teaspoon of the salt. Stir until well blended. Cover the surface with plastic wrap and set aside.

3. In a small bowl, combine the cumin, chili powder, pepper, and the remaining ¼ teaspoon salt. Rub over the salmon. Place in the prepared baking pan and bake for 7 minutes, or until opaque. Remove and turn off the oven. Place the tortillas in the oven for 3 minutes, or until warmed.

4. Unwrap the tortillas. Flake the salmon into a bowl. Divide the lettuce evenly among the tortillas. Divide the salmon and place over the lettuce. Top with the avocado mixture.

Serves 4

♥ **Heart healthy ingredients: 8**

Per serving: 480 calories, 185 calories from fat, 21 g total fat, 3 g saturated fat, 9 g monounsaturated fat, 5 g polyunsaturated fat, 94 mg cholesterol, 488 mg sodium, 36 g carbohydrates, 6 g fiber, 2 g sugar, 37 g protein

194

Grilled Shrimp with Mango Salsa

Sweet, juicy mangos are loaded with vitamins, minerals, antioxidants, and fiber. Similar to papayas—another bright orange tropical fruit—mangos also contain an enzyme with stomach-soothing capabilities that aid digestion.

½ pound peeled and deveined large shrimp

♥ 2 teaspoons chili powder

1 teaspoon ground cumin

♥ ¼ teaspoon ground red pepper

♥ 2 mangos, peeled, seeded, and chopped

♥ ½ small red onion, finely chopped

⅓ cup chopped cilantro

♥ 1 clove garlic, minced

♥ 1 tablespoon minced chile pepper

♥ 3 tablespoons lime juice

1. Preheat the grill or broiler. In a large bowl, combine the shrimp, chili powder, cumin, and ground red pepper. Set aside.

2. *To make the salsa:* In a medium bowl, combine the mangos, onion, cilantro, garlic, chile pepper, and lime juice. Toss to coat and set aside.

3. *To make the shrimp:* Place the shrimp in a grill basket or on a broiler pan. Grill or broil the shrimp 6" from the heat, turning once, for 4 minutes, or until opaque. Serve with the reserved salsa.

Serves 4

♥ **Heart healthy ingredients: 7**

Per serving: 129 calories, 10 calories from fat, 1 g total fat, 0 g saturated fat, 0 g monounsaturated fat, 1 g polyunsaturated fat, 84 mg cholesterol, 123 mg sodium, 22 g carbohydrates, 3 g fiber, 16 g sugar, 10 g protein

Grilled Tuna with Wasabi Cream

Wasabi, also known as Japanese horseradish, has a fiery, pungent flavor that mellows nicely when blended with sour cream. Look for wasabi paste or wasabi powder (which you mix with water to make a paste) in the Asian section of your supermarket. To make this dish part of a heart healthy meal, serve with Barley Edamame Salad (page 119).

2 tablespoons reduced-sodium soy sauce

2 tablespoons rice wine vinegar

1 tablespoon sugar

½ teaspoon toasted sesame oil

½ teaspoon ground ginger

♥ 1½ pounds tuna steaks

¼ cup reduced-fat sour cream

½ teaspoon wasabi paste

1. In a large shallow dish, combine the soy sauce, vinegar, sugar, oil, and ginger. Stir until the sugar dissolves. Add the tuna, turning to coat. Cover and marinate in the refrigerator for 30 minutes, turning occasionally.

2. Coat the grill rack or broiler rack with cooking spray. Preheat the grill or broiler. In a small bowl, combine the sour cream and wasabi paste.

3. Remove the tuna from the dish and discard the marinade. Place the tuna on the grill or broiler rack and grill or broil, turning once, for 6 minutes for medium-rare. Serve with the wasabi cream.

Serves 6

♥ **Heart healthy ingredients: 1**

Per serving: 194 calories, 64 calories from fat, 7 g total fat, 2 g saturated fat, 2 g monounsaturated fat, 2 g polyunsaturated fat, 47 mg cholesterol, 227 mg sodium, 4 g carbohydrates, 0 g fiber, 2 g sugar, 27 g protein

Tuna Tetrazzini

This low-fat version of the classic family-friendly casserole is sure to please. When switching to whole wheat pasta, start by using half whole wheat and half regular, gradually increasing to all whole wheat pasta as your family gets used to it.

♥ 1 pound whole wheat spaghetti, broken in half

♥ 2 tablespoons extra-virgin olive oil

♥ 6 scallions, chopped

♥ 4 ounces shiitake mushrooms, stemmed and sliced

♥ ½ teaspoon dried thyme, crushed

3 cups reduced-fat milk

1 cup fat-free, reduced-sodium chicken broth

¼ cup cornstarch

1 cup (4 ounces) grated Parmesan cheese

♥ 3 cans (6 ounces each) solid white tuna, drained and broken up

♥ 2 tablespoons wheat germ

1. Preheat the oven to 375°F. Coat a 13" × 9" baking pan with cooking spray.

2. Prepare the pasta according to package directions. Drain and return to the pot.

3. Meanwhile, heat the oil in a medium saucepan over medium heat. Add the scallions, mushrooms, and thyme and cook, stirring occasionally, for 5 minutes, or until lightly browned. In a measuring cup or small bowl, whisk together the milk, broth, and cornstarch. Stir into the mushroom mixture and bring to a simmer over medium heat. Add ¾ cup of the cheese and cook for 3 minutes, or until the sauce thickens.

4. Pour the mushroom mixture over the pasta in the pot. Add the tuna and toss to coat. Scrape into the prepared pan and sprinkle with the wheat germ and the remaining ¼ cup cheese. Bake for 35 minutes, or until bubbling in the center.

Serves 8

♥ **Heart healthy ingredients: 7**

Per serving: 436 calories, 100 calories from fat, 11 g total fat, 4 g saturated fat, 5 g monounsaturated fat, 2 g polyunsaturated fat, 43 mg cholesterol, 446 mg sodium, 55 g carbohydrates, 8 g fiber, 8 g sugar, 32 g protein

MAKEOVER MAGIC

Tetrazzini classically includes a rich cream sauce made from butter, flour, and whole milk. By switching to reduced-fat milk and thickening it with just cornstarch, the fat grams are cut almost in half—yet the dish is still a creamy, delicious delight. The tuna adds heart healthy omega-3 fatty acids.

	Traditional Tetrazzini Recipe	Tuna Tetrazzini
Calories	559	436
Fat (g)	21	11
Percent calories from fat	34	23

Crab Cakes

Serve these flavorful cakes on a bed of baby salad greens with either the Black Bean Salad (page 120) or Corn Salsa (page 265).

¼ cup reduced-fat canola mayonnaise

1 egg white

1 teaspoon grated lime peel

♥ 1 tablespoon lime juice

½ teaspoon ground cumin

♥ 8 drops hot-pepper sauce

1 pound fresh jumbo lump crabmeat, picked over

♥ ½ small red onion, finely chopped

¼ cup chopped cilantro

3 tablespoons + ½ cup dried low-sodium bread crumbs

1. In a large bowl, whisk together the mayonnaise, egg white, lime peel, lime juice, cumin, and hot-pepper sauce. Add the crabmeat, onion, cilantro, and 3 tablespoons of the bread crumbs. Gently toss with a rubber spatula until well blended. Shape into 4 cakes.

2. Place the remaining ½ cup bread crumbs on a plate. Dredge the cakes in the crumbs, pressing to coat. Place on a parchment-lined baking sheet and chill, uncovered, for at least 30 minutes.

3. Heat a nonstick skillet coated with cooking spray over medium heat. Place the crab cakes in the skillet and cook, turning once, for 10 minutes, or until heated through.

Serves 4

♥ **Heart healthy ingredients: 3**

Per serving: 166 calories, 46 calories from fat, 5 g total fat, 0 g saturated fat, 3 g monounsaturated fat, 2 g polyunsaturated fat, 89 mg cholesterol, 491 mg sodium, 5 g carbohydrates, 1 g fiber, 1 g sugar, 22 g protein

Salmon Cakes

Salmon packed in a pouch can vary greatly in the amount of sodium per serving, so be sure to read labels and select the brand with the lowest sodium. Serve the cakes on whole wheat buns or with Fruited Rice Pilaf (page 150) and steamed asparagus.

2 egg whites

¼ cup reduced-fat canola mayonnaise

♥ ¼ jarred roasted red pepper, patted dry and chopped

♥ 1 teaspoon lemon juice

♥ ½ teaspoon dried thyme, crushed

¼ teaspoon capers

♥ 2 pouches (7 ounces each) salmon, patted dry

♥ 1 cup fresh whole wheat bread crumbs

1. In a medium bowl, whisk the egg whites. Stir in the mayonnaise, pepper, lemon juice, thyme, and capers. Add the salmon and bread crumbs and gently toss with a rubber spatula until well blended. Shape the mixture into 4 cakes and place on a parchment-lined baking sheet. Chill, uncovered, for at least 30 minutes.

2. Heat a nonstick skillet coated with cooking spray over medium heat. Place the cakes in the skillet and cook, turning once, for 6 minutes, or until browned and crisp.

Serves 4

♥ **Heart healthy ingredients: 5**

Per serving: 248 calories, 100 calories from fat, 11 g total fat, 2 g saturated fat, 5 g monounsaturated fat, 3 g polyunsaturated fat, 44 mg cholesterol, 472 mg sodium, 7 g carbohydrates, 0 g fiber, 1 g sugar, 26 g protein

Hoisin Halibut with Bok Choy

Halibut is a good source of omega-3 fatty acids, which improve the ratio of "good" and "bad" cholesterol, decrease blood clots and inflammation of the arteries, and relax veins and arteries to improve bloodflow.

2 tablespoons hoisin sauce

♥ 1 tablespoon orange juice

♥ 4 halibut fillets (5 ounces each), skinned

♥ 4 heads baby bok choy, halved

1. Preheat the oven to 400°F. Coat a baking sheet with sides (jelly-roll pan) with cooking spray.

2. In a small bowl, stir together the hoisin sauce and orange juice. Place the halibut and bok choy on the prepared baking sheet. Brush both with the glaze. Bake for 10 minutes, or until the fish flakes easily when tested with a fork.

Serves 4

♥ **Heart healthy ingredients: 3**

Per serving: 199 calories, 29 calories from fat, 3 g total fat, 0 g saturated fat, 1 g monounsaturated fat, 1 g polyunsaturated fat, 45 mg cholesterol, 440 mg sodium, 14 g carbohydrates, 3 g fiber, 6 g sugar, 32 g protein

Oven-Fried Fish and Chips

While all cold-water fatty fish have been shown to promote heart health due to omega-3 fatty acids and B vitamins, many other fish are worthy, too. For those wary of strong "fishy" flavors, cod is a good place to start, as its mild-tasting white flesh easily picks up the seasonings from sauces or rubs.

♥ 4 medium sweet potatoes, scrubbed

♥ 2 tablespoons extra-virgin olive oil

¼ teaspoon salt

¼ cup dry bread crumbs

¼ cup cornmeal

♥ ⅛ teaspoon ground red pepper

1 egg white

4 fresh or thawed frozen cod or other fish fillets (4 ounces each)

1. Preheat the oven to 450°F. Coat 2 baking sheets with sides (jelly-roll pans) with cooking spray.

2. Cut the potatoes lengthwise into 8 wedges. Place on 1 baking sheet (the largest if sizes vary) and toss with the oil and salt. Bake, turning once, for 20 minutes, or until lightly browned and tender.

3. In a shallow dish, combine the bread crumbs, cornmeal, and pepper. In another shallow dish, beat the egg white. Dip the fillets into the egg white and then dredge in the crumb mixture. Place on the remaining prepared baking sheet. Spray the fillets with cooking spray.

4. Bake the fish, turning once, for 6 minutes for each ½" thickness of fish, or until the fish flakes easily when tested with a fork. Serve with the sweet potatoes.

Serves 4

♥ **Heart healthy ingredients: 3**

Per serving: 324 calories, 73 calories from fat, 8 g total fat, 1 g saturated fat, 5 g monounsaturated fat, 1 g polyunsaturated fat, 42 mg cholesterol, 367 mg sodium, 37 g carbohydrates, 5 g fiber, 6 g sugar, 25 g protein

MAKEOVER MAGIC

Traditionally, this British fast food is deep-fried. Here we've eliminated all the bad fats by oven-frying the fish and potatoes. To increase the nutritional benefits even more, antioxidant-rich sweet potatoes replace baking potatoes.

	Traditional Fish and Chips	Oven-Fried Fish and Chips
Calories	492	324
Fat (g)	18	8
Percent calories from fat	33	22

CHAPTER 9

Please 'Em with Poultry

Tandoori Chicken

Heart healthy yogurt is the base of the spicy marinade in this Indian-inspired grilled chicken. Garam masala, a warming blend of spices, is a common ingredient in northern Indian cuisine. The pungent blend lowers cholesterol and triglycerides, improves glycemic control and insulin sensitivity, and reduces blood clots.

- ♥ 1 cup low-fat plain yogurt
- ♥ 4 cloves garlic, minced
- ♥ 1 tablespoon minced fresh ginger
- ♥ 1 tablespoon lemon juice

  1 teaspoon honey
- ♥ 1 teaspoon garam masala or curry powder
- ♥ ½ teaspoon chili powder

  ½ teaspoon salt

  6 boneless, skinless chicken breast halves (about 3 ounces each)

1. In a large bowl, whisk together the yogurt, garlic, ginger, lemon juice, honey, garam masala or curry powder, chili powder, and salt. Place the chicken on a cutting board and, with a small knife, cut ½"-deep slashes, about 1" apart, into the chicken. Place the chicken in the yogurt mixture and toss to coat. Cover the bowl and refrigerate for 4 hours.

2. Coat a grill rack or broiler pan with cooking spray. Preheat the grill or broiler. Remove the chicken from the marinade, discarding the marinade. Place the chicken on the grill rack or broiler pan. Grill or broil 6" from the heat source, turning once, for 15 minutes, or until a thermometer inserted in the thickest portion registers 160°F and the juices run clear.

Serves 6

♥ **Heart healthy ingredients: 6**

Per serving: 135 calories, 16 calories from fat, 16 g total fat, 2 g saturated fat, 1 g monounsaturated fat, 0 g polyunsaturated fat, 52 mg cholesterol, 281 mg sodium, 6 g carbohydrates, 0 g fiber, 4 g sugar, 22 g protein

Cilantro-Broiled Chicken Breasts

If you want to reduce saturated fat in your diet, skinless chicken breasts are one way to go. The minced garlic in this recipe will help lower cholesterol and blood pressure, improve bloodflow, and reduce clots.

4 boneless, skinless chicken breast halves (about 3 ounces each)

♥ 3 cloves garlic, minced

2 tablespoons minced cilantro

♥ 2 teaspoons extra-virgin olive oil

2 teaspoons grated lime peel

1 teaspoon ground cumin

1. Preheat the broiler. Place the chicken on a baking sheet.

2. In a small bowl, combine the garlic, cilantro, oil, lime peel, and cumin. Evenly divide among the chicken pieces, pressing into each breast and covering the top. Broil 6" from the heat source for 15 minutes, or until a thermometer inserted in the thickest portion registers 160°F and the juices run clear.

Serves 4

♥ **Heart healthy ingredients: 2**

Per serving: 126 calories, 31 calories from fat, 4 g total fat, 1 g saturated fat, 2 g monounsaturated fat, 1 g polyunsaturated fat, 49 mg cholesterol, 58 mg sodium, 2 g carbohydrates, 0 g fiber, 3 g sugar, 2 g protein

Chicken and Vegetables in Cream Sauce

Reduced-fat sour cream adds tang and creaminess—but not a lot of saturated fat—to this easy one-pot dinner starring chicken breasts and asparagus. A healthy and delicious sign of spring, bright green asparagus can reduce blood pressure, cholesterol, and plaque buildup and neutralize the effects of oxidation. And with just 4 calories a spear, it's also great for weight loss.

- ♥ 1 tablespoon extra-virgin olive oil
- ♥ 1 red onion, cut into wedges
- ♥ 1 orange bell pepper, cut into thin strips
- ♥ 1 pound asparagus, cut into 2" pieces
- ♥ 1 teaspoon dried thyme

  4 boneless, skinless chicken breast halves (about 3 ounces each)

  1½ cups fat-free, reduced-sodium chicken broth

  ½ cup dry sherry or broth

  2 tablespoons all-purpose flour

  ½ cup reduced-fat sour cream

1. Heat the oil in a large nonstick skillet over medium-high heat. Add the onion, pepper, and asparagus and cook, stirring occasionally, for 5 minutes, or until crisp-tender. Remove to a plate and keep warm.

2. Rub the thyme into the chicken. Heat the same skillet over medium heat. Add the chicken and cook, turning once, for 10 minutes, or until well browned.

3. In a measuring cup, whisk together the broth, sherry, and flour. Stir in the sour cream. Add to the skillet and bring to a simmer. Simmer for 5 minutes, or until the sauce is thickened and a thermometer inserted in the thickest portion of the chicken registers 160°F and the juices run clear.

4. Evenly divide the vegetables among 4 plates. Top each serving with a chicken breast and one-fourth of the sauce.

Serves 4

♥ Heart healthy ingredients: 5

Per serving: 255 calories, 72 calories from fat, 8 g total fat, 3 g saturated fat, 4 g monounsaturated fat, 1 g polyunsaturated fat, 61 mg cholesterol, 418 mg sodium, 19 g carbohydrates, 4 g fiber, 6 g sugar, 24 g protein

ROOTING FOR RUTIN

Asparagus is an excellent source of an especially powerful type of flavonoid called rutin. Studies have demonstrated that rutin can protect cell membranes from free-radical damage (which leads to hardening of the arteries), strengthen capillaries, and lower "bad" LDL cholesterol. Rutin has also been shown to have a preventative effect against diabetes. So become a rutin fan—your heart will thank you.

Chicken Ragout

Ragout is a rich stew of meat, poultry, or fish bathed in a thick, flavorful sauce. This version packs plenty of fiber-, vitamin-, and mineral-rich vegetables.

♥ 2 tablespoons extra-virgin olive oil

4 boneless, skinless chicken breast halves (about 3 ounces each)

♥ 1 onion, chopped

1 small bulb fennel, chopped

♥ 3 tomatoes, seeded and chopped

♥ 2 cloves garlic, minced

½ cup fat-free, reduced-sodium chicken broth

♥ ¼ cup dry red wine

♥ 1 cup canned white beans, rinsed and drained

♥ ¼ cup kalamata olives, pitted and chopped

1. Heat 1 tablespoon of the oil in a large skillet over medium-high heat. Add the chicken and cook, turning once, for 5 minutes, or until browned. Remove to a plate.

2. Add the remaining 1 tablespoon oil to the skillet and cook the onion and fennel, stirring, for 4 minutes, or until lightly browned. Add the tomatoes and garlic and cook for 1 minute longer. Stir in the broth and wine and bring to a simmer. Return the chicken and any accumulated juices to the skillet, along with the beans and olives. Cover and simmer for 15 minutes, or until a thermometer inserted in the thickest portion of the chicken registers 160°F and the juices run clear.

Serves 4

♥ **Heart healthy ingredients: 7**

Per serving: 292 calories, 87 calories from fat, 10 g total fat, 1 g saturated fat, 6 g monounsaturated fat, 1 g polyunsaturated fat, 49 mg cholesterol, 242 mg sodium, 24 g carbohydrates, 6 g fiber, 6 g sugar, 25 g protein

Spicy Oven-Fried Chicken

A tangy, slightly spicy buttermilk marinade is the secret to perfect (and perfectly healthy) oven-fried chicken. Genuine buttermilk is the liquid left from churning butter from full-fat milk. Naturally low-fat cultured buttermilk, the kind in supermarkets, is milk that has been soured with lactic acid. If you don't have buttermilk on hand, you can make sour milk by adding ½ teaspoon lemon juice or vinegar to ½ cup milk. A curdled look is typical.

½ cup buttermilk

♥ 1 clove garlic, minced

♥ ½ teaspoon hot-pepper sauce

4 skinless chicken breasts on the bone (about 9 ounces each)

♥ ½ cup whole wheat pastry flour

♥ 2 tablespoons ground flaxseed

1 teaspoon baking powder

♥ ¼ teaspoon ground red pepper

¼ teaspoon salt

1. In a shallow baking dish, combine the buttermilk, garlic, and hot-pepper sauce. Add the chicken, turn to coat, and place breast side down. Cover and marinate in the refrigerator for 30 minutes or up to 8 hours.

2. Preheat the oven to 425°F. Place a rack in a baking sheet with sides (jelly-roll pan) and coat with cooking spray.

3. In a large zip-top bag, combine the flour, flaxseed, baking powder, ground red pepper, and salt. Remove 1 chicken breast from the marinade, shaking off any excess. Place in the bag, seal, and shake to coat. Place on the rack and repeat with the remaining chicken. Coat the chicken with cooking spray.

4. Bake for 45 minutes, or until a thermometer inserted in the thickest portion registers 170°F and the juices run clear.

Serves 4

♥ **Heart healthy ingredients: 5**

Per serving: 381 calories, 52 calories from fat, 6 g total fat, 1 g saturated fat, 1 g monounsaturated fat, 2 g polyunsaturated fat, 150 mg cholesterol, 492 mg sodium, 16 g carbohydrates, 3 g fiber, 2 g sugar, 63 g protein

Chicken Parmigiana

The chicken in our lightened-up Parmigiana is baked in the oven rather than sautéed in a lot of oil. Be careful when choosing bread crumbs, which can be loaded with sodium. Always go for a low-sodium option when available.

♥ 1 cup dried whole wheat bread crumbs, preferably low-sodium

¼ cup grated Parmesan cheese

♥ 2 cloves garlic, minced

2 egg whites

1 tablespoon water

1¼ pounds chicken breast cutlets

♥ 2 cups fat-free jarred marinara sauce

1. Preheat the oven to 400°F. Coat a baking sheet with sides (jelly-roll pan) with cooking spray.

2. On a plate, combine the bread crumbs, cheese, and garlic. In a pie plate, whisk the egg whites with the water. Dip the cutlets into the egg white mixture and then dredge in the bread crumb mixture, pressing to coat. Place the cutlets on the prepared pan and coat with cooking spray.

3. Bake the cutlets, turning once, for 6 minutes, or until browned. Top with the marinara sauce and bake for 3 minutes longer, or until the chicken is no longer pink and the juices run clear.

Serves 4

♥ **Heart healthy ingredients: 3**

Per serving: 273 calories, 33 calories from fat, 4 g total fat, 1 g saturated fat, 1 g monounsaturated fat, 1 g polyunsaturated fat, 87 mg cholesterol, 428 mg sodium, 17 g carbohydrates, 2 g fiber, 9 g sugar, 37 g protein

Roast Chicken and Vegetables

An orange glaze adds a sweet touch to roasted chicken breasts. All the veggies here are terrific for your heart, including parsnips, a root vegetable related to carrots and similar in size. They have a golden color and a stronger flavor than carrots, but they're just as sweet. Parsnips are a source of vitamin C, folate, and potassium and can be used in place of potatoes in recipes.

3 parsnips, peeled and cut into 2" pieces

♥ 2 large sweet potatoes, peeled and cut into 2" pieces

♥ 2 large red onions, cut into wedges

♥ 4 cloves garlic, minced

♥ 2 tablespoons extra-virgin olive oil

¼ teaspoon salt

4 skinless chicken breasts on the bone (about 9 ounces each)

3 tablespoons all-fruit orange marmalade

♥ ½ teaspoon ground cinnamon

1. Preheat the oven to 375°F. Coat a large roasting pan with cooking spray.

2. Place the parsnips, potatoes, onions, garlic, oil, and salt in the pan and toss to coat well. Push to the perimeter of pan. Place the chicken, skinned sides down, in the center of the pan. Roast for 20 minutes.

3. In a small bowl, stir together the marmalade and cinnamon. Remove the pan from the oven, turn over the chicken, and coat with the marmalade mixture. Roast for 25 minutes longer, or until a thermometer inserted in the center of the chicken registers 170°F and the meat is no longer pink.

Serves 4

♥ **Heart healthy ingredients: 5**

Per serving: 506 calories, 84 calories from fat, 10 g total fat, 2 g saturated fat, 6 g monounsaturated fat, 2 g polyunsaturated fat, 99 mg cholesterol, 326 mg sodium, 62 g carbohydrates, 9 g fiber, 21 g sugar, 44 g protein

Revamped Chicken Potpie

Here's a classic—but lighter—version of chicken potpie, right down to the peas and carrots. To vary the dish, use any blend of frozen vegetables—such as broccoli, green beans, peppers, and onions—and season with basil or oregano instead of thyme.

1 cup reduced-fat milk

2 tablespoons cornstarch

♥ 1 tablespoon extra-virgin olive oil

♥ 1 red onion, chopped

♥ 2 cloves garlic, minced

♥ ½ teaspoon dried thyme, crushed

1 pound boneless, skinless chicken breasts, cut into 1" pieces

1 cup fat-free, reduced-sodium chicken broth

♥ 1 box (10 ounces) frozen peas and carrots

1 package (11 ounces) refrigerated soft breadstick dough

1. Preheat the oven to 375°F. Coat a 9" baking pan with cooking spray. In a small bowl, whisk together the milk and cornstarch.

2. Heat the oil in a large nonstick skillet over medium-high heat. Add the onion, garlic, and thyme and cook, stirring occasionally, for 3 minutes. Add the chicken and cook, stirring occasionally, for 4 minutes longer, or until lightly browned. Add the broth and peas and carrots and bring to a simmer. Stir the milk mixture and add to the skillet. Cook, stirring constantly, for 1 minute, or until thickened. Scrape the mixture into the prepared pan.

3. Arrange 6 of the breadsticks in one direction over the mixture. Arrange the remaining 6 breadsticks in the opposite direction, forming a lattice top. Bake for 15 to 18 minutes, or until the breadsticks are golden brown and cooked through.

Serves 8

♥ **Heart healthy ingredients: 5**

Per serving: 239 calories, 45 calories from fat, 5 g total fat, 1 g saturated fat, 2 g monounsaturated fat, 1 g polyunsaturated fat, 35 mg cholesterol, 428 mg sodium, 28 g carbohydrates, 2 g fiber, 5 g sugar, 19 g protein

MAKEOVER MAGIC

Piecrust is usually loaded with saturated fat and calories. By topping the pie with breadstick dough and making our own low-fat sauce, we've cut the calories almost in half and eliminated 80 percent of the fat!

	Traditional Potpie	Revamped Chicken Potpie
Calories	462	239
Fat (g)	26	5
Percent calories from fat	51	19

Chicken-Zucchini Pasta Toss

Here's a quick pasta dish that's sure to please. Put five heart healthy foods (whole grain pasta, olive oil, onion, garlic, and tomatoes) together, and you've got a meal that does it all, from reducing blood pressure and cholesterol to preventing plaque buildup and diabetes.

- 8 ounces whole wheat penne pasta
- 2 tablespoons extra-virgin olive oil
- 1 onion, chopped

  1 medium zucchini, halved lengthwise and cut into 1" pieces

  ¾ pound boneless, skinless chicken breasts, cut into 2" strips
- 1 clove garlic, minced

  ½ teaspoon dried basil, crushed
- 2 large tomatoes, chopped

  ½ cup fat-free, reduced-sodium chicken broth

1. Prepare the pasta according to package directions. Drain and place in a large serving bowl.

2. Meanwhile, heat the oil in a large skillet over medium heat. Add the onion and zucchini and cook, stirring occasionally, for 5 minutes, or until lightly browned. Add the chicken, garlic, and basil and cook, stirring, for 3 minutes longer, or until lightly browned. Stir in the tomatoes and broth and bring to a simmer.

3. Simmer, uncovered, for 10 minutes, or until the flavors blend and the chicken is cooked through. Pour over the pasta and toss to mix.

Serves 4

Heart healthy ingredients: 5

Per serving: 406 calories, 80 calories from fat, 9 g total fat, 1 g saturated fat, 6 g monounsaturated fat, 1 g polyunsaturated fat, 49 mg cholesterol, 132 mg sodium, 51 g carbohydrates, 7 g fiber, 6 g sugar, 29 g protein

Curried Chicken Salad

This satisfying main dish salad incorporates lots of heart healthy foods. When grilling or broiling chicken breasts, always throw a few more on the fire to have on hand for this quick dinner. Once cooled, store cooked chicken in a zip-top bag in the refrigerator for up to 3 days.

¼ cup reduced-fat mayonnaise

♥ ¼ cup low-fat yogurt

2 tablespoons mango chutney

♥ 2 teaspoons curry powder

½ pound cooked chicken breast, chopped

2 ribs celery, chopped

♥ 2 scallions, chopped

♥ 1 cup red grapes, halved

♥ 1 head red or green leaf lettuce

♥ ½ cup almonds, toasted and chopped

1. In a large bowl, whisk together the mayonnaise, yogurt, chutney, and curry powder. Stir in the chicken, celery, scallions, and grapes.

2. Evenly divide the lettuce among 4 plates. Top with the chicken salad and sprinkle each serving with 2 tablespoons of the almonds.

Serves 4

♥ Heart healthy ingredients: 6

Per serving: 269 calories, 100 calories from fat, 11 g total fat, 1 g saturated fat, 5 g monounsaturated fat, 2 g polyunsaturated fat, 50 mg cholesterol, 234 mg sodium, 20 g carbohydrates, 4 g fiber, 13 g sugar, 23 g protein

THAT'S NUTTY

Almonds, Brazil nuts, cashews, and pistachios are actually fruit seeds. Macadamia nuts and walnuts are kernels. And a peanut isn't a nut at all: It's both a legume and a seed. One more thing: All "nuts" are fruits. Isn't that nutty?

Turkey Cutlets with Avocado Salsa

Because avocados are so high in fat, recipes often use just half of one. To keep the remaining half from browning, remove the seed and spray the flesh with cooking spray, then wrap in plastic wrap and refrigerate for up to 3 days.

- ❦ 1 cup grape tomatoes, halved
- ❦ ½ avocado, halved, pitted, and chopped
- ❦ 4 scallions, chopped
- ❦ 1 tablespoon extra-virgin olive oil
- ❦ 1 tablespoon lime juice
- ½ teaspoon ground cumin
- 1 pound turkey breast cutlets
- ¼ teaspoon salt
- ¼ teaspoon ground black pepper

1. In a small bowl, combine the tomatoes, avocado, scallions, oil, lime juice, and cumin. Set aside.

2. Season the cutlets with the salt and pepper. Heat a large nonstick skillet coated with cooking spray over medium heat. Add half of the cutlets and cook, turning once, for 3 minutes, or until browned and no longer pink. Remove to a plate and repeat with remaining cutlets. Top with the reserved avocado mixture.

Serves 4

❦ **Heart healthy ingredients: 5**

Per serving: 201 calories, 69 calories from fat, 8 g total fat, 1 g saturated fat, 5 g monounsaturated fat, 1 g polyunsaturated fat, 45 mg cholesterol, 250 mg sodium, 4 g carbohydrates, 2 g fiber, 1 g sugar, 29 g protein

Turkey Burgers

Serving these low-fat turkey burgers on a whole wheat bun with lettuce and tomato can lower blood pressure and cholesterol, as well as the risk for heart attack and stroke. They taste great, too.

1 pound ground turkey breast

♥ 4 scallions, chopped

♥ 1 clove garlic, minced

♥ ¼ cup prepared low-fat salsa, drained well

¼ cup (1 ounce) shredded reduced-fat pepper Jack cheese

♥ 4 whole wheat buns

♥ 4 lettuce leaves

♥ 4 slices tomato

1. Coat the grill rack or broiler pan with cooking spray. Preheat the grill or broiler.

2. In a medium bowl, combine the turkey, scallions, garlic, salsa, and cheese. Shape into 4 burgers. Grill or broil 4" from the heat source, turning once, for 12 minutes, or until a thermometer inserted in the center registers 165°F and the meat is no longer pink.

3. Line the bottom of each bun with a lettuce leaf and tomato slice. Top each with a burger and the top of the bun.

Serves 4

♥ **Heart healthy ingredients: 6**

Per serving: 262 calories, 37 calories from fat, 4 g total fat, 1 g saturated fat, 1 g monounsaturated fat, 1 g polyunsaturated fat, 46 mg cholesterol, 379 mg sodium, 25 g carbohydrates, 4 g fiber, 5 g sugar, 34 g protein

MAKEOVER MAGIC

Drop those beef burgers! By switching from beef to lean turkey breast and using reduced-fat cheese, you'll shrink the fat by more than 80 percent and the calories by almost half.

	Traditional Burger	Turkey Burger
Calories	466	262
Fat (g)	26	4
Percent calories from fat	50	14

Turkey Picadillo

Traditionally made with beef or pork, picadillo—a kind of hash made with ground meat, flavor-packed vegetables, and tomatoes—is a favorite in many Spanish-speaking countries. Our heart healthy version uses low-fat turkey plus garlic, onions, olives, and raisins. Serve alongside Black Beans and Rice (page 155) or use as a filling for whole grain tortillas.

- ♥ 1 tablespoon extra-virgin olive oil
- ♥ 1 onion, chopped
- ♥ 1 red bell pepper, chopped
- ♥ 2 cloves garlic, minced

  1 pound ground turkey breast
- ♥ 1 can (14½ ounces) no-salt-added whole tomatoes, chopped
- ♥ ¼ cup no-salt-added tomato sauce

  ¼ cup raisins
- ♥ ¼ cup pimiento-stuffed green olives, chopped

  ½ teaspoon ground cumin
- ♥ ¼ cup sliced almonds

1. Heat the oil in a nonstick skillet over medium-high heat. Add the onion and pepper and cook, stirring occasionally, for 5 minutes.

2. Add the garlic and turkey and cook, stirring occasionally, for 5 minutes longer, or until the turkey is no longer pink.

3. Add the tomatoes, tomato sauce, raisins, olives, and cumin. Bring to a boil over medium-high heat.

4. Reduce the heat to low, partially cover, and simmer for 10 minutes, or until slightly thickened. Top with the almonds.

Serves 6

♥ **Heart healthy ingredients: 8**

Per serving: 189 calories, 59 calories from fat, 6 g total fat, 1 g saturated fat, 4 g monounsaturated fat, 1 g polyunsaturated fat, 30 mg cholesterol, 266 mg sodium, 14 g carbohydrates, 2 g fiber, 9 g sugar, 22 g protein

Herb-Roasted Turkey Breast

Not just for the holidays, roasted turkey is delicious year-round. Serve with seasonal vegetables or a salad, such as Greens with Strawberries and Kiwifruit (page 110) and Vegetable Quinoa (page 146) in the spring, or Brown Rice with Greens and Feta (page 151) and corn on the cob in the summer.

♥ 3 tablespoons orange juice

♥ 2 tablespoons extra-virgin olive oil

♥ 2 garlic cloves, minced

1 tablespoon fresh rosemary, minced, or 1 teaspoon dried crushed

♥ 1 tablespoon fresh thyme, minced, or 1 teaspoon dried crushed

1 teaspoon grated orange peel

½ teaspoon salt

½ teaspoon ground black pepper

1 bone-in turkey breast (6 pounds)

1. Preheat the oven to 350°F. In a small bowl, combine 1 tablespoon of the orange juice, 1 tablespoon of the oil, the garlic, rosemary, thyme, orange peel, salt, and pepper. In another small bowl, combine the remaining 2 tablespoons orange juice and 1 tablespoon oil and set aside.

2. Place the turkey on a rack in a roasting pan. Loosen the skin with your fingers, leaving it attached along the bottom edges. Spread the herb mixture under the turkey skin.

3. Roast the turkey for 2½ to 3 hours, or until a thermometer inserted in the thickest portion registers 170°F and the juices run clear, basting every 30 minutes with the reserved orange juice mixture. Let stand for 10 minutes before carving. Discard the skin and carve.

Serves 12

♥ **Heart Healthy Ingredients: 4**

Per serving: 150 calories, 27 calories from fat, 3 g total fat, 1 g saturated fat, 2 g monounsaturated fat, 0 g polyunsaturated fat, 70 mg cholesterol, 153 mg sodium, 1 g carbohydrates, 0 g fiber, 0 g sugar, 28 g protein

CHAPTER 10

Accent with Meat

Beef Tenderloin with Cranberry Port Sauce

A product of Portugal, port is a sweet fortified wine often consumed after a meal. Here, it helps offset tart cranberries in a robust sauce for tenderloin. Vintage ports are the highest quality and most expensive. Ruby ports are less expensive and work well for cooking because they are slightly lower quality. Serve with a side of Garlic Smashed Potatoes (page 144) for a wonderful combination.

1 teaspoon extra-virgin olive oil

2 cloves garlic, minced

1½ teaspoons dried basil, crushed

1½ teaspoons dried thyme, crushed

½ teaspoon coarsely ground black pepper

1 center-cut beef tenderloin roast (2 pounds), well trimmed

2 cups fat-free, reduced-sodium beef broth

2 cups ruby port

4 large shallots, minced

¾ cup dried cranberries

1. Preheat the oven to 425°F. In a small bowl, combine the oil, garlic, basil, thyme, and pepper.

2. Place the beef on a rack in a large roasting pan. Rub the herb mixture over the beef. Roast for 35 minutes, or until a thermometer inserted in the center registers 145°F for medium-rare or, if desired, for 45 minutes for medium (160°F) to 55 minutes for well-done (165°F). Let stand for 10 minutes before slicing.

3. Meanwhile, in a medium saucepan over medium-high heat, combine the broth, port, shallots, and cranberries. Bring to a boil and boil for 25 minutes, or until reduced to 2 cups. Set aside.

4. Skim the fat from the roasting pan and add the juices to the reserved port sauce. Serve the tenderloin with the sauce.

Serves 12

Heart healthy ingredients: 6

Per serving: 189 calories, 48 calories from fat, 5 g total fat, 2 g saturated fat, 2 g monounsaturated fat, 0 g polyunsaturated fat, 51 mg cholesterol, 120 mg sodium, 10 g carbohydrates, 1 g fiber, 6 g sugar, 17 g protein

Spicy Fajitas

An abundance of vegetables contributes both flavor and heart healthy nutrients to the traditional Mexican wrap, the fajita. Jalapeño and other chile peppers are filled with capsaicin, especially in the seeds and membranes. When seeding and chopping, it's best to wear rubber gloves to avoid burning your skin.

1 teaspoon ground cumin

♥ ¼ teaspoon ground red pepper

¼ teaspoon salt

1 flank steak (about ¾ pound)

♥ 6 scallions, cut into 2" pieces

♥ 1 red bell pepper, cut into thin strips

♥ 1 jalapeño chile pepper, seeded and finely chopped (optional)

♥ 1 large tomato, seeded and chopped

♥ 2 tablespoons lime juice

♥ 4 (6") whole wheat flour tortillas

1. In a small bowl, combine the cumin, ground red pepper, and salt. Rub over both sides of the steak.

2. Heat a nonstick skillet coated with cooking spray over medium-high heat. Add the steak and cook, turning once, for 5 minutes, or until a thermometer inserted in the center registers 145°F for medium-rare or, if desired, for 7 minutes for medium (160°F) or 9 minutes for well-done (165°F). Place on a cutting board and let stand for 10 minutes. Slice against the grain into bite-size pieces.

3. Meanwhile, recoat the skillet with cooking spray and heat over medium heat. Add the scallions, bell pepper, and chile pepper, if using. Cook, stirring occasionally, for 8 minutes, or until well browned and very tender. Add the tomato and lime juice and cook, stirring to loosen brown bits, for 2 minutes.

4. Place 1 tortilla on each of 4 plates. Top with the sliced steak and then the vegetable mixture.

Serves 4

♥ **Heart healthy ingredients: 7**

Per serving: 222 calories, 49 calories from fat, 5 g total fat, 2 g saturated fat, 2 g monounsaturated fat, 0 g polyunsaturated fat, 28 mg cholesterol, 408 mg sodium, 26 g carbohydrates, 3 g fiber, 3 g sugar, 22 g protein

Beef and Vegetable Stroganoff

Instead of the traditional egg noodles, our hearty combo of beef, vegetables, and sour cream is served atop heart healthy quinoa. Shiitake mushrooms provide another twist. Besides being an abundant source of antioxidants, shiitakes have been found to reduce cholesterol.

2 cups water

♥ 1 cup quinoa, well rinsed

½ pound beef top round or sirloin steak, cut into thin strips

♥ 1 large onion, cut into thin wedges

♥ 1 red bell pepper, cut into thin strips

♥ 8 ounces shiitake mushrooms, stemmed and sliced

♥ 4 cloves garlic, minced

♥ ¼ cup red wine

1¼ cups fat-free, reduced-sodium beef broth

1 teaspoon Dijon mustard

¼ teaspoon ground black pepper

½ cup fat-free sour cream

1. In a medium saucepan, bring the water to a boil. Stir in the quinoa, reduce the heat to medium-low, cover, and simmer for 20 minutes, or until most of the water is absorbed. Remove from the heat and let stand for 10 minutes.

2. Meanwhile, heat a large nonstick skillet coated with cooking spray over high heat. In batches, add the beef and cook, stirring frequently, for 1½ minutes, or until no longer pink. Remove to a plate.

3. Recoat the skillet with cooking spray and cook the onion, bell pepper, and mushrooms for 5 minutes, or until lightly browned. Add the garlic and cook for 1 minute longer. Add the wine and cook for 1 minute longer. Add the broth, mustard, and black pepper and bring to a boil. Return the beef to the skillet and cook just until heated through. Remove from the heat.

4. Slowly stir a spoonful of the beef sauce into the sour cream, then stir the sour cream into the beef mixture. Serve the stroganoff over the quinoa.

Serves 4

♥ **Heart healthy ingredients: 6**

Per serving: 334 calories, 49 calories from fat, 5 g total fat, 1 g saturated fat, 3 g monounsaturated fat, 2 g polyunsaturated fat, 34 mg cholesterol, 230 mg sodium, 46 g carbohydrates, 5 g fiber, 8 g sugar, 24 g protein

MAKEOVER MAGIC

Rich and creamy, this classic dish is made much healthier by using less meat than the traditional and pumping up the protein with shiitakes and quinoa. Fat-free sour cream reduces the fat even more.

	Traditional Stroganoff	Beef and Vegetable Stroganoff
Calories	492	334
Fat (g)	15	5
Percent calories from fat	27	13

Beef and Asparagus Stir-Fry

Beefy sirloin steak and woodsy asparagus have a natural affinity for each other, and this stir-fry brings out the best in both ingredients. Several cuts of beef are quite low in fat—in fact, ounce for ounce, they have less fat than skinless chicken thighs. So reach for these beef cuts when shopping: eye round, sirloin tip, top round, sirloin, or brisket.

1 cup fat-free, reduced-sodium beef broth

♥ 1½ tablespoons lemon juice

2 teaspoons reduced-sodium soy sauce

2 teaspoons cornstarch

♥ 1 clove garlic, minced

♥ 4 teaspoons extra-virgin olive oil

1 sirloin steak (about 8 ounces), cut into thin strips

♥ 1 red onion, cut into thin wedges

♥ 1 pound asparagus, cut into 2" pieces

♥ 2 cups hot cooked brown rice

1. In a measuring cup or small bowl, whisk together the broth, lemon juice, soy sauce, cornstarch, and garlic. Set aside.

2. Heat 2 teaspoons of the oil in a large nonstick skillet over medium-high heat. Add half of the beef and cook, stirring constantly, for 3 minutes, or until just browned. Using a slotted spoon, remove the beef to a plate. Add the remaining 2 teaspoons oil to the skillet and repeat with the remaining beef.

3. Add the onion and asparagus to the skillet and cook, stirring constantly, for 4 minutes. Stir the broth mixture and add to the skillet, along with the beef and any accumulated juices. Cook, stirring constantly, for 4 minutes, or until the sauce thickens and the asparagus is tender-crisp.

4. Evenly divide the rice among 4 plates. Top each serving with one-fourth of the beef mixture.

Serves 4

♥ **Heart healthy ingredients: 6**

Per serving: 275 calories, 69 calories from fat, 8 g total fat, 2 g saturated fat, 5g monounsaturated fat, 1 g polyunsaturated fat, 24 mg cholesterol, 240 mg sodium, 34 g carbohydrates, 5 g fiber, 5 g sugar, 18 g protein

Souped-Up Sloppy Joes

It's believed that sloppy joes were invented in the 1930s in a café in Iowa. The chef, named Joe, added sauce to ground meat to stretch the meat, which was then in short supply because of the Depression. We've stretched it even further—and made it much healthier—by adding lots of vegetables.

- ♥ 1 onion, finely chopped
- ♥ 1 carrot, finely chopped
- 1 rib celery, finely chopped
- ♥ 1 small red bell pepper, finely chopped
- ♥ 1 clove garlic, minced
- ¾ pound extra-lean ground beef
- ♥ 2 cans (8 ounces each) no-salt-added tomato sauce
- ¼ cup barbecue sauce
- ♥ 4 whole wheat buns

1. Heat a large nonstick skillet coated with cooking spray over medium-high heat. Add the onion, carrot, celery, and pepper and cook, stirring occasionally, for 5 minutes, or until softened.

2. Add the garlic and beef and cook, stirring occasionally, for 8 minutes, or until the beef is browned and no longer pink. Stir in the tomato sauce and barbecue sauce. Bring to a simmer. Cover and simmer, stirring occasionally, for 10 minutes, or until the flavors blend.

3. Place the bottom of each bun on 4 plates. Evenly divide the meat mixture among the buns and top with the lids.

Serves 4

♥ **Heart healthy ingredients: 6**

Per serving: 321 calories, 60 calories from fat, 7 g total fat, 2 g saturated fat, 2 g monounsaturated fat, 2 g polyunsaturated fat, 45 mg cholesterol, 471 mg sodium, 44 g carbohydrates, 7 g fiber, 17 g sugar, 23 g protein

MAKEOVER MAGIC

Going with extra-lean ground beef (95 percent lean or more) and substituting vegetables for some of the beef, this family favorite fits beautifully into a heart healthy meal plan. Opting for whole wheat buns increases the health benefits even more.

	Traditional Sloppy Joes	Souped-Up Sloppy Joes
Calories	462	321
Fat (g)	22	7
Percent calories from fat	43	20

Makeover Veal Marsala

Heart healthy olive oil takes the place of sat-fat-loaded butter, and the addition of shiitake mushrooms further increases the heart friendliness of this elegant but easy dish.

1 pound veal cutlets

¼ teaspoon salt

¼ teaspoon ground black pepper

¼ cup fat-free, reduced-sodium chicken broth

2 teaspoons all-purpose flour

♥ 1 tablespoon extra-virgin olive oil

♥ 4 ounces shiitake mushrooms, stemmed and sliced

4 ounces white mushrooms, sliced

♥ 2 cloves garlic, minced

♥ ¼ cup Marsala wine

1. Season the veal with the salt and pepper. In a small measuring cup or bowl, whisk together the broth and flour.

2. Heat the oil in a large nonstick skillet over medium-high heat. Add the veal and cook, turning once, for 3 minutes, or until browned. Remove to a serving plate.

3. Add the shiitakes, white mushrooms, and garlic to the skillet and cook, stirring occasionally, for 5 minutes, or until the liquid has evaporated and the mushrooms are browned. Stir the broth mixture and add to the skillet, along with the wine and any accumulated juices from the veal. Bring to a boil and cook, stirring, for 3 minutes, or until thickened. Pour over the veal.

Serves 4

♥ **Heart healthy ingredients: 4**

Per serving: 204 calories, 61 calories from fat, 7 g total fat, 2 g saturated fat, 4 g monounsaturated fat, 1 g polyunsaturated fat, 94 mg cholesterol, 276 mg sodium, 6 g carbohydrates, 1 g fiber, 2 g sugar, 25 g protein

Orange-Ginger Pork Chops

Breaded pork chops have always been a family-pleasing dinner. We jazz them up by adding orange and ginger to the coating—and lighten them up by baking in the oven instead of frying. For the healthiest bread crumbs possible, make your own using whole grain bread: Toast the slices, let cool, then pulse in the food processor until fine crumbs form. Store in an airtight container in the freezer for up to 4 months.

1 orange

1½ cups fresh whole grain bread crumbs

1 tablespoon grated fresh ginger

¼ teaspoon salt

2 egg whites

4 boneless top loin pork chops (about 1 pound), trimmed of any visible fat

1. Preheat the oven to 425°F. Coat a baking sheet with cooking spray.

2. Grate the peel from the orange to measure ½ teaspoon and squeeze the juice to measure ¼ cup. Combine the peel, bread crumbs, ginger, and salt in a shallow bowl. Whisk the egg whites and orange juice in another shallow bowl.

3. Dip the chops into the egg white mixture, then dredge in the bread crumb mixture, pressing the crumbs onto the chops. Place the chops on the prepared baking sheet and coat with cooking spray. Bake, turning once, for 15 minutes, or until a thermometer inserted in the centers of the chops reaches 160°F.

Serves 4

Heart healthy ingredients: 3

Per serving: 222 calories, 58 calories from fat, 6.4 g total fat, 2 g saturated fat, 3 g monounsaturated fat, 0.6 g polyunsaturated fat, 62 mg cholesterol, 284 mg sodium, 13 g carbohydrates, 4 g fiber, 4 g sugar, 28 g protein

Ginger-Roasted Pork with Sweet Potatoes

Sweet potatoes are an unbelievably heart healthy food, with a wealth of nutrients to lower "bad" cholesterol, high blood pressure, and plaque buildup in arteries. They also regulate blood sugar and insulin resistance in people with type 2 diabetes—and may even help you lose weight.

- ♥ 2 large sweet potatoes, peeled and cut into 2" pieces
- ♥ 1 large onion, cut into wedges
- ♥ 1 large red bell pepper, cut into 2" pieces
- ♥ 2 tablespoons extra-virgin olive oil
- ½ teaspoon salt
- ♥ 1 teaspoon ground ginger
- ½ teaspoon ground allspice
- ♥ ½ teaspoon ground cinnamon
- 1 boneless pork loin roast (about 2 pounds)

1. Preheat the oven to 400°F. Place the potatoes, onion, and pepper in a large roasting pan. Drizzle with the oil, sprinkle with ¼ teaspoon of the salt, and toss to coat well. Push to the perimeter of the roasting pan.

2. In a small bowl, combine the ginger, allspice, cinnamon, and the remaining ¼ teaspoon salt, stirring to blend well. Rub the spice mixture over the pork.

3. Place the pork in the center of the roasting pan. Roast for 1 hour, or until the vegetables are tender and a thermometer inserted in the center of the pork reaches 155°F and the juices run clear. Let stand for 10 minutes before slicing.

Serves 10

♥ **Heart healthy ingredients: 6**

Per serving: 199 calories, 65 calories from fat, 7 g total fat, 2 g saturated fat, 4 g monounsaturated fat, 1 g polyunsaturated fat, 57 mg cholesterol, 199 mg sodium, 11 g carbohydrates, 2 g fiber, 4 g sugar, 21 g protein

SWEET POTATO OR YAM?

How do you tell the difference between a sweet potato and a yam? Truth be told, yams aren't particularly common at your average grocery store. However, they're readily available in both Asian and Caribbean grocery stores, if you're lucky enough to live near either of those. The trick to telling them apart is simply knowing what to look for.

- Sweet potatoes have light, smooth, thin skins and tapered ends.
- Yams have dark, rough, thick, scaly skin; are cylindrical; and are often really, really big. They can grow up to 7 feet long and weigh up to 150 pounds!

Properly cooked sweet potatoes are creamy, moist, and sweet, while cooked yams are drier, starchy, slippery, and almost never sweet (making them far better suited for more savory dishes)—but you can't tell that from looking at them in the store.

Balsamic-Rosemary Pork Kebabs

Red wine and olive oil, two heart health standouts, combine with balsamic vinegar and fresh rosemary for a flavorful marinade for pork kebabs. Heart-friendly garlic, bursting with antioxidants, is in there as well. To save time, look for peeled garlic in the refrigerator section of supermarkets. Store it in an airtight container in the refrigerator for up to 2 weeks.

- ¼ cup dry red wine
- 2 tablespoons extra-virgin olive oil
- 2 tablespoons balsamic vinegar
- 2 tablespoons fresh chopped rosemary or 2 teaspoons dried crushed
- 2 cloves garlic, minced
- ¼ teaspoon salt
- ¼ teaspoon cracked black pepper
- 1 pork tenderloin (about 1 pound), cut into 2" pieces
- 1 large red bell pepper, cut into 2" pieces
- 1 large sweet onion, cut into thick wedges

1. In a large glass bowl or zip-top bag, combine the wine, oil, vinegar, rosemary, garlic, salt, and black pepper. Add the pork and toss to coat. Cover the bowl or seal the bag and refrigerate, tossing occasionally, for 4 hours or overnight.

2. Coat the grill rack or broiler pan with cooking spray. Preheat the grill or broiler.

3. Alternately thread the pork, bell pepper, and onion onto 4 metal skewers. Discard the marinade. Grill or broil the kebabs 5" from the heat source, turning occasionally, for 10 minutes, or until the pork is no longer pink.

Serves 4

Heart healthy ingredients: 5

Per serving: 227 calories, 87 calories from fat, 10 g total fat, 2 g saturated fat, 6 g monounsaturated fat, 1 g polyunsaturated fat, 55 mg cholesterol, 193 mg sodium, 13 g carbohydrates, 2 g fiber, 2 g sugar, 19 g protein

Quick White Bean Stew

Serve this hearty stew with warm, crusty whole grain bread and Grape and Fennel Salad (page 109). Finish the simple meal with Quick and Easy Rice Pudding (page 243). With even more vitamin C than oranges, red bell peppers are rich in just about everything you need for heart health. They lower "bad" cholesterol and high blood pressure, ease bloodflow, reduce artery-clogging plaque, and help with glycemic control.

½ pound reduced-fat pork sausage, cut into ½" slices

🍂 1 onion, chopped

🍂 1 red bell pepper, chopped

🍂 4 cloves garlic, minced

1 tablespoon fresh chopped rosemary or 1 teaspoon dried

🍂 1 can (15 ounces) cannellini beans, rinsed and drained

2 cups fat-free, reduced-sodium chicken broth

🍂 2 tomatoes, chopped

1. In a large saucepan over medium-high heat, cook the sausage, stirring occasionally, for 5 minutes, or until browned and cooked through. With a slotted spoon, remove to a plate lined with paper towels. Discard all but 1 tablespoon of the drippings.

2. Add the onion and pepper to the drippings remaining in the saucepan and cook, stirring occasionally, for 5 minutes, or until lightly browned. Add the garlic and rosemary and cook, stirring frequently, for 1 minute longer. Stir in the beans, broth, and tomatoes and bring to a boil. Reduce the heat to medium, cover, and simmer for 10 minutes. Stir in the sausage and heat through.

Serves 4

🍂 **Heart healthy ingredients: 5**

Per serving: 202 calories, 25 calories from fat, 3 g total fat, 1 g saturated fat, 1 g monounsaturated fat, 0 g polyunsaturated fat, 14 mg cholesterol, 417 mg sodium, 31 g carbohydrates, 6 g fiber, 6 g sugar, 13 g protein

CHAPTER 11

Snack to Your Heart's Content

Toasted Trail Mix

There will be happy trails for you with this fruity, nutty mix. The heart healthy foods here are loaded with fiber to lower blood pressure and cholesterol. The concentration of antioxidants and nutrients in dried fruits may be even higher than in fresh. But try to eat less because the calories are higher, too.

1 egg white

♥ ½ cup whole wheat mini pretzels

♥ ½ cup toasted oat cereal

♥ ½ cup pecans

♥ ½ cup almonds

½ cup unsweetened dried pears or apples

♥ ½ cup dried cherries

2 tablespoons brown sugar

♥ 2 teaspoons ground ginger

1. Preheat the oven to 350°F. Line two baking sheets with sides (jelly-roll pans) with parchment paper.

2. In a large bowl, whisk the egg white. Add the pretzels, cereal, pecans, almonds, pears or apples, and cherries. With a rubber spatula, toss to coat well. Sprinkle with the sugar and ginger and toss until well blended. Spread in the prepared pans and bake, turning occasionally, for 20 minutes, or until browned.

Makes 12 servings (3 cups)

♥ **Heart healthy ingredients: 6**

Per serving: 135 calories, 53 calories from fat, 6 g total fat, 1 g saturated fat, 3 g monounsaturated fat, 2 g polyunsaturated fat, 0 mg cholesterol, 33 mg sodium, 19 g carbohydrates, 3 g fiber, 9 g sugar, 3 g protein

Peanut Bars

Here's a healthful, peanutty take on those sweet marshmallow-laden rice-crisp bars. Natural peanut butter has a tendency to separate. The best way to incorporate the oil is to leave the unopened jar upside down for a day, then open and stir completely. Store in the refrigerator (right side up) to keep emulsified.

♥ ½ cup natural peanut butter

½ cup honey

1 tablespoon pure vanilla extract

♥ 4 cups toasted oat cereal

♥ ⅓ cup flaxseed, ground

1. In a large saucepan over medium heat, combine the peanut butter, honey, and vanilla extract. Cook, stirring, for 4 minutes, or until melted. Remove from the heat and stir in the cereal and flaxseed until well blended.

2. Coat a glass 8" or 9" baking dish with cooking spray. Spread the cereal mixture into the pan with a rubber spatula. Refrigerate for 30 minutes or until firm. Cut into 24 pieces.

Makes 24

♥ **Heart healthy ingredients: 3**

Per serving: 80 calories, 30 calories from fat, 3 g total fat, 1 g saturated fat, 2 g monounsaturated fat, 0 g polyunsaturated fat, 0 mg cholesterol, 73 mg sodium, 12 g carbohydrates, 1 g fiber, 7 g sugar, 2 g protein

Fruit with Creamy Chocolate Dip

Apples and bananas are both excellent sources of fiber, antioxidants, and potassium that reduce cholesterol and lower blood pressure. This scrumptious dip, with cream cheese and yogurt for added protein, is perfect for an after-school or late-night snack.

4 ounces fat-free cream cheese

¼ cup confectioners' sugar

🍃 2 tablespoons unsweetened cocoa powder

🍃 ¼ teaspoon ground cinnamon

🍃 ½ cup low-fat vanilla yogurt

🍃 1 apple

🍃 1 banana

1. In a medium bowl with an electric mixer on medium speed, beat the cream cheese, sugar, cocoa, and cinnamon until smooth and creamy. Beat in the yogurt. Place in a serving bowl, cover, and refrigerate for at least 30 minutes.

2. Just before serving, core and cut the apple into wedges. Peel and cut the banana into thick slices. Serve with the chocolate dip.

Serves 2

🍃 **Heart healthy ingredients: 5**

Per serving: 259 calories, 22 calories from fat, 2 g total fat, 1 g saturated fat, 1 g monounsaturated fat, 0 g polyunsaturated fat, 8 mg cholesterol, 353 mg sodium, 51 g carbohydrates, 6 g fiber, 38 g sugar, 13 g protein

Quick No-Bake Apple-Cherry Crisp

No need to turn on the oven to get that wonderful fruit-and-oat combo of a classic fruit crisp. Granola sprinkled on applesauce and cherries does the trick. Cherries are bursting with antioxidants, fiber, omega-3 fatty acids, and other nutrients, making them a delicious and nutritious addition to your meals. They lower blood pressure and cholesterol, reduce plaque buildup and blood clots, and reduce the risk of heart disease overall.

🍃 ¾ cup unsweetened applesauce

🍃 ¼ cup cherries, pitted and halved

🍃 Pinch of ground cinnamon

🍃 ⅓ cup low-fat granola

In a serving bowl, stir together the applesauce, cherries, and cinnamon. Sprinkle with the granola.

Serves 1

🍃 **Heart healthy ingredients: 4**

Per serving: 239 calories, 20 calories from fat, 2 g total fat, 1 g saturated fat, 1 g monounsaturated fat, 0 g polyunsaturated fat, 0 mg cholesterol, 93 mg sodium, 55 g carbohydrates, 5 g fiber, 33 g sugar, 4 g protein

Harvest Cookies

You can increase your intake of good fats by using olive oil instead of butter or margarine in baked recipes. Be sure to use light olive oil, as it lacks the rich flavor of virgin or extra-virgin and will go unnoticed in baked goods.

- ♥ ¾ cup canned plain pumpkin puree
- 1 cup packed dark brown sugar
- 2 large eggs
- ♥ ¼ cup light olive oil
- ♥ ⅔ cup whole wheat pastry flour
- ⅔ cup all-purpose flour
- 1 teaspoon baking powder
- ¼ teaspoon baking soda
- 1½ teaspoons pumpkin pie spice
- ¼ teaspoon salt
- ♥ ½ cup chopped walnuts
- ♥ ½ cup dried cranberries

1. Preheat the oven to 350°F. Line a baking sheet with parchment paper.

2. In a medium bowl, whisk together the pumpkin, brown sugar, eggs, and oil. In a large bowl, whisk together the pastry flour, all-purpose flour, baking powder, baking soda, pumpkin pie spice, and salt. Make a well in the center and stir in the pumpkin mixture. Add the walnuts and cranberries and stir until well blended.

3. Drop dough by level tablespoonfuls about 1½" apart onto the prepared baking sheet. Bake for 10 minutes, or until the cookies are lightly browned and firm to the touch. Remove to a rack to cool completely. Repeat with the remaining dough.

Makes 36

♥ **Heart healthy ingredients: 5**

Per cookie: 75 calories, 26 calories from fat, 3 g total fat, 1 g saturated fat, 1 g monounsaturated fat, 1 g polyunsaturated fat, 12 mg cholesterol, 47 mg sodium, 11 g carbohydrates, 1 g fiber, 7 g sugar, 1 g protein

Mocha Coffee

To make this a mocha café au lait, place the soy milk in a small saucepan and heat over medium heat until bubbles form around the edges. Whisk briefly to make foamy and add to the cup with coffee.

- ♥ ½ ounce bittersweet (60% cocoa or more) chocolate, grated
- ♥ ¼ teaspoon ground cinnamon
- 1 cup hot coffee
- ♥ ½ cup vanilla soy milk

Place the chocolate and cinnamon in a large coffee cup. Gradually add the coffee and soy milk. Stir to melt the chocolate.

Serves 1

♥ **Heart healthy ingredients: 3**

Per serving: 141 calories, 51 calories from fat, 6 g total fat, 3 g saturated fat, 2 g monounsaturated fat, 1 g polyunsaturated fat, 0 mg cholesterol, 48 mg sodium, 20 g carbohydrates, 1 g fiber, 15 g sugar, 4 g protein

Fat-Free Applesauce Oatmeal Cookies

"I served these delicious and healthy cookies at our first WomenHeart luncheon for our employees. Many people at the luncheon made the cookies at home and had very positive results. I heard comments like 'So easy to make,' 'I didn't know heart healthy cookies could taste so good,' and 'My 2-year old daughter loves them!' I am thrilled to share this tasty and healthy recipe with you to enjoy and share with your friends and family!"

GAIL C., LA CROSSE, WISCONSIN

- ♥ 3 cups quick-cooking oats
- ♥ 1 cup whole wheat pastry flour
- 1 teaspoon baking soda
- ♥ ¼ teaspoon ground nutmeg
- ♥ ½ teaspoon ground cinnamon
- ♥ 1½ cups unsweetened applesauce
- 1 cup sugar
- 1 teaspoon pure vanilla extract
- ♥ ⅔ cup dried cranberries or cherries

1. Preheat the oven to 350°F.

2. In a large bowl, combine the oats, flour, baking soda, nutmeg, and cinnamon. Add the applesauce, sugar, and vanilla extract and stir until well blended. Stir in the cranberries or cherries.

3. With wet hands, roll the dough into 1" balls and place on a non-stick baking sheet or sheets. (If the dough is too sticky, place in the freezer for a few minutes.) Using the bottom of a glass dipped in sugar, flatten the cookies.

4. Bake for 20 minutes, or until lightly browned. Cool on the sheet for 3 minutes. Remove to a rack to cool completely.

Makes 48

♥ **Heart healthy ingredients: 6**

Per cookie: 51 calories, 3 calories from fat, 0 g total fat, 0 g saturated fat, 0 g monounsaturated fat, 0 g polyunsaturated fat, 0 mg cholesterol, 27 mg sodium, 11 g carbohydrates, 1 g fiber, 6 g sugar, 1 g protein

175 FAMILY-PLEASING, HEART-PROTECTING RECIPES

Chocolate Almond Biscotti

Here's a terrific way to enjoy chocolate's heart healthy flavonoids. Cocoa and bittersweet chocolate (with at least 60 percent cocoa) do more than improve the ratio between "good" and "bad" cholesterol; they also lower blood pressure, reduce the risk of type 2 diabetes, and relax blood vessels.

1½ cups all-purpose flour

♥ ⅓ cup unsweetened cocoa powder

1½ teaspoons baking powder

♥ ½ teaspoon ground cinnamon

6 tablespoons butter, softened

¾ cup sugar

2 eggs

1 tablespoon pure vanilla extract

♥ ½ cup chopped slivered almonds

♥ 2 ounces bittersweet (60% cocoa or more) chocolate, chopped

1. Preheat the oven to 400°F. Line a baking sheet with parchment paper.

2. In a small bowl, stir together the flour, cocoa, baking powder, and cinnamon. In a large bowl, with an electric mixer on high speed, cream the butter and sugar until fluffy. Beat in the eggs, one at a time. Beat in the vanilla extract. Add the flour mixture and beat on low just until combined. Fold in the almonds and chocolate.

3. Place the dough on the prepared baking sheet and shape into a loaf about 9" × 5". Bake for 20 minutes, or until the top springs back when lightly touched. Remove to a rack to cool, about 15 minutes.

4. Reduce the oven temperature to 300°F. Cut the loaf crosswise into 18 (½"-thick) slices. Place the slices cut side down on the baking sheet. Bake, turning once, for 25 minutes, or until dry and crisp. Remove to a rack to cool completely.

Makes 18

♥ **Heart healthy ingredients: 4**

Per serving: 145 calories, 65 calories from fat, 7 g total fat, 3 g saturated fat, 2 g monounsaturated fat, 1 g polyunsaturated fat, 34 mg cholesterol, 81 mg sodium, 19 g carbohydrates, 1 g fiber, 10 g sugar, 3 g protein

Frozen Berry Pops

If you don't have frozen-pop molds, use paper cups with wooden sticks. Here's how: Evenly divide the mixture into 4 paper cups and freeze for about 30 minutes, or until starting to set. Insert a stick into the center of each cup and freeze completely.

- 1 cup frozen strawberries (not in syrup)
- 1 small ripe banana, quartered
- 1 cup fat-free vanilla yogurt

  ½ teaspoon lime zest
- 1 teaspoon lime juice

In a blender, combine the strawberries, banana, yogurt, lime zest, and lime juice. Blend until smooth. Pour into 4 frozen-pop molds. Freeze at least 4 hours.

Makes 4

Heart healthy ingredients: 4

Per serving: 90 calories, 1 calorie from fat, 0 g total fat, 0 g saturated fat, 0 g monounsaturated fat, 0 g polyunsaturated fat, 1 mg cholesterol, 43 mg sodium, 20 g carbohydrates, 2 g fiber, 16 g sugar, 3 g protein

Tropical Fruit Pops

In addition to being delicious, mangos are rich in antioxidants, potassium, and fiber, making them a good heart healthy addition to anyone's meals.

- 2 ripe mangos, peeled, pitted, and chopped
- 1 small ripe banana, quartered
- ½ cup orange juice

In a blender, combine the mangos, banana, and orange juice. Blend until smooth. Pour into 4 frozen-pop molds. Freeze at least 4 hours.

Makes 4

Heart healthy ingredients: 3

Per serving: 102 calories, 3 calories from fat, 0 g total fat, 0 g saturated fat, 0 g monounsaturated fat, 0 g polyunsaturated fat, 2 mg cholesterol, 2 mg sodium, 26 g carbohydrates, 3 g fiber, 19 g sugar, 1 g protein

CHAPTER 12

Just for Dessert

Quick and Easy Rice Pudding

This delicious dessert comes together in minutes with the help of the microwave and already cooked rice. You can vary the flavors by using walnuts, dried cranberries, and orange extract (just ½ teaspoon) or almonds, raisins, and a pinch of cinnamon.

- 1½ cups vanilla soy milk
- 3 egg yolks
- ¼ cup sugar
- 3 tablespoons cornstarch
- 1 teaspoon pure vanilla extract
- 2 cups cooked brown rice
- ½ cup shelled pistachio nuts, toasted
- ¼ cup dried cherries

In a 1½-quart microwavable bowl, whisk together the milk, egg yolks, sugar, cornstarch, and vanilla extract. Microwave on high, stirring every 2 minutes, for 8 minutes, or until thickened. Remove from the microwave and stir in the rice, pistachios, and cherries. Cover and let stand for 5 minutes before serving.

Serves 6

Heart healthy ingredients: 4

Per serving: 267 calories, 76 calories from fat, 8 g total fat, 2 g saturated fat, 4 g monounsaturated fat, 2 g polyunsaturated fat, 102 mg cholesterol, 31 mg sodium, 41 g carbohydrates, 3 g fiber, 16 g sugar, 7 g protein

Chocolate Almond Pudding

Often thought of just for pasta dishes, ricotta cheese is delicious when combined with a bit of sugar, turning it from savory cheese to sweet treat. And it's a great way to create a lovely no-cook chocolate pudding.

- 1½ cups fat-free ricotta cheese
- ½ cup low-fat vanilla yogurt
- ½ cup unsweetened cocoa powder
- ¼ cup confectioners' sugar
- 2 teaspoons pure vanilla extract
- ¼ teaspoon almond extract
- 4 tablespoons sliced almonds, toasted

In a food processor, combine the ricotta, yogurt, cocoa, sugar, vanilla extract, and almond extract. Pulse just until smooth. Evenly divide among 4 dessert dishes and sprinkle each serving with 1 tablespoon of the almonds.

Serves 4

Heart healthy ingredients: 3

Per serving: 196 calories, 44 calories from fat, 5 g total fat, 1 g saturated fat, 3 g monounsaturated fat, 1 g polyunsaturated fat, 17 mg cholesterol, 120 mg sodium, 26 g carbohydrates, 4 g fiber, 15 g sugar, 12 g protein

Peach-Blueberry Shortcakes

Here's a nice variation of strawberry shortcake, using the delicious combination of peaches and blueberries. Any fruits will work: Try nectarines and raspberries or, for a tropical twist, mango and kiwifruit.

6 peaches, peeled, pitted, and sliced

♥ 2 cups blueberries

2 tablespoons brown sugar

♥ 2½ cups whole wheat pastry flour

⅓ cup granulated sugar

1 tablespoon baking powder

⅛ teaspoon salt

⅓ cup cold butter, cut into small pieces

1 cup fat-free milk

♥ 3 cups low-fat vanilla yogurt

1. Heat the oven to 400°F. Line a baking sheet with parchment paper. In a medium bowl, toss the peaches, blueberries, and brown sugar until well combined. Set aside.

2. In a large bowl, combine the flour, granulated sugar, baking powder, and salt. Cut in the butter until it resembles coarse meal. Add the milk and stir just until blended. Place on a lightly floured surface and knead 7 times or until a soft dough forms. Pat the dough ½" thick and cut out 12 rounds with a 2½" cutter.

3. Place the rounds on the prepared baking sheet. Bake for 12 minutes, or until golden brown. Transfer the sheet to a cooling rack for 15 minutes.

4. Split the shortcakes in half. Place 1 shortcake bottom on each of 12 plates. Evenly divide the peach mixture over the shortcakes. Top each with ¼ cup of the yogurt and the other half of the shortcake.

Serves 12

♥ Heart healthy ingredients: 3

Per serving: 257 calories, 57 calories from fat, 6 g total fat, 4 g saturated fat, 2 g monounsaturated fat, 0 g polyunsaturated fat, 17 mg cholesterol, 254 mg sodium, 44 g carbohydrates, 5 g fiber, 23 g sugar, 7 g protein

MAKEOVER MAGIC

Traditionally, shortcakes are full of butter and topped with whipped cream, adding a lot of artery-clogging fats. Using a small amount of butter for flavor and substituting yogurt for the whipped cream reduces the calories by half and the fat by 80 percent!

	Traditional Shortcake	Peach-Blueberry Shortcake
Calories	497	257
Fat (g)	32	6
Percent calories from fat	58	21

Lemon-Lime Pudding Cake

Pudding cakes are magical dessert treats—as the cake bakes, the bottom becomes a rich, sublime pudding and the top turns into a flavorful sponge cake. Be sure to use freshly squeezed juice for the best flavor.

⅓ cup all-purpose flour

¾ cup granulated sugar

⅛ teaspoon salt

🌿 1 cup vanilla soy milk

2 teaspoons grated lemon and/or lime peel

🌿 ¼ cup lemon juice

🌿 ¼ cup lime juice

2 tablespoons butter, melted

3 eggs, separated

Confectioners' sugar for garnish

🌿 2 cups fresh raspberries

1. Preheat the oven to 350°F. Bring 6 cups water to a boil. Coat an 8" glass baking dish with cooking spray.

2. In a medium bowl, whisk together the flour, ½ cup of the granulated sugar, and salt. Add the milk, peel, lemon juice, lime juice, butter, and egg yolks and whisk until smooth.

3. Beat the egg whites in a large bowl with an electric mixer on high until soft peaks form. Gradually add the remaining ¼ cup granulated sugar while beating; beat until stiff glossy peaks form. Fold the egg whites into the milk mixture. The batter will be lumpy and thin. Scrape into the prepared baking dish.

4. Place the baking dish in a large (13" × 9" × 2") roasting pan. Fill the roasting pan with the boiling water until it reaches halfway up the baking dish. Bake for 35 minutes, or until the cake is puffed and lightly browned. Cool on a wire rack for 15 minutes. Dust the cake with confectioners' sugar and serve with the raspberries.

Serves 8

🌿 **Heart healthy ingredients: 4**

Per serving: 175 calories, 45 calories from fat, 5 g total fat, 2 g saturated fat, 2 g monounsaturated fat, 0 g polyunsaturated fat, 87 mg cholesterol, 104 mg sodium, 31 g carbohydrates, 0 g fiber, 21 g sugar, 4 g protein

Orange Pistachio Cake

Pistachios are helpful to heart health. A recent study found that they lower LDL ("bad") cholesterol levels and lipoprotein ratios.

♥ ¾ cup shelled natural pistachios

1¼ cups all-purpose flour

¼ teaspoon salt

6 eggs, separated

½ teaspoon cream of tartar

1½ cups sugar

1 teaspoon grated orange peel

♥ ½ cup orange juice

⅔ cup all-fruit orange marmalade spread

♥ ½ cup dried cherries, chopped

1. Preheat the oven to 325°F. Coarsely chop ½ cup of the pistachios and set aside. Finely chop the remaining ¼ cup and place in a large bowl. Add the flour and salt and whisk until well blended. Set aside.

2. In a large bowl, beat the egg whites and cream of tartar with an electric mixer at high speed until soft peaks form. Gradually add ¾ cup of the sugar, beating until stiff peaks form. Set aside.

3. Place the yolks in another large bowl and beat with the same beaters for 3 minutes or until very thick and light in color. With the mixer running, add the remaining ¾ cup sugar, 1 tablespoon at a time, until thick. Add the orange peel and orange juice and beat until smooth. Fold in the reserved flour mixture. Fold in one-fourth of the beaten whites. Gently fold in the remaining egg whites just until blended.

4. Scrape the batter into an ungreased 10" tube pan and smooth the top. Bake for 55 minutes, or until the cake springs back when lightly touched. Invert the pan over a narrow-neck bottle to cool completely. Run a knife around the sides and center tube of the pan and invert the cake onto a plate.

5. Heat the marmalade in a small saucepan over medium heat until melted. Pour over the cake, allowing it to be absorbed into the cake. Top with the reserved chopped pistachios and dried cherries.

Serves 12

♥ **Heart healthy ingredients: 3**

Per serving: 283 calories, 56 calories from fat, 6 g total fat, 1 g saturated fat, 3 g monounsaturated fat, 1 g polyunsaturated fat, 106 mg cholesterol, 89 mg sodium, 51 g carbohydrates, 1 g fiber, 36 g sugar, 7 g protein

Raspberry Buckle

Ah, raspberries. This succulent fruit is a great source of fiber and antioxidants that lower blood pressure, control cholesterol, and prevent diabetes. And this homey dessert is a great way to enjoy the precious berries. As the buckle bakes, the batter rises to the top, creating a delicious puddinglike creation that is irresistible!

♥ 1 cup whole wheat pastry flour

¾ cup sugar

2 teaspoons baking powder

¼ teaspoon salt

♥ ¾ cup vanilla soy milk

2 tablespoons butter, melted

♥ 2 bags (10 ounces each) frozen raspberries

2 teaspoons grated orange peel

1. Preheat the oven to 350°F. Coat an 8" glass baking dish with cooking spray.

2. In a large bowl, whisk together the flour, sugar, baking powder, and salt. Add the milk and butter and stir until well blended. Scrape into the prepared dish.

3. Sprinkle the raspberries and orange peel over the batter. Bake for 60 minutes, or until a toothpick inserted in the center comes out clean. Let stand 15 minutes before serving.

Serves 12

♥ **Heart healthy ingredients: 3**

Per serving: 137 calories, 23 calories from fat, 3 g total fat, 1 g saturated fat, 1 g monounsaturated fat, 0 g polyunsaturated fat, 5 mg cholesterol, 159 mg sodium, 28 g carbohydrates, 4 g fiber, 17 g sugar, 2 g protein

Apple-Cranberry Crisp

Prepared low-fat granola creates delicious crunch in this crisp—without the added fat of a traditional butter-laden topping.

♥ 5 apples, peeled, cored, and cut into ½" slices (about 4 cups)

♥ 1 cup cranberries

½ cup packed brown sugar

♥ 1 tablespoon chopped crystallized ginger

♥ 1 tablespoon lemon juice

♥ 2 cups low-fat granola with almonds

3 tablespoons pure maple syrup

1. Preheat the oven to 350°F. In a large bowl, combine the apples and cranberries. Add the brown sugar, ginger, and lemon juice and toss to blend well. Scrape into an 8" baking dish.

2. In a small bowl, toss the granola with the maple syrup. Sprinkle over the apple mixture. Bake for 35 minutes, or until the apples are tender and the crisp is bubbling in the center.

Serves 6

♥ **Heart healthy ingredients: 5**

Per serving: 311 calories, 17 calories from fat, 2 g total fat, 1 g saturated fat, 1 g monounsaturated fat, 0 g polyunsaturated fat, 0 mg cholesterol, 98 mg sodium, 75 g carbohydrates, 7 g fiber, 48 g sugar, 3 g protein

Fruit 'n' Nut Coffee Cake

This lightened-up coffee cake is specked with heart healthy cranberries and almonds. Whole wheat flour ups the fiber count.

♥ 1 cup low-fat plain yogurt

1 cup sugar

3 eggs

⅓ cup canola oil

1 tablespoon pure vanilla extract

½ teaspoon ground cardamom

1½ teaspoons baking powder

1 teaspoon baking soda

½ teaspoon salt

♥ 2¼ cups whole wheat pastry flour

♥ ½ cup dried cranberries

♥ ½ cup almonds, toasted and chopped

1 teaspoon grated orange peel

1. Preheat the oven to 350°F. Coat a small Bundt pan with cooking spray.

2. In a large bowl, whisk together the yogurt, sugar, eggs, oil, vanilla extract, and cardamom. Stir in the baking powder, baking soda, and salt. Add the flour and whisk until well blended. Fold in the cranberries, almonds, and orange peel.

3. Scrape the batter into the prepared pan. Bake for 30 minutes, or until a toothpick inserted in the center comes out clean. Cool on a rack for 10 minutes. Invert the cake onto the rack and cool completely.

Serves 12

♥ **Heart healthy ingredients: 4**

Per serving: 278 calories, 90 calories from fat, 10 g total fat, 1 g saturated fat, 6 g monounsaturated fat, 33 g polyunsaturated fat, 54 mg cholesterol, 302 mg sodium, 41 g carbohydrates, 4 g fiber, 22 g sugar, 6 g protein

MAKEOVER MAGIC

Using just a little oil (instead of lots of butter) and low-fat yogurt (instead of sour cream) means this delicious cake is now a healthy treat the whole family can enjoy.

	Traditional Coffee Cake	Fruit 'n' Nut Coffee Cake
Calories	464	278
Fat (g)	28	10
Percent calories from fat	54	32

175 Family-Pleasing, Heart-Protecting Recipes

Flourless Chocolate Cake

This rich cake is loaded with antioxidants from red wine and chocolate, as well as fiber and omega-3 fatty acids from walnuts. Together they help control cholesterol and blood pressure, reduce plaque buildup, and improve bloodflow.

❦ 1½ cups walnuts

1 cup granulated sugar

❦ 6 ounces bittersweet chocolate (60% cocoa or more)

6 eggs, separated

❦ ¼ cup unsweetened cocoa powder

❦ ⅓ cup dry red wine

Confectioners' sugar for garnish

1. Preheat the oven to 350°F. Coat a 10" springform pan with cooking spray. Place the walnuts and ½ cup of the granulated sugar in a food processor and pulse until finely ground. Add the chocolate and pulse until the chocolate is ground. Set aside.

2. In a large bowl with an electric mixer on high, beat the egg whites until foamy. Beat until stiff glossy peaks form, gradually adding the remaining ½ cup granulated sugar while beating.

3. In another large bowl, with the same beaters, beat the egg yolks for 4 minutes, or until thick. Add the cocoa and wine and beat until well blended. Fold in the chocolate mixture. Fold in one-fourth of the egg whites, then the remaining egg whites in 2 batches.

4. Scrape the batter into the pan. Bake for 40 minutes, or until a knife inserted in the center comes out clean. Cool the cake completely in the pan on a rack for 2 hours. Run a knife around the sides of the pan and release the sides. Dust with the confectioners' sugar before serving.

Serves 16

❦ **Heart healthy ingredients: 4**

Per serving: 159 calories, 69 calories from fat, 8 g total fat, 3 g saturated fat, 2 g monounsaturated fat, 2 g polyunsaturated fat, 79 mg cholesterol, 28 mg sodium, 21 g carbohydrates, 1 g fiber, 19 g sugar, 4 g protein

Chocolate Angel Food Cake

Adding cocoa to low-fat angel food cake adds decadence without fat. The cake is delicious with fruit, or, for a more elegant look, drizzle it with melted bittersweet chocolate, being sure to use antioxidant-rich chocolate with 60 percent cocoa or more.

1 cup all-purpose flour

1¾ cups + 2 tablespoons sugar

♥ ¼ cup unsweetened cocoa powder

♥ ½ teaspoon ground cinnamon

¼ teaspoon salt

12 egg whites, at room temperature

2 teaspoons cream of tartar

♥ 1 quart strawberries, hulled and sliced

♥ 1 cup low-fat vanilla yogurt

1. Preheat the oven to 350°F. In a medium bowl, whisk together the flour, ¾ cup of the sugar, the cocoa, cinnamon, and salt. Set aside.

2. In a large bowl with an electric mixer on medium speed, beat the egg whites until frothy. Add the cream of tartar and increase the speed to high. Gradually add 1 cup of the remaining sugar while beating and beat until stiff glossy peaks form. Gently fold in one-third of the flour mixture. Fold in the remaining flour mixture just until blended.

3. Spoon the batter into an ungreased 10" tube pan with a removable bottom. Bake for 40 minutes, or until a toothpick inserted in the center comes out clean. Invert the pan over a narrow-neck bottle to cool completely. Run a knife around the sides of the pan and invert the cake onto a serving plate.

4. Thirty minutes before serving, toss the strawberries with the remaining 2 tablespoons sugar. To serve, slice the cake into 12 pieces. Top each slice with some berries and a dollop of the yogurt.

Serves 12

♥ **Heart healthy ingredients: 4**

Per serving: 210 calories, 6 calories from fat, 1 g total fat, 0 g saturated fat, 0 g monounsaturated fat, 0 g polyunsaturated fat, 1 mg cholesterol, 276 mg sodium, 47 g carbohydrates, 2 g fiber, 37 g sugar, 6 g protein

Tropical Phyllo Cups

Delicate layers of phyllo make a lovely base for quick-broiled bananas and mango. Try other fillings as well, such as Chocolate Almond Pudding (page 243) or frozen yogurt with a drizzle of melted raspberry all-fruit jam.

4 sheets (12" × 17") frozen phyllo dough, thawed

🍂 ⅓ cup walnuts, finely chopped

🍂 2 bananas, cut into 1" slices

🍂 1 mango, peeled, pitted, and chopped

2 tablespoons brown sugar

1 tablespoon grated lime peel

1. Preheat the oven to 325°F. Coat four 6-ounce custard cups with butter-flavored cooking spray.

2. Place 1 sheet of phyllo on a work surface. Coat with butter-flavored cooking spray and sprinkle with one-fourth of the walnuts. Top with another sheet of phyllo. Coat with cooking spray and sprinkle with one-third of the remaining walnuts. Repeat with the remaining sheets of phyllo and walnuts. With a sharp knife, cut the phyllo stack into 4 equal rectangles. Press into the prepared custard cups.

3. Place the cups on a baking sheet and bake for 8 minutes, or until golden brown. Cool on a rack.

4. Preheat the broiler and place the oven rack on the top shelf. Coat a baking sheet with sides (jelly-roll pan) with cooking spray.

5. In a medium bowl, combine the bananas, mango, sugar, and lime zest. Spread out on the prepared baking sheet. Broil for 5 minutes, or until the fruit is tender and lightly browned. Place a phyllo cup on each of 4 dessert plates. Evenly divide the banana mixture among the cups.

Serves 4

🍂 **Heart healthy ingredients: 3**

Per serving: 226 calories, 60 calories from fat, 7 g total fat, 1 g saturated fat, 1 g monounsaturated fat, 4 g polyunsaturated fat, 0 mg cholesterol, 96 mg sodium, 41 g carbohydrates, 4 g fiber, 25 g sugar, 3 g protein

YES, WE HAVE BANANAS

How long have bananas been around? No one knows for sure. Some horticulturists maintain that the very first fruit on earth was a banana. We do know that records dating back to 327 BC suggest that Alexander the Great "discovered" bananas when he invaded India. Bananas were introduced to Americans in 1876, during our country's first centennial celebration in Philadelphia. The exotic delicacies were carefully wrapped in foil and sold for 10 cents each to the thoroughly intrigued public.

Flavorful Fruit Tart

A creamy, Marsala-flavored filling of ricotta cheese and yogurt is topped with heart healthy fruit in this lovely tart. Marsala hails from Italy and is a fortified wine, meaning that brandy has been added to it, giving it a rich, smoky flavor. It adds a nice richness to cream-based desserts. And the easy crust—made with walnuts and whole wheat flour—is good for you, too.

- ¼ cup walnuts
- ¾ cup whole wheat pastry flour
- 2 tablespoons granulated sugar
- ⅛ teaspoon salt
- 3 tablespoons light olive oil
- 2 ounces bittersweet (60% cocoa or more) chocolate, melted
- 1 cup fat-free ricotta cheese
- ⅓ cup confectioners' sugar
- 2 tablespoons Marsala wine
- 1 cup low-fat vanilla yogurt
- 3 kiwifruit, peeled, halved, and sliced
- 1 cup red grapes, sliced
- 2 tablespoons all-fruit apple jelly, melted

1. Place the walnuts in a food processor and pulse until ground. Add the flour, granulated sugar, and salt and pulse until blended. With the motor running, gradually add the oil until a dough forms. Wrap the dough in plastic and refrigerate for 30 minutes.

2. Preheat the oven to 425°F. Press the dough onto the bottom and up the sides of a 9" tart pan with a removable bottom. Bake for 10 minutes, or until lightly browned. Cool completely on a rack. Spread the chocolate over the bottom of the shell.

3. In a medium bowl, with an electric mixer on medium speed, beat the ricotta, confectioners' sugar, and wine until smooth. Add the yogurt and beat 1 minute. Pour into the tart shell. Arrange the kiwifruit and grapes over the filling and brush with the jelly.

Serves 12

Heart healthy ingredients: 6

Per serving: 187 calories, 74 calories from fat, 8 g total fat, 2 g saturated fat, 3 g monounsaturated fat, 2 g polyunsaturated fat, 6 mg cholesterol, 65 mg sodium, 25 g carbohydrates, 1 g fiber, 17 g sugar, 4 g protein

Chocolate Berry Crepes

Crepes are paper-thin pancakes that are best filled with fruits for dessert or a savory mixture for an entrée. You can make your own crepes, but it's much easier to find them in the refrigerated section of your market.

- ♥ 1½ cups strawberries, sliced
- ♥ 1 cup blueberries
- ♥ 1 cup raspberries

  1 tablespoon brown sugar
- ♥ 1½ cups low-fat vanilla yogurt
- ♥ 2 tablespoons + 1 teaspoon unsweetened cocoa powder

  4 (7") ready-to-use refrigerated crepes

1. In a large bowl, toss the strawberries, blueberries, raspberries, and brown sugar to combine well. In a medium bowl, stir together the yogurt and 2 tablespoons of the cocoa.

2. Place 1 crepe on each of 4 serving plates. Evenly divide the yogurt mixture down the center of each crepe and top with one-fourth of the berry mixture. Roll up the crepes, jelly-roll style. Sprinkle with the remaining 1 teaspoon cocoa.

Serves 4

♥ **Heart healthy ingredients: 5**

Per serving: 153 calories, 24 calories from fat, 3 g total fat, 1 g saturated fat, 1 g monounsaturated fat, 0 g polyunsaturated fat, 11 mg cholesterol, 117 mg sodium, 29 g carbohydrates, 3 g fiber, 17 g sugar, 7 g protein

Cran-Raspberry Ice

Known as granité in France and granita in Italy, an ice is a frozen mixture of juice, wine, or coffee and sugar that is stirred often during freezing to form coarse crystals. It's a delicious—and healthy—way to end a summer meal.

- ♥ 2 cups cranberry-raspberry juice (100% juice)
- ♥ ¼ cup orange juice

  2 tablespoons sugar
- ♥ 1½ cups low-fat vanilla yogurt

1. In a 9" square metal baking pan, whisk together the cranberry-raspberry juice, orange juice, and sugar until the sugar dissolves. Freeze for 1 hour. Stir to blend in any frozen portions. Freeze again, stirring every 45 minutes, for about 4 hours, or until the mixture has a uniform slushy consistency and ice crystals form.

2. To serve, scrape into 6 serving bowls and top each serving with ¼ cup of the yogurt.

Serves 6

♥ **Heart healthy ingredients: 3**

Per serving: 113 calories, 7 calories from fat, 1 g total fat, 1 g saturated fat, 0 g monounsaturated fat, 0 g polyunsaturated fat, 3 mg cholesterol, 44 mg sodium, 23 g carbohydrates, 0 g fiber, 22 g sugar, 3 g protein

Summer Fruit Compote

What could be better than summer's best fruits, steeped in heart healthy red wine? A cherry pitter makes simple work of pitting cherries, but if you don't have one, try this method: Stem the cherries, then insert a sturdy drinking straw through the stem end and push the pit out the bottom of the cherry.

- 2 cups red wine, such as Pinot Noir, Merlot, or Shiraz

  ¾ cup sugar

- 3 cinnamon sticks

- 1 tablespoon minced crystallized ginger

  4 peaches, quartered and pitted

- 2 cups pitted cherries, halved

- 1 pint raspberries

1. In a medium saucepan, combine the wine, sugar, cinnamon, and ginger over medium-high heat. Bring to a boil, stirring occasionally. Add the peaches and cook for 2 minutes.

2. Remove to a heat-safe glass bowl and stir in the cherries and raspberries. Discard the cinnamon sticks. Serve at room temperature or chilled.

Serves 6

Heart healthy ingredients: 5

Per serving: 238 calories, 4 calories from fat, 1 g total fat, 0 g saturated fat, 0 g monounsaturated fat, 0 g polyunsaturated fat, 0 mg cholesterol, 3 mg sodium, 47 g carbohydrates, 2 g fiber, 36 g sugar, 1 g protein

CHAPTER 13

Dressings, Salsas, Sauces, and Spreads

Tofu Mayonnaise

Here's a great way to add soy to your diet while enjoying a healthy alternative to prepared mayonnaise, which is naturally high in fat and sodium. Vary the flavor by adding fresh herbs, garlic, or roasted red peppers.

- 6 ounces reduced-fat silken tofu, well drained
- ¼ cup extra-virgin olive oil
- 1 tablespoon lemon juice
- 2 teaspoons Dijon mustard
- 2 teaspoons honey
- ¼ teaspoon salt

In a food processor, combine the tofu and oil and process until smooth. Add the lemon juice, mustard, honey, and salt and process until smooth. Refrigerate for up to 1 week until ready to serve.

Makes 1 cup (8 servings)

Heart healthy ingredients: 3

Per serving: 69 calories, 55 calories from fat, 8 g total fat, 1 g saturated fat, 5 g monounsaturated fat, 1 g polyunsaturated fat, 0 mg cholesterol, 123 mg sodium, 2 g carbohydrates, 0 g fiber, 2 g sugar, 2 g protein

Creamy Garlic Dressing

When using yogurt in dressings, sauces, or salads, it's best to first drain it for 2 to 12 hours. This reduces the water, providing a creamy base for your dressing. To drain, place a coffee filter or white paper towel in a sieve placed over a bowl and fill with the yogurt. Refrigerate while draining.

- ½ cup low-fat plain yogurt, drained for 2 hours (see above)
- 1 tablespoon extra-virgin olive oil
- 1 tablespoon white wine vinegar
- 1 clove garlic, minced
- 1 tablespoon minced fresh herb, such as basil, cilantro, oregano, or parsley
- ⅛ teaspoon salt

In a small bowl, whisk together the yogurt, oil, vinegar, garlic, herb, and salt. Refrigerate for up to 1 week until ready to serve.

Makes 1 cup (16 servings)

Heart healthy ingredients: 3

Per serving: 15 calories, 8 calories from fat, 1 g total fat, 0 g saturated fat, 1 g monounsaturated fat, 0 g polyunsaturated fat, 1 mg cholesterol, 29 mg sodium, 1 g carbohydrates, 0 g fiber, 1 g sugar, 0 g protein

Tomato-Basil Vinaigrette

So versatile, this vinaigrette is great for pasta, bean, or green salads. Give it a Tex-Mex flavor by substituting cilantro for the basil and adding a dash of hot-pepper sauce.

- ½ cup low-sodium tomato or vegetable juice
- ¼ cup white balsamic vinegar
- 2 tablespoons extra-virgin olive oil
- 2 tablespoons chopped fresh basil
- 1 clove garlic, minced
- ⅛ teaspoon salt

In a small jar, combine the tomato or vegetable juice, vinegar, oil, basil, garlic, and salt. Cover and shake to combine. Refrigerate for up to 1 week until ready to serve.

Makes 1 cup (16 servings)

Heart healthy ingredients: 3

Per serving: 20 calories, 15 calories from fat, 2 g total fat, 0 g saturated fat, 1 g monounsaturated fat, 0 g polyunsaturated fat, 0 mg cholesterol, 29 mg sodium, 1 g carbohydrates, 1 g fiber, 0 g sugar, 0 g protein

Citrus Vinaigrette

Chives are in the herb section of the produce aisle and are also available frozen or freeze-dried. Use this dressing for pasta salad, roasted-beet salad, or tossed with baby spinach leaves.

- ½ cup orange juice
- 2 tablespoons lime juice
- 2 tablespoons sherry or white wine vinegar
- 2 tablespoons extra-virgin olive oil
- 2 tablespoons chopped chives
- 1 teaspoon sugar
- ⅛ teaspoon salt

In a small jar, combine the orange juice, lime juice, sherry or vinegar, oil, chives, sugar, and salt. Cover and shake to combine. Refrigerate until ready to serve.

Makes 1 cup (16 servings)

Heart healthy ingredients: 4

Per serving: 22 calories, 15 calories from fat, 2 g total fat, 0 g saturated fat, 1 g monounsaturated fat, 0 g polyunsaturated fat, 0 mg cholesterol, 35 mg sodium, 2 g carbohydrates, 0 g fiber, 0 g sugar, 0 g protein

Herb-Dijon Vinaigrette

To get the most juice from a lemon, roll it firmly on the countertop with the palm of your hand before cutting in two. This will burst the membranes and soften the lemon. Use this vinaigrette over steamed asparagus or grilled salmon, or use it to replace the mayonnaise in potato salad.

½ teaspoon grated lemon peel

⅓ cup fresh lemon juice

⅓ cup water

2 tablespoons extra-virgin olive oil

2 tablespoons honey or sugar

1 tablespoon white wine vinegar

1 tablespoon Dijon mustard

1 shallot, minced

1 teaspoon fresh chopped herb such as dill, thyme, basil, or parsley

⅛ teaspoon salt

In a small jar, combine the lemon peel, lemon juice, water, oil, honey or sugar, vinegar, mustard, shallot, herb, and salt. Cover and shake to combine. Refrigerate until ready to serve.

Makes 1 cup (16 servings)

Heart healthy ingredients: 3

Per serving: 26 calories, 15 calories from fat, 2 g total fat, 0 g saturated fat, 1 g monounsaturated fat, 0 g polyunsaturated fat, 0 mg cholesterol, 36 mg sodium, 3 g carbohydrates, 0 g fiber, 3 g sugar, 0 g protein

Updated Cheese Sauce

Use this healthier version of cheese sauce as the base for a pasta sauce or as a topping for steamed vegetables, chicken, or fish.

♥ 2 cups plain low-fat soy milk

2 tablespoons cornstarch

♥ 1 shallot, minced

♥ 1 clove garlic, minced

1 cup (4 ounces) shredded reduced-fat cheese such as Cheddar, Monterey Jack, or Jarlsberg

1. In a measuring cup or small bowl, whisk together the milk and cornstarch. Set aside.

2. Heat a small saucepan coated with cooking spray over medium heat. Add the shallot and garlic and cook, stirring constantly, for 4 minutes, or until very tender. Stir the milk mixture and pour into the pan, whisking constantly. Cook for 5 minutes, or until the mixture thickens. Add the cheese and cook, stirring constantly, for 3 minutes longer, or until the cheese melts.

Makes 12 servings (3 cups)

♥ **Heart healthy ingredients: 3**

Per serving: 40 calories, 8 calories from fat, 1 g total fat, 0 g saturated fat, 0 g monounsaturated fat, 0 g polyunsaturated fat, 2 mg cholesterol, 73 mg sodium, 5 g carbohydrates, 0 g fiber, 1 g sugar, 3 g protein

MAKEOVER MAGIC

No need for butter in this delicious creamy sauce! The fat and calories have been slashed by using low-fat soy milk thickened with cornstarch instead of full-fat (whole) cow's milk thickened with a butter/flour roux. Reduced-fat cheese lowers the counts even more.

	Traditional Cheese Sauce	Updated Cheese Sauce
Calories	79	40
Fat (g)	6	1
Percent calories from fat	68	23

Corn Salsa

For the tastiest salsa, cover and refrigerate for a few hours or overnight before serving.

1 tablespoon red wine vinegar

♥ 1 tablespoon lime juice

♥ 1 tablespoon extra-virgin olive oil

♥ 1 teaspoon mashed canned chipotle chile in adobo sauce with 2 teaspoons sauce

2 packages (10 ounces each) frozen corn kernels, thawed

♥ 2 large tomatoes, seeded and finely chopped

♥ 1 orange bell pepper, finely chopped

♥ 6 scallions, chopped

In a large bowl, whisk together the vinegar, lime juice, oil, and chipotle and adobo sauce. Stir in the corn, tomatoes, pepper, and scallions.

Serves 8
♥ **Heart healthy ingredients: 6**

Per serving: 96 calories, 23 calories from fat, 3 g total fat, 0 g saturated fat, 1 g monounsaturated fat, 0 g polyunsaturated fat, 0 mg cholesterol, 304 mg sodium, 17 g carbohydrates, 3 g fiber, 4 g sugar, 3 g protein

Soy Delicious Guacamole

Here's a brilliant green blend of two nutritional powerhouse ingredients—avocado and edamame.

♥ 1 cup fresh or frozen shelled edamame (green soybeans)

♥ ¼ cup low-fat plain yogurt

♥ 2 cloves garlic

♥ 1 avocado, halved and pitted

♥ 1 large tomato, seeded and chopped

¼ cup chopped cilantro

♥ 2 tablespoons fresh lime juice

1. Cook the edamame according to package directions. Drain and cool completely.

2. Place the edamame, yogurt, and garlic in a food processor and pulse until almost smooth.

3. Scoop the avocado from the shell and place in a medium bowl. Mash with a fork until almost smooth. Stir in the edamame mixture, tomato, cilantro, and lime juice.

Serves 6
♥ **Heart healthy ingredients: 6**

Per serving: 108 calories, 56 calories from fat, 6 g total fat, 1 g saturated fat, 3 g monounsaturated fat, 1 g polyunsaturated fat, 1 mg cholesterol, 98 mg sodium, 10 g carbohydrates, 4 g fiber, 2 g sugar, 4 g protein

Garlicky Hummus

Lemons and probiotic yogurt (yogurt with health-promoting bacteria) help lower cholesterol. Lemons alone lower blood pressure and reduce the risk of diabetes. Serve this hearty dip with warmed whole wheat pita bread.

- 1 can (15 ounces) garbanzo beans (chickpeas), rinsed and drained
- ¼ cup low-fat plain yogurt
- 2 cloves garlic
- 3 tablespoons tahini (sesame paste)
- 3 tablespoons fresh lemon juice
- 1 tablespoon extra-virgin olive oil
- ⅛–¼ teaspoon ground red pepper

In a food processor, combine the beans, yogurt, garlic, tahini, lemon juice, oil, and pepper. Process until smooth.

Serves 6

Heart healthy ingredients: 7

Per serving: 110 calories, 53 calories from fat, 6 g total fat, 1 g saturated fat, 3 g monounsaturated fat, 2 g polyunsaturated fat, 1 mg cholesterol, 71 mg sodium, 11 g carbohydrates, 3 g fiber, 2 g sugar, 4 g protein

Basic Tomato Sauce

For a change of pace and to increase the vegetables in this sauce, add finely chopped mushrooms, carrots, and celery along with the onion. During the summer, stir chopped fresh basil into the sauce after cooking.

- 2 tablespoons extra-virgin olive oil
- 1 large onion, chopped
- 2 cloves garlic, minced
- 2 teaspoons dried Italian seasoning, crushed
- ½ cup red wine
- 2 cans (14½ ounces each) no-salt-added whole tomatoes with juice
- 1 can (6 ounces) no-salt-added tomato paste

Heat the oil in a large saucepan over medium heat. Add the onion and cook, stirring occasionally, for 5 minutes, or until lightly browned. Add the garlic and seasoning and cook for 2 minutes longer. Add the wine and cook, stirring occasionally, for 5 minutes longer. Stir in the tomatoes and tomato paste and bring to a simmer. Reduce the heat to low, cover, and cook for 20 minutes to blend flavors.

Serves 8

Heart healthy ingredients: 6

Per serving: 96 calories, 31 calories from fat, 4 g total fat, 1 g saturated fat, 2 g monounsaturated fat, 0 g polyunsaturated fat, 0 mg cholesterol, 25 mg sodium, 12 g carbohydrates, 4 g fiber, 7 g sugar, 3 g protein

CHAPTER 14

Party Hearty

A Spring Cocktail Party

Here's a great way to catch up with family and friends in a relaxed setting. These delicious appetizers go well with wines but are also delectable with healthy "mocktails," such as a pomegranate spritzer: Fill a tall glass with 2 tablespoons antioxidant-rich pomegranate juice. Top with unflavored seltzer water and a squeeze of lime. So refreshing!

175 FAMILY-PLEASING, HEART-PROTECTING RECIPES

Indian Chicken Skewers

♥ ½ cup low-fat plain yogurt

2 tablespoons mango chutney

♥ 1 clove garlic, minced

♥ 1 tablespoon fresh lime juice

♥ ¾ teaspoon garam masala (Indian spice mix)

1 pound boneless, skinless chicken breasts, cut into 1" cubes

1 bunch scallions, cut into 1" pieces

1. Soak 20 (6") wooden skewers in water for 1 hour.

2. In a large zip-top bag, combine the yogurt, chutney, garlic, lime juice, and garam masala. Add the chicken and toss to coat. Seal the bag, pressing out the air, and refrigerate for 45 minutes.

3. Coat a grill rack or broiler pan with cooking spray. Preheat the grill or broiler.

4. Drain the skewers. Thread 3 chicken cubes onto each skewer, alternating with the scallion pieces. Discard the marinade. Place the skewers on the grill rack or broiler pan. Grill or broil 6" from the heat, turning once, for 6 minutes, or until no longer pink.

Serves 10
♥ **Heart healthy ingredients: 4**

Per serving: 65 calories, 7 calories from fat, 1 g total fat, 0 g saturated fat, 0 g monounsaturated fat, 0 g polyunsaturated fat, 27 mg cholesterol, 39 mg sodium, 3 g carbohydrates, 0 g fiber, 2 g sugar, 11 g protein

Warm Artichoke Dip

2 packages (10 ounces each) frozen artichoke hearts, thawed, drained, and squeezed dry

♥ 1 jar (7 ounces) roasted red peppers, drained and patted dry

♥ 3 cloves garlic

4 ounces fat-free cream cheese

1 cup (4 ounces) grated Parmesan cheese

¼ cup reduced-fat mayonnaise

♥ 1 tablespoon lemon juice

1. Preheat the oven to 400°F. Coat a 1-quart baking dish with cooking spray.

2. In a food processor, combine the artichokes, peppers, and garlic and pulse until chopped. Transfer to the prepared dish.

3. To the processor, add the cream cheese, ¾ cup of the Parmesan, the mayonnaise, and lemon juice. Process until smooth. Scrape into the dish with the artichokes and stir to blend well. Sprinkle with the remaining ¼ cup Parmesan. Bake for 15 minutes or until hot and bubbling. Serve with fat-free crackers and crudités.

Serves 12

♥ **Heart healthy ingredients: 3**

Per serving: 87 calories, 37 calories from fat, 4 g total fat, 2 g saturated fat, 1 g monounsaturated fat, 0 g polyunsaturated fat, 9 mg cholesterol, 340 mg sodium, 7 g carbohydrates, 2 g fiber, 2 g sugar, 6 g protein

MAKEOVER MAGIC

A favorite treat in restaurants, artichoke dip usually has full-fat mayonnaise as the base. We use reduced-fat mayo in ours and mix it with fat-free cream cheese—and also pump up the nutrition by adding healthy peppers with the artichokes.

	Traditional Artichoke Dip	Warm Artichoke Dip
Calories	296	87
Fat (g)	25	4
Percent calories from fat	76	41

Stuffed Mushrooms

36 medium white mushrooms

♥ 1 tablespoon extra-virgin olive oil

♥ 1 large onion, finely chopped

2 ounces Canadian bacon, chopped

♥ 2 cloves garlic, minced

♥ 1 tablespoon chopped fresh thyme or 1 teaspoon dried crushed

$\frac{1}{3}$ cup dry white wine or fat-free, reduced-sodium chicken broth

♥ $\frac{1}{2}$ cup fresh whole grain bread crumbs

$\frac{1}{2}$ cup (2 ounces) grated Romano cheese, divided

1. Preheat the oven to 400°F. Stem the mushrooms. Chop the stems and set aside. Place the caps, gill sides down, on a large baking sheet with sides (jelly-roll pan). Coat well with cooking spray. Turn the mushrooms over, coat with cooking spray again, and set aside.

2. Heat the oil in a nonstick skillet over medium heat. Add the onion, Canadian bacon, and reserved mushroom stems and cook, stirring, for 5 minutes, or until lightly browned. Add the garlic and thyme and cook for 1 minute longer. Add the wine or broth and cook for another minute. Scrape into a bowl. Add the bread crumbs and $\frac{1}{4}$ cup of the cheese and stir until well blended.

3. Evenly divide the bread crumb mixture among the mushroom caps. Sprinkle with the remaining $\frac{1}{4}$ cup cheese. Bake for 10 minutes, or until lightly browned and heated through.

Serves 6

♥ **Heart healthy ingredients: 5**

Per serving: 56 calories, 25 calories from fat, 3 g total fat, 1 g saturated fat, 1 g monounsaturated fat, 0 g polyunsaturated fat, 6 mg cholesterol, 157 mg sodium, 4 g carbohydrates, 1 g fiber, 1 g sugar, 3 g protein

A Summer Barbecue Celebration

Gather the neighbors and fire up the grill! Here's a heart healthy cookout so flavorful, no one will know it's good for them. Ground beef for hamburgers is cut with whole grain bulgur to trim the fat and calories. The creamiest, healthiest potato salad around uses reduced-fat sour cream and yogurt blended with fat-free mayonnaise. (If you'd like to pump up the nutrients, use half sweet potatoes and half red potatoes.) The meal ends with frozen yogurt topped with delicious summer fruits cooked in healthy red wine—a perfect finale.

Best Burgers

- ⅔ cup bulgur wheat

  1 cup warm water

  1½ pounds lean ground beef (97% fat free)

- ¼ cup reduced-sodium tomato paste

  ¼ cup sweet pickle relish

  ½ teaspoon ground black pepper

- 8 whole wheat hamburger buns

- 8 romaine lettuce leaves

- 1 large tomato, cut into 8 slices

  ¼ cup fat-free Russian or Thousand Island dressing

1. In a small bowl, combine the bulgur with the water. Let stand for 30 minutes, or until the bulgur is tender and the water is absorbed.

2. Coat the grill rack or broiler rack with cooking spray. Preheat the grill or broiler.

3. In a medium bowl, combine the bulgur, beef, tomato paste, relish, and pepper, mixing just until combined. Shape into 8 patties.

4. Grill the burgers over high heat or broil, turning once, for 10 minutes, or until a thermometer inserted in the center registers 160°F and the meat is no longer pink.

5. Place 1 bun bottom on each of 8 plates. Top with a lettuce leaf, tomato slice, burger, and ½ tablespoon of the dressing.

Serves 8

Heart healthy ingredients: 5

Per serving: 283 calories, 51 calories from fat, 6 g total fat, 2 g saturated fat, 2 g monounsaturated fat, 1 g polyunsaturated fat, 45 mg cholesterol, 369 mg sodium, 38 g carbohydrates, 6 g fiber, 8 g sugar, 22 g protein

Creamy Potato Salad

3 pounds red potatoes, cut into ¾" pieces

¼ cup fat-free mayonnaise

¼ cup reduced-fat sour cream

♥ ¼ cup low-fat plain yogurt

3 tablespoons red wine vinegar

2 tablespoons prepared mustard

♥ 8 scallions, chopped

♥ 1 red bell pepper, chopped

1 rib celery, chopped

1. Place the potatoes in a large saucepan and cover with water. Bring to a boil over high heat. Reduce the heat to low and simmer for 12 minutes, or until tender. Drain and cool completely.

2. In a large bowl, whisk together the mayonnaise, sour cream, yogurt, vinegar, and mustard. Add the potatoes, scallions, pepper, and celery and toss to coat well.

Serves 8

♥ **Heart healthy ingredients: 3**

Per serving: 74 calories, 11 calories from fat, 1 g total fat, 1 g saturated fat, 0 g monounsaturated fat, 0 g polyunsaturated fat, 4 mg cholesterol, 136 mg sodium, 11 g carbohydrates, 5 g fiber, 4 g sugar, 4 g protein

Frozen Yogurt with Fruit Wine Sauce

1 cup sugar

♥ 1 cup dry red wine

½ cup water

♥ ⅓ cup lemon juice

3 tablespoons cornstarch

4 peaches, peeled, pitted, and cut into thin strips

♥ 1½ cups fresh blueberries

¼ teaspoon ground nutmeg

♥ 1 quart reduced-fat vanilla frozen yogurt

1. In a medium saucepan, whisk together the sugar, wine, water, lemon juice, and cornstarch until well blended. Bring to a boil over medium heat. Stir in the peaches, blueberries, and nutmeg and cook, stirring constantly, for 5 minutes, or until thickened. Cool at least 10 minutes or up to 1 hour before serving.

2. Evenly divide the frozen yogurt among 8 bowls. Top with the fruit sauce.

Serves 8

♥ **Heart healthy ingredients: 4**

Per serving: 387 calories, 42 calories from fat, 5 g total fat, 3 g saturated fat, 0 g monounsaturated fat, 0 g polyunsaturated fat, 65 mg cholesterol, 57 mg sodium, 73 g carbohydrates, 2 g fiber, 53 g sugar, 10 g protein

A Thanksgiving Feast

Thanksgiving is often a time of overindulgence. With these flavorful recipes, you can stay on a healthy meal plan and never miss the traditional fat-laden dressing and mashed spuds. We'll leave the turkey to you, but be sure to have about 3 ounces (the size of the palm of your hand) turkey breast and go easy on the gravy—it's full of fat. The pumpkin pie will polish off the meal beautifully.

Herbed Bread Dressing

- 1½ pounds whole grain bread, cut into 1½" cubes
- 2 tablespoons extra-virgin olive oil
- 2 large onions, chopped
- 2 large carrots, chopped
- 2 ribs celery, chopped
- 8 ounces shiitake mushrooms, stemmed and sliced
- ½ cup minced fresh parsley
- 1 tablespoon chopped fresh thyme or 1 teaspoon dried
- 1 tablespoon chopped fresh sage or 1 teaspoon dried
- ¼ teaspoon freshly ground black pepper
- 2 cups fat-free, reduced-sodium chicken broth

1. Preheat the oven to 400°F. Coat a 13" × 9" baking dish with cooking spray.

2. Arrange the bread cubes in a single layer on 2 baking sheets with sides (jelly-roll pans) and bake for 10 minutes, or until toasted. Reduce the oven temperature to 350°F.

3. Meanwhile, heat the oil in a large skillet over medium-high heat. Add the onions, carrots, and celery and cook, stirring occasionally, for 5 minutes. Add the mushrooms and cook, stirring occasionally, for 8 minutes longer, or until the liquid has evaporated and the mushrooms are browned. Stir in the parsley, thyme, sage, and pepper.

4. In a large bowl, combine the bread cubes and onion mixture. Add the broth and toss to coat well. Spread in the prepared dish and bake for 45 minutes, or until lightly browned.

Serves 12

♥ Heart healthy ingredients: 6

Per serving: 149 calories, 28 calories from fat, 3 g total fat, 1 g saturated fat, 2 g monounsaturated fat, 0 g polyunsaturated fat, 0 mg cholesterol, 0 mg sodium, 29 g carbohydrates, 10 g fiber, 5 g sugar, 5 g protein

Pumpkin Pie in Nut Crust

¾ cup whole wheat pastry flour

¾ cup all-purpose flour

3 tablespoons ground walnuts or pecans

¼ teaspoon salt

3 tablespoons cold butter, cut into small pieces

2 tablespoons light olive oil

1 teaspoon lemon juice

4–5 tablespoons ice cold water

1 can (15 ounces) plain pumpkin puree

1 cup fat-free evaporated milk

½ cup packed brown sugar

2 egg whites

1 egg

1½ teaspoons pumpkin pie spice

1 teaspoon pure vanilla extract

1. In a food processor, combine the pastry flour, all-purpose flour, nuts, and salt. Pulse until blended. Add the butter, oil, and lemon juice and pulse until the mixture resembles fine meal. Add the water as needed, 1 tablespoon at a time, and pulse just until the dough forms large clumps. Place on a piece of plastic wrap and form into a ball. Flatten into a disk and wrap in the plastic wrap. Refrigerate for at least 1 hour.

2. Preheat the oven to 425°F. Coat a 9" pie plate with cooking spray.

3. Place the dough between 2 pieces of waxed paper and roll into a 12" circle. Remove the top piece of paper and invert the dough into the pie plate. Peel off the second piece of paper. Press the dough into the pie plate and up onto the rim, patching if necessary. Turn the edge under and flute. Place in the refrigerator.

4. In a large bowl, whisk the pumpkin, milk, sugar, egg whites, egg, pumpkin pie spice, and vanilla extract until smooth. Pour into the crust. Bake for 15 minutes. Reduce the temperature to 350°F. Bake for 25 minutes longer, or until a knife inserted in the center comes out clean. Cool on a rack for 2 hours. Cover and refrigerate.

Serves 12

Heart healthy ingredients: 5

Per serving: 192 calories, 62 calories from fat, 7 g total fat, 3 g saturated fat, 3 g monounsaturated fat, 1 g polyunsaturated fat, 30 mg cholesterol, 109 mg sodium, 26 g carbohydrates, 2 g fiber, 12 g sugar, 5 g protein

Mashed Root Vegetables

- 3 pounds sweet potatoes, peeled and cut into 2" pieces

- 3 pounds parsnips, peeled and cut into 2" pieces

- 2 tablespoons extra-virgin olive oil

- 1 onion, chopped

- 2 cloves garlic, minced

- ⅓ cup reduced-fat milk

1. Place 2" of water in the bottom of a skillet. Add a steamer basket and place the sweet potatoes and parsnips in the basket. Cover and bring to a boil over high heat. Reduce the heat to medium and simmer for 15 minutes, or until the vegetables are very tender.

2. Meanwhile, heat the oil in a large nonstick skillet over medium heat. Add the onion and cook, stirring, for 5 minutes, or until lightly browned. Add the garlic and cook, stirring frequently, for 1 minute longer.

3. Drain the vegetables and place in a large bowl. Add the onion mixture and milk and mash with a potato masher until smooth.

Serves 12

Heart healthy ingredients: 4

Per serving: 197 calories, 24 calories from fat, 3 g total fat, 1 g saturated fat, 2 g monounsaturated fat, 0 g polyunsaturated fat, 0 mg cholesterol, 72 mg sodium, 42 g carbohydrates, 8 g fiber, 10 g sugar, 3 g protein

A Super Bowl Blowout

A Super Bowl party offers a terrific reason to get out in the dead of winter and have some fun! Our casual gathering makes entertaining a breeze because all the dishes can be made ahead of time: Chili prepared in the slow cooker is sure to please and needs no work during the party. The nachos can be prepared up to step 2 then finished off in the oven just before the guests arrive. Make the tasty snack cake the day before for a delicious half-time treat.

Slow-Cooked Chili Con Carne

1 pound ground turkey breast

♥ 2 large onions, chopped

♥ 3 cloves garlic, minced

♥ 3 red or orange bell peppers, chopped

♥ 2 cans (14½ ounces each) no-salt-added whole tomatoes in juice, undrained and cut up

♥ 1 can (8 ounces) no-salt-added tomato sauce

♥ 1 can (15 ounces) red kidney beans, rinsed and drained

♥ 1 can (15 ounces) pinto beans, rinsed and drained

♥ 1 tablespoon chili powder

1 teaspoon ground cumin

♥ ¼ teaspoon red-pepper flakes

1 package (10 ounces) frozen corn kernels, thawed

½ cup reduced-fat sour cream

½ cup shredded reduced-fat Cheddar cheese

1. Place the turkey, onions, and garlic in a large nonstick skillet over medium-high heat. Cook, stirring to break up the turkey, for 5 minutes, or until the turkey is no longer pink. Place in a 5½-quart or larger slow cooker. Stir in the bell peppers, tomatoes with their juice, tomato sauce, kidney beans, pinto beans, chili powder, cumin, and pepper flakes.

2. Cover and cook on high for 4 to 5 hours or low for 6 to 8 hours. Stir in the corn during the last 30 minutes of cooking.

3. Evenly divide the chili among 8 bowls and top each serving with 1 tablespoon of the sour cream and 1 tablespoon of the cheese.

Serves 10

♥ **Heart healthy ingredients: 7**

Per serving: 215 calories, 38 calories from fat, 4 g total fat, 2 g saturated fat, 1 g monounsaturated fat, 0 g polyunsaturated fat, 27 mg cholesterol, 191 mg sodium, 27 g carbohydrates, 7 g fiber, 8 g sugar, 20 g protein

Piled-High Nachos

- 2 large onions, chopped
- 2 red bell peppers, chopped
- 4 ounces shiitake mushrooms, stemmed and chopped
- 2 cloves garlic, minced
- 2 tablespoons extra-virgin olive oil

  10 (6") corn tortillas
- 1 can (16 ounces) fat-free refried beans

  1 cup (4 ounces) shredded reduced-fat sharp Cheddar cheese
- 1½ cups fat-free salsa

1. Preheat the oven to 375°F. Coat a baking sheet with sides (jelly-roll pan) with cooking spray. Place the onions, peppers, mushrooms, and garlic in the pan. Drizzle with the oil and toss to coat well. Roast, turning once, for 20 minutes, or until browned and tender. Without turning off the oven, remove the onion mixture and place in a bowl and set aside.

2. Cut each tortilla into 8 wedges. Arrange in a single layer on 2 baking sheets with sides and coat with cooking spray. Bake for 10 minutes, or until lightly browned.

3. Top the chips with the beans. Sprinkle the reserved vegetables on top, and then the cheese. Bake for 10 minutes, or until the cheese melts. Serve with the salsa.

Serves 10

❦ Heart healthy ingredients: 7

Per serving: 206 calories, 60 calories from fat, 7 g total fat, 2 g saturated fat, 2 g monounsaturated fat, 1 g polyunsaturated fat, 8 mg cholesterol, 343 mg sodium, 30 g carbohydrates, 5 g fiber, 5 g sugar, 7 g protein

MAKEOVER MAGIC

Your family will love these hearty nachos. Healthy roasted vegetables top the chips, eliminating the need for ground beef, and baked chips and reduced-fat cheese are just as delicious as full-fat versions—but with a lot fewer calories!

	Traditional Nachos	Piled-High Nachos
Calories	551	206
Fat (g)	35	7
Percent calories from fat	57	31

Chocolate Snack Cake

½ cup all-purpose flour

♥ ⅓ cup unsweetened cocoa powder

¼ teaspoon baking powder

¼ teaspoon salt

¾ cup granulated sugar

♥ ¼ cup light olive oil

♥ ¼ cup fat-free plain yogurt

1 teaspoon pure vanilla extract

½ teaspoon almond extract

3 large egg whites

1½ cups confectioners' sugar

2½ tablespoons fat-free milk

♥ ¼ cup sliced almonds

1. Preheat the oven to 375°F. Coat a 9" square pan with cooking spray.

2. In a small bowl, combine the flour, cocoa, baking powder, and salt. In a large bowl, with an electric mixer at medium speed, beat the granulated sugar, oil, yogurt, vanilla extract, almond extract, and egg whites until well blended. Add the flour mixture and beat just until blended.

3. Scrape the batter into the prepared pan. Bake for 25 minutes, or until a wooden pick inserted in the center comes out clean. Cool on a rack for 10 minutes. Remove from the pan and cool completely on a rack.

4. In a small bowl, whisk together the confectioners' sugar and milk until smooth. Place the cake on a serving plate and drizzle with the icing. Sprinkle with the almonds.

Serves 10

♥ **Heart healthy ingredients: 4**

Per serving: 231 calories, 63 calories from fat, 7 g total fat, 1 g saturated fat, 5 g monounsaturated fat, 1 g polyunsaturated fat, 0 mg cholesterol, 95 mg sodium, 41 g carbohydrates, 1 g fiber, 34 g sugar, 3 g protein

INDEX

Underscored page references indicate boxed text. **Boldface** references indicate photographs.

A

Acorn squash, 60
Acute coronary syndrome, olive oil reducing, 39
Age, as heart disease risk factor, vii
Alcohol. *See also* Wine
    mortality and, 71
Almonds
    Brussels Sprouts Amandine, 136, **137**
    Chocolate Almond Biscotti, **238**, 239
    Chocolate Almond Pudding, 243
    Chocolate Almond Scones, 84, **85**
    Fruit 'n' Nut Coffee Cake, 249
    Simple Salmon with Almonds, 190
    Toasted Trail Mix, 233
    Wild Rice with Almonds and Currants, 151
Alpha-carotene
    heart health benefits of, 4
    in winter squash, 59
Alpha-linolenic acid, sources of, 51
    beans, 13
    flaxseed, 23
Anaheim peppers, 46
Aneurysm, xiii
Angina, ix
Antioxidants. *See also specific antioxidants*
    for diabetes control, xvi
    heart health benefits of, 4–6
    oxygen and, 178
    sources of
        apples, 7, 8
        asparagus, 9
        berries, 14
        carrots, 18
        cruciferous vegetables, 21–22
        dark leafy greens, 27
        garlic, 24, 166
        herbs, 29
        olives and olive oil, 39
        onions, 125
        oranges, 42
        sea vegetables, 53

        shiitake mushrooms, 34, 35
        sweet potatoes, 48
        tropical fruits, 66
Apples, 7–8
    Apple and Jicama Slaw, 108
    Apple-Cranberry Crisp, 248
    best uses for, 8
    Fruit with Creamy Chocolate Dip, 234, **235**
    for ripening bananas, 11
Applesauce
    Fat-Free Applesauce Oatmeal Cookies, 237
    Quick No-Bake Apple-Cherry Crisp, 234
Apricot marmalade
    Apricot Asparagus and Carrots, **132**, 133
Arame, 53
Arrhythmias, x
Arterial blockage, viii
Arterial narrowing (stenosis), viii
Arterial plaque. *See also* Atherosclerosis
    effects of, ix, viii
    flavonoids and, 5
    increasing blood pressure, xii
    omega-3 fatty acids and, 2
Artichokes
    Warm Artichoke Dip, **268**, 270
Arugula
    Arugula Tabbouleh, **152**, 153
    Garlic-Roasted Sweet Potatoes with Arugula, **142**, 143
    Quick Arugula and Shrimp Salad, 126
Asian-style dishes
    Asian Slaw with Chicken, 123
    Hoisin Halibut with Bok Choy, 199
    Peanut Noodle Salad, 116
    Soba Noodle Salad, 117
    Sweet-and-Sour Shrimp Soup, 102
    Tofu and Bok Choy Stir-Fry, 166
    Vegetable Noodle Bowl, 182, **183**
Asparagus, 9
    Apricot Asparagus and Carrots, **132**, 133
    Asparagus Frittata, **78**, 79
    Asparagus Salad with Goat Cheese, 111

Asparagus *(cont.)*
    Beef and Asparagus Stir-Fry, 224
    Chicken and Vegetables in Cream Sauce, 204
    choosing, 133
    growing time of, 9
    rutin in, 204
    storing, 133
    thick vs. thin, 79
Atherosclerosis. *See also* Arterial plaque
    angina with, ix
    effects of, viii
    foods affecting
        cranberries, 15
        oats, 38
        tea, 61–62
    from free radical damage, 6
    homocysteine and, ix
    oxidative stress and, xvi
    vitamin C and, 5
Atrial fibrillation, x
Avocados, 10–11
    choosing, 10
    preserving, 10
    Soy Delicious Guacamole, **264**, 265
    storing, 10
    Turkey Cutlets with Avocado Salsa, 214, **215**

B

Balsamic vinegar
    Balsamic-Rosemary Pork Kebabs, 230
Bananas, 11–12
    Berry Smoothie, 94
    choosing, 12
    Frozen Berry Pops, 240, **241**
    Fruit with Creamy Chocolate Dip, 234, **235**
    history of, 253
    ripening of, 11, 12
    Tropical Fruit Pops, 240, **241**
    Tropical Phyllo Cups, 253
    uses for, 12
Barbecue celebration menu, 272
    Best Burgers, **272**, 273
    Creamy Potato Salad, **272**, 274
    Frozen Yogurt with Fruit Wine Sauce, 274
Barley
    Barley Edamame Salad, 119
    Broccoli-Barley Pilaf, 154
    food label health claims on, 68

Basil
    Tomato-Basil Vinaigrette, 260, **261**
Beans, 13–14. *See also* Lentils
    Better-for-You Black Bean Chili, 163
    Black Bean Salad, 120, **121**
    Black Beans and Rice, 155
    Broccoli Rabe and Chickpea Soup, 101
    cooking times for, 164
    Curried Vegetables with Beans, 162
    Escarole and Bean Soup, 100
    Garlicky Hummus, 266
    Grandma's Baked Beans, 164
    Italian Three Bean Salad, 122
    measurements of, 158
    planted with corn and beans, 174
    Quick White Bean Stew, 231
    Slow-Cooked Chili Con Carne, 280
    soaking, for reducing gas, 13
    Spinach and Cannellini Beans, 160, **161**
    Tex-Mex Beans and Rice, 158
    Vegetarian Gumbo, 157
Beef
    Beef and Asparagus Stir-Fry, 224
    Beef and Vegetable Stroganoff, 223
    Beef Tenderloin with Cranberry Port Sauce, **220**, 221
    Best Burgers, **272**, 273
    Souped-Up Sloppy Joes, 225
    Spicy Fajitas, 222
    Warm Steak and Orange Salad, 128, **129**
Bell peppers. *See* Peppers, bell
Belly fat
    heart disease risk from, 73
    yogurt for losing, 74
Berries, 14–16. *See also* Blackberries; Blueberries; Cranberries; Raspberries; Strawberries
    washing, 15
Beta-carotene. *See also* Beta-carotene supplements
    heart health benefits of, 4, 5, 18
    sources of
        bell peppers, 4, 44
        carrots, 4, 18
        cruciferous vegetables, 21
        dark leafy greens, 4, 27
        kiwifruit, 30
        sea vegetables, 53
        seeds, 55
        spinach, 58
        sweet potatoes, 4, 48, 143

tropical fruits, 66
winter squash, 4, 59
Beta-carotene supplements, 4
Betaine
in spinach, 58
in sweet potatoes, 48
Beverages. *See also* Smoothies; Wine
Mocha Coffee, 236
pomegranate spritzer, 268
Biscotti
Chocolate Almond Biscotti, **238**, 239
Blood clots
cause of, viii
inhibiting, with
cranberries, 15
fruits and vegetables, 6
garlic, 25
kiwifruit, 30, 31
red wine, 70–71
resveratrol, 5
tomato juice, 63
Blood glucose
controlling or lowering, with
capsaicin, 46
cinnamon, 29–30
exercise, xv
fiber, 3, 68
spinach, 58
sweet potatoes, 48
foods affecting, xvi
healthy ranges of, xv
insulin and, 48
Blood pressure. *See also* High blood
pressure
definition of, xii
lowering, with
chocolate, 20
omega-3 fatty acids, 2
vitamin C, 5
whole grains, 68
meaning of readings of, xii
oral contraceptives increasing, xiv
Blood sugar. *See* Blood glucose
Blueberries
Berry Smoothie, 94
Chocolate Berry Crepes, 256
Frozen Yogurt with Fruit Wine Sauce, 274
Fruit and Bran Muffins, 87
Fruited Granola, 83

Lemon Blueberry Muffins, **88**, 89
Peach-Blueberry Shortcakes, 244, **245**
BMI, xvi, xviii
Body fat
avocado reducing, 10–11
heart disease risk from, 73
yogurt for reducing, 74
Body mass index, xvi, xviii
Bok choy
Hoisin Halibut with Bok Choy, 199
Tofu and Bok Choy Stir-Fry, 166
Bowel regularity, fiber for, 3, 68
Bradycardia, x
Brain health, blood sugar and, xvi
Bran, 16–17
Fruit and Bran Muffins, 87
types of, 87
Breads
Broccoli and Cheese Strata, 77
French Toast with Orange Cream, 82
Herbed Bread Dressing, 276
quick
Cherry Corn Muffins, 90
Chocolate Almond Scones, 84, **85**
Cinnamon-Raisin Quick Bread, 91
Fruit and Bran Muffins, 87
Gingered Carrot Loaf, 92
Lemon Blueberry Muffins, **88**, 89
Breakfasts
Asparagus Frittata, **78**, 79
Baked Oatmeal Pudding, 86
Berry Smoothie, 94
Broccoli and Cheese Strata, 77
Cherry Corn Muffins, 90
Chocolate Almond Scones, 84, **85**
Cinnamon-Raisin Quick Bread, 91
French Toast with Orange Cream, 82
Fruit and Bran Muffins, 87
Fruited Granola, 83
Gingered Carrot Loaf, 92
Gingered Fruit Salad, 93
Green Tea–Oatmeal Pancakes, 80, **81**
Lemon Blueberry Muffins, **88**, 89
Peach Melba Smoothie, 94
Broccoli, 21, 22
Broccoli and Cheese Strata, 77
Broccoli-Barley Pilaf, 154
Curried Vegetables with Beans, 162
Happy Heart Pasta Primavera, 175

Broccoli (*cont.*)
　introducing children to, 22
　Orange-Glazed Broccoli, 135
　Quick Vegetable Mac 'n' Cheese, 172, **173**
Broccoli rabe
　Broccoli Rabe and Chickpea Soup, 101
Brussels sprouts, 21
　Brussels Sprouts Amandine, 136, **137**
Buckwheat, 67, 68
Bulgur wheat
　Arugula Tabbouleh, **152**, 153
　Bulgur-Stuffed Roasted Peppers, **168**, 169
Burgers
　Best Burgers, **272**, 273
　Turkey Burgers, 216
Butternut squash, 60
　Penne with Roasted Autumn Vegetables, 174
　Roasted Winter Vegetables, 141
B vitamins. *See also* Folate
　heart health benefits of, ix, 6
　sources of
　　sweet potatoes, 48
　　tomatoes, 63
　　tropical fruits, 66

C

Cabbage, 21. *See also* Coleslaw mix
CAD, characteristics of, viii, ix–x
Cakes
　Chocolate Angel Food Cake, 252
　Chocolate Snack Cake, 282
　Flourless Chocolate Cake, **250**, 251
　Fruit 'n' Nut Coffee Cake, 249
　Lemon-Lime Pudding Cake, 246
　Orange Pistachio Cake, 247
　Peach-Blueberry Shortcakes, 244, **245**
Calorie burning, from physical activities, xiii
Cancer, oxidative stress and, xvi
Capsaicin, in chile peppers, 46–47, 47
Carotenoids
　avocados for absorption of, 10
　converted to vitamin A, 4
　heart health benefits of, 4–5
　sources of, 4, 4
　　bananas, 11–12
　　bell peppers, 44
　　cherries, 26
　　grapes, 26
　　tomatoes, 63

　tropical fruits, 66
　winter squash, 59
Carrots, 18–19
　Apricot Asparagus and Carrots, **132**, 133
　Carrot and Sweet Potato Puree, 140
　Creamy Carrot Soup, 96, **97**
　Curried Vegetables with Beans, 162
　Gingered Carrot Loaf, 92
　Happy Heart Pasta Primavera, 175
　Quick Vegetable Mac 'n' Cheese, 172, **173**
　sugar myth about, 96
　Vegetable Quinoa, 146, **147**
　vitamin A in, 18
Cascabel peppers, 46
Cauliflower, 21
　Curry-Roasted Cauliflower, 141
　Quick Vegetable Mac 'n' Cheese, 172, **173**
Cayenne peppers, 46
Celery
　Vegetarian Gumbo, 157
CHD. *See* Coronary heart disease
Cheese
　Asparagus Salad with Goat Cheese, 111
　Broccoli and Cheese Strata, 77
　Brown Rice with Greens and Feta, 151
　Chicken Parmigiana, 208
　Updated Cheese Sauce, 263
Cherries, 26–27
　Cherry Corn Muffins, 90
　Fruited Granola, 83
　Quick No-Bake Apple-Cherry Crisp,
　　234
　Summer Fruit Compote, 257
Chicken
　Asian Slaw with Chicken, 123
　Chicken and Eggplant Pasta Salad, 130
　Chicken and Vegetables in Cream Sauce,
　　204
　Chicken Parmigiana, 208
　Chicken Ragout, 205
　Chicken-Zucchini Pasta Toss, 212
　Cilantro-Broiled Chicken Breasts, 203
　Curried Chicken Salad, 213
　Curry Chicken and Rice Salad, 127
　Indian Chicken Skewers, **268**, 269
　Quick Chicken Noodle Soup, 104
　Revamped Chicken Potpie, **210**, 211
　Roast Chicken and Vegetables, 209
　Spicy Oven-Fried Chicken, 206, **207**
　Tandoori Chicken, 202

Chickpeas
    Broccoli Rabe and Chickpea Soup, 101
    Garlicky Hummus, 266
Children
    introducing cruciferous vegetables to, 22
    overweight, xviii
Chili
    Better-for-You Black Bean Chili, 163
    Slow-Cooked Chili Con Carne, 280
Chipotle peppers, 46
Chocolate
    Chocolate Almond Biscotti, **238**, 239
    Chocolate Almond Pudding, 243
    Chocolate Almond Scones, 84, **85**
    Chocolate Angel Food Cake, 252
    Chocolate Berry Crepes, 256
    Chocolate Snack Cake, 282
    dark, 19–21
    Flourless Chocolate Cake, **250**, 251
    as fruit, 19
    Fruit with Creamy Chocolate Dip, 234,
        235
    melting temperature of, 20
    Mocha Coffee, 236
Cholesterol, blood
    free radicals and, 4
    function of, xi
    high
        heart disease risk from, vii, xi
        from overweight or obesity, xviii
    lowering, with
        fiber, viii, 3–4, 67
        garlic, 25
        shiitake mushrooms, 34, 35
        soy foods, 56
        turmeric, 30
        yogurt, 73
    meaning of levels of, xi
    types of (*see* HDL cholesterol; LDL cholesterol)
Chowder
    Zesty Clam Chowder, 103
Chromium, 41, 41
Cilantro
    Cilantro-Broiled Chicken Breasts, 203
Cinnamon, 29–30
    Cinnamon-Raisin Quick Bread, 91
Clams
    Coquille St. Jacques, 187
    Paella, **188**, 189
    Zesty Clam Chowder, 103

Cocktail party menu, 268
    Indian Chicken Skewers, **268**, 269
    Stuffed Mushrooms, 271
    Warm Artichoke Dip, **268**, 270
Cod
    Oven-Fried Fish and Chips, 200
Coffee
    Mocha Coffee, 236
Coleslaw mix
    Asian Slaw with Chicken, 123
    Coleslaw with Lemon Dressing, 108
    Vegetable Noodle Bowl, 182, **183**
Collard greens, 27, 27, 28
Compote
    Summer Fruit Compote, 257
Cookies
    Fat-Free Applesauce Oatmeal Cookies, 237
    Harvest Cookies, 236
Corn
    Corn Salsa, **264**, 265
    planted with corn and beans, 174
    Zesty Succotash Salad, **106**, 107
Cornmeal
    Cherry Corn Muffins, 90
Coronary arteries, healthy vs. obstructed, viii
Coronary artery disease (CAD), characteristics of,
        viii, ix–x
Coronary heart disease (CHD)
    flavonoids and, 5, 41
    food label claims about, 56
    garlic and, 24–25
    preventing, with
        beans, 13
        carotenoids, 4
        fiber, 3
        grapes, 26
        lentils, 33
        nuts, 36
        olive oil, 39
        onions, 41
        quinoa, 49–50
        sea vegetables, 53
        yogurt, 73
    preventing death from
        broccoli for, 22
        lentils for, 33
        nuts for, 36
Couscous
    Curried Couscous, 149
    Peppered Couscous, 149

Crab
  Crab Cakes, 198
Cranberries
  Apple-Cranberry Crisp, 248
  Beef Tenderloin with Cranberry Port Sauce, **220**, 221
  Fruit and Bran Muffins, 87
  Fruited Granola, 83
  Fruited Rice Pilaf, 150
  Fruit 'n' Nut Coffee Cake, 249
Cranberry-raspberry juice
  Cran-Raspberry Ice, 256
Cream cheese
  French Toast with Orange Cream, 82
Crepes
  Chocolate Berry Crepes, 256
Crisps
  Apple-Cranberry Crisp, 248
  Quick No-Bake Apple-Cherry Crisp, 234
Cruciferous vegetables, 21–22. *See also* Broccoli; Brussels sprouts; Cabbage; Cauliflower
  introducing children to, 22
  preparing, 21
Cucumbers
  Sesame Salmon with Spicy Cucumber Salad, 191
Cultures, in yogurt, 72–73, 73
Currants
  Wild Rice with Almonds and Currants, 151
Curry paste
  Curried Vegetables with Beans, 162
  Curry Chicken and Rice Salad, 127
Curry powder, 29
  Curried Chicken Salad, 213
  Curried Couscous, 149
  Curried Vegetables with Beans, 162
  Curry-Roasted Cauliflower, 141

D

Desserts
  Apple-Cranberry Crisp, 248
  Chocolate Almond Pudding, 243
  Chocolate Angel Food Cake, 252
  Chocolate Berry Crepes, 256
  Chocolate Snack Cake, 282
  Cran-Raspberry Ice, 256
  Flavorful Fruit Tart, 254, **255**
  Flourless Chocolate Cake, **250**, 251
  Frozen Yogurt with Fruit Wine Sauce, 274

  Fruit 'n' Nut Coffee Cake, 249
  Lemon-Lime Pudding Cake, 246
  Orange Pistachio Cake, 247
  Peach-Blueberry Shortcakes, 244, **245**
  Pumpkin Pie in Nut Crust, **275**, 277
  Quick and Easy Rice Pudding, 243
  Raspberry Buckle, 248
  Summer Fruit Compote, 257
  Tropical Phyllo Cups, 253
Diabetes
  controlling, with
    chromium, 41
    exercise, xv
    fish oil, 48
    foods, xvi
    sweet potatoes, 48
  description of, xv
  from free radical damage, 6
  heart disease and, xv–xvi
  insulin and, 48
  from overweight or obesity, xviii
  reducing blood clots from, 63
  reducing risk of, with
    capsaicin, 46
    magnesium-rich foods, 68
    physical activity and weight loss, xvi
Diastolic blood pressure, xii, xiv
Dijon mustard
  Herb-Dijon Vinaigrette, **261**, 262
Dips
  Fruit with Creamy Chocolate Dip, 234, **235**
  Warm Artichoke Dip, **268**, 270
Doctor approval, when starting new diet, 2
Dressing, bread
  Herbed Bread Dressing, 276
Dressings, salad
  Citrus Vinaigrette, 260, **261**
  Creamy Garlic Dressing, 259, **261**
  Herb-Dijon Vinaigrette, **261**, 262
  Tomato-Basil Vinaigrette, 260, **261**

E

Edamame, 55–56
  Barley Edamame Salad, 119
  Edamame Pilaf, 150
  Soy Delicious Guacamole, **264**, 265
  Vegetable Noodle Bowl, 182, **183**

Eggplant
    Chicken and Eggplant Pasta Salad, 130
    Eggplant Lasagna, 167
Eggs
    Asparagus Frittata, **78**, 79
    Broccoli and Cheese Strata, 77
Escarole
    Escarole and Bean Soup, 100
Exercise
    calories burned by, xiii
    government Web site on, xviii
    health benefits from, xv, xvi

F

Fajitas
    Spicy Fajitas, 222
Family history, as heart disease risk factor,
        vii
Fat, body
    avocado reducing, 10–11
    heart disease risk from, 73
    yogurt reducing, 74
Fats, dietary
    function of, xi–xii
    reducing, in meal makeovers, xvii
    saturated, xii, 2
    unsaturated, xii (*see also* Monounsaturated fats;
        Polyunsaturated fats)
Fennel
    Grape and Fennel Salad, 109
Fiber
    for diabetes control, xvi
    heart health benefits of, 3–4
        cholesterol reduction, xvi, 3, 67–68
        plaque prevention, viii
    recommended intake of, 3
    sources of, 3, 3
        apples, 7, 8
        asparagus, 9
        avocados, 10
        bananas, 11
        beans, 13
        berries, 15
        bran, 16
        carrots, 18
        cherries, 26
        dark leafy greens, 28
        flaxseed, 23

        grapes, 26
        kiwifruit, 30
        lentils, 33
        nuts, 36
        oats, 38
        onions, scallions, and shallots, 41
        oranges, 42, 43
        quinoa, 50
        sea vegetables, 53
        seeds, 54
        shiitake mushrooms, 34
        soy foods, 56
        soy nuts, 55
        spinach, 58
        sweet potatoes, 48
        tomatoes, 63
        tropical fruits, 66
        whole grains, 67–68, 67
        winter squash, 60
Fish
    Grilled Tuna with Wasabi Cream, 196
    Hoisin Halibut with Bok Choy, 199
    omega-3 fatty acids in, 51, 51
    Oven-Fried Fish and Chips, 200
    Salmon Cakes, 199
    Sesame Salmon with Spicy Cucumber Salad,
        191
    Simple Salmon with Almonds, 190
    Spiced Salmon Tacos, 192, **193**
    Tuna Tetrazzini, 197
Fish oil
    for diabetes patients, 52
    heart health benefits of, 2, 51
Flavonoids
    heart health benefits of, 5
    sources of, 5, 5
        apples, 7, 7, 8
        asparagus, 204
        cherries, 26
        cruciferous vegetables, 21–22
        dark chocolate, 19
        grapes, 26
        kiwifruit, 30
        red wine, 70–71
        tea, 61
Flaxseed, 23–24
    crushing, 23
    omega-3 fatty acids in, 2
    uses for, 23

Flaxseed oil, 23–24
    omega-3 fatty acids in, 2
    uses for, 23
Folate
    heart health benefits of, ix, 6
    sources of, 6, 6
        asparagus, 9
        avocados, 10
        beans, 13
        garlic, 24
        kiwifruit, 30
        lentils, 33
        onions, 41
        oranges, 42, 43
        quinoa, 50
        sea vegetables, 53
        seeds, 54
        soy foods, 56
        spinach, 58
        tea, 61
        tomatoes, 63
        tropical fruits, 66
        winter squash, 60
        yogurt, 72
Food labels
    checking sodium on, xiv
    health claims on, 56, 68
    sodium claims on, xiv
Food preparation tips, for meal makeovers, xvii
Free radicals
    antioxidants and, 4, 5–6
    diseases from, 6
    oxidative stress from, xvi
French paradox, 70
French toast
    French Toast with Orange Cream, 82
Fresh foods, for reducing sodium intake, xiv
Frittata
    Asparagus Frittata, **78**, 79
Fruits. *See also specific fruits*
    dried
        Fruited Granola, 83
        Fruited Rice Pilaf, 150
        Toasted Trail Mix, 233
    fiber in, 3
    Flavorful Fruit Tart, 254, **255**
    Frozen Yogurt with Fruit Wine Sauce, 274
    Fruit and Bran Muffins, 87
    Fruit 'n' Nut Coffee Cake, 249

Fruit with Creamy Chocolate Dip, 234, **235**
Gingered Fruit Salad, 93
Summer Fruit Compote, 257
tropical, 66
    Tropical Fruit Pops, 240, **241**

G

Garam masala, 29
Garlic, 24–25
    antioxidants in, 4, 166
    Creamy Garlic Dressing, 259, **261**
    Garlicky Hummus, 266
    Garlic-Roasted Sweet Potatoes with Arugula, **142**, 143
    Garlic Smashed Potatoes, 144
Gas, from beans, reducing, 13
Genetics, as heart disease risk factor, vii
Ginger, 29
    Gingered Carrot Loaf, 92
    Gingered Fruit Salad, 93
    Ginger-Roasted Pork with Sweet Potatoes, 228, **229**
    Orange-Ginger Pork Chops, 227
Gluten-free whole grains, 68
Grains. *See also* Whole grains
    barley
        Barley Edamame Salad, 119
        Broccoli-Barley Pilaf, 154
        food label health claims on, 68
    bulgur wheat
        Arugula Tabbouleh, **152**, 153
        Bulgur-Stuffed Roasted Peppers, **168**, 169
    couscous
        Curried Couscous, 149
        Peppered Couscous, 149
    Fruited Granola, 83
    oats, 38
        Baked Oatmeal Pudding, 86
        Fat-Free Applesauce Oatmeal Cookies, 237
        Green Tea–Oatmeal Pancakes, 80, **81**
    quinoa, 49–50, 49, 50
        Quinoa Florentine, 148
        Vegetable Quinoa, 146, **147**
    rice
        Black Beans and Rice, 155
        brown, 67, 68
        Brown Rice with Greens and Feta, 151
        Curry Chicken and Rice Salad, 127

Edamame Pilaf, 150
Fruited Rice Pilaf, 150
Paella, **188**, 189
Quick and Easy Rice Pudding, 243
Tex-Mex Beans and Rice, 158
Vegetarian Gumbo, 157
wild rice
Wild Rice with Almonds and Currants, 151
Granola
Fruited Granola, 83
Grape juice, <u>26</u>, <u>71</u>
Grapes, 26–27
cardio-protective effects of, <u>71</u>
Flavorful Fruit Tart, 254, **255**
Grape and Fennel Salad, 109
Green beans
Chopped Niçoise Salad, **124**, 125
Greens
Brown Rice with Greens and Feta, 151
dark leafy, 27–28
flavor of, <u>27</u>
Greens with Strawberries and Kiwifruit, 110
Sauteéd Bitter Greens, 134
Green tea, <u>61</u>
Green Tea–Oatmeal Pancakes, 80, **81**
Guacamole
Soy Delicious Guacamole, **264**, 265
Guajillo peppers, <u>46</u>
Guavas, 66
Gumbo
Vegetarian Gumbo, 157

H

Habanero peppers, <u>46</u>
Halibut
Hoisin Halibut with Bok Choy, 199
Ham
Healthy Chef's Salad, 126
Hardening of the arteries, viii, xiii, xix. *See also*
Atherosclerosis
HDL cholesterol
function of, xi
increasing, with
avocados, 10
omega-3 fatty acids, 2
turmeric, 30
yogurt, 74
meaning of levels of, <u>xi</u>

Heart arrhythmias, x
Heart attack risk calculator, <u>xviii</u>
Heart attacks, ix–x
from free radical damage, 6
preventing, with
beans, 13
beta-carotene, 5, 18
carrots, 18
fiber, 3
fish, 51
folate, 6
lentils, <u>33</u>
lycopene-rich foods, 66
nuts, 36
olive oil, 39
omega-3 fatty acids, 2
tea, 61
triglycerides and, <u>xii</u>
Heart disease. *See also* Coronary artery
disease (CAD); Coronary heart
disease (CHD); Heart attacks;
Heart failure
flavonoids and, 5
from free radical damage, 6
incidence of, <u>viii</u>
as leading cause of death, vii
preventing, with
alpha-linolenic acid, 23
beans, 13
berries, 15
chocolate, 20
fiber, 3
food and exercise, xviii
omega-3 fatty acids, 2
red wine, 70–71
tomatoes, 63–64
vitamin C, 5
whole grains, 16–17
risk factors for, vii, x–xviii
types of, viii–x
Heart failure, x, xiii
Heart health, foods promoting,
vii–viii
Herbs, 28–30. *See also specific herbs*
Herb-Dijon Vinaigrette, **261**, 262
Herbed Bread Dressing, 276
Herb-Roasted Turkey Breast, 218
old, discarding, <u>29</u>
Hesperitin, in oranges, 5, 42–43

High blood pressure. *See also* Blood pressure
  cause of, xii
  effects of, xiii
  from free radical damage, 6
  lowering, with
    folate, 6
    potassium, xiv–xv, 6–7
    sodium restriction, xiii–xiv, 6–7
    spinach, 58
  from overweight or obesity, xviii
  oxidative stress and, xvi
High-density lipoproteins. *See* HDL cholesterol
Hijiki, 53
Hoisin sauce
  Hoisin Halibut with Bok Choy, 199
Homocysteine, ix
  sweet potatoes lowering, 48
Honeydew melon
  Gingered Fruit Salad, 93
Hummus
  Garlicky Hummus, 266
Hypertension. *See* Blood pressure; High blood pressure

I

Ice
  Cran-Raspberry Ice, 256
Ice pops
  Frozen Berry Pops, 240, **241**
  Tropical Fruit Pops, 240, **241**
Indian-style dishes. *See also* Curry paste; Curry powder
  Indian Chicken Skewers, **268**, 269
  Tandoori Chicken, 202
Ingredient substitutions, for recipes, xvii
Insulin. *See also* Insulin resistance; Insulin sensitivity
  diabetes and, 48
Insulin resistance
  fiber improving, xvi
  sweet potatoes lowering, 48
Insulin sensitivity, 20
Iron, in spinach, 58
Italian-style dishes
  Broccoli Rabe and Chickpea Soup, 101
  Chicken Parmigiana, 208
  Italian Three Bean Salad, 122

J

Jicama
  Apple and Jicama Slaw, 108

K

Kale, 27, 27
  Warm Kale Salad, 109
Kebabs
  Balsamic-Rosemary Pork Kebabs, 230
Kelp, 53
Kiwifruit, 30–31
  choosing, 31
  Flavorful Fruit Tart, 254, **255**
  Gingered Fruit Salad, 93
  Greens with Strawberries and Kiwifruit, 110
  origin and naming of, 110
  preparing, 31

L

Labels, food, health claims on, 56, 68
Lactobacillus acidophilus, in yogurt, 73
Lasagna
  Eggplant Lasagna, 167
LDL cholesterol
  effects of, xi
  lowering, with
    avocados, 10
    cranberries, 15
    fiber, xvi, 3
    grapes, 26
    kiwifruit, 31
    oats, 38
    omega-3 fatty acids, 2
    soy foods, 56
    sweet potatoes, 48
    tomato juice, 63–64
  meaning of levels of, xi
Lemon balm, 29
Lemons, 32
  Coleslaw with Lemon Dressing, 108
  juicing and grating, 180
  Lemon Blueberry Muffins, **88**, 89
  Lemon-Lime Pudding Cake, 246
  uses for, 180
Lentils, 33–34
  Braised Lentils with Spinach, 159
  Spicy Red Lentil Soup, 99
  types of, 99
Lignans
  in sea vegetables, 53
  in seeds, 55

Lima beans
  Zesty Succotash Salad, **106**, 107
Lime juice
  Citrus Vinaigrette, 260, **261**
  for preserving avocados, 10
Limes, 32. *See also* Lime juice
  juicing and grating, 180
  Lemon-Lime Pudding Cake, 246
  uses for, 180
Linguine
  Linguine with Walnut Pesto, 180
  Spinach Linguine with Fresh Tomatoes and Pork,
    185
Live active cultures, in yogurt, 72–73, 73
Low-density lipoproteins. *See* LDL cholesterol
Lutein, sources of
  bell peppers, 44
  cruciferous vegetables, 22
  dark leafy greens, 27
  kiwifruit, 30
  spinach, 58
  winter squash, 59
Lycopene, sources of
  red peppers, 44
  tomatoes, 4, 63, 63, 64
  tropical fruits, 66

M

Macaroni
  Quick Vegetable Mac 'n' Cheese, 172, **173**
Magnesium, sources of
  lentils, 33
  quinoa, 49, 50
  salmon, 51
  sea vegetables, 53
  seeds, 55
  tea, 61
  tomatoes, 63
  whole grains, 68
Main dishes
  meat
    Balsamic-Rosemary Pork Kebabs, 230
    Beef and Asparagus Stir-Fry, 224
    Beef and Vegetable Stroganoff, 223
    Beef Tenderloin with Cranberry Port Sauce,
      220, 221
    Best Burgers, **272**, 273
    Ginger-Roasted Pork with Sweet Potatoes, 228,
      229

    Makeover Veal Marsala, 226
    Orange-Ginger Pork Chops, 227
    Quick White Bean Stew, 231
    Souped-Up Sloppy Joes, 225
    Spicy Fajitas, 222
  meatless
    Better-for-You Black Bean Chili, 163
    Braised Lentils with Spinach, 159
    Bulgur-Stuffed Roasted Peppers, **168**, 169
    Curried Vegetables with Beans, 162
    Eggplant Lasagna, 167
    Sesame-Seared Tofu, 165
    Tex-Mex Beans and Rice, 158
    Tofu and Bok Choy Stir-Fry, 166
    Vegetarian Gumbo, 157
  pasta
    Baked Pasta and Spinach, 171
    Greek-Inspired Pasta, **176**, 177
    Happy Heart Pasta Primavera, 175
    Linguine with Walnut Pesto, 180
    Mediterranean Pasta with Shrimp, 184
    Orzo Pilaf, 178
    Penne with Alfredo Sauce, 181
    Penne with Roasted Autumn Vegetables, 174
    Quick Vegetable Mac 'n' Cheese, 172, **173**
    Spaghetti with Puttanesca Sauce, 179
    Spinach Linguine with Fresh Tomatoes and
      Pork, 185
    Vegetable Noodle Bowl, 182, **183**
  poultry
    Chicken and Vegetables in Cream Sauce, 204
    Chicken Parmigiana, 208
    Chicken Ragout, 205
    Chicken-Zucchini Pasta Toss, 212
    Cilantro-Broiled Chicken Breasts, 203
    Curried Chicken Salad, 213
    Herb-Roasted Turkey Breast, 218
    Revamped Chicken Potpie, **210**, 211
    Roast Chicken and Vegetables, 209
    Slow-Cooked Chili Con Carne, 280
    Spicy Oven-Fried Chicken, 206, **207**
    Tandoori Chicken, 202
    Turkey Burgers, 216
    Turkey Cutlets with Avocado Salsa, 214, **215**
    Turkey Picadillo, 217
  seafood
    Coquilles St. Jacques, 187
    Crab Cakes, 198
    Grilled Shrimp with Mango Salsa, **194**, 195
    Grilled Tuna with Wasabi Cream, 196

Main dishes (*cont.*)
  seafood (*cont.*)
    Hoisin Halibut with Bok Choy, 199
    Oven-Fried Fish and Chips, 200
    Paella, **188**, 189
    Salmon Cakes, 199
    Scallops Fra Diavolo, 190
    Sesame Salmon with Spicy Cucumber Salad, 191
    Simple Salmon with Almonds, 190
    Spiced Salmon Tacos, 192, **193**
    Tuna Tetrazzini, 197
Mangos, 66
  Gingered Fruit Salad, 93
  Grilled Shrimp with Mango Salsa, **194**, 195
  Tropical Fruit Pops, 240, **241**
  Tropical Phyllo Cups, 253
Mayonnaise
  Tofu Mayonnaise, 259
Meal makeover tips, xvii
Meatless main dishes. *See* Main dishes, meatless
Meats. *See* Beef; Pork; Veal
Medications, foods interacting with, 2
Melons
  Gingered Fruit Salad, 93
Mexican-style dishes
  Piled-High Nachos, **279**, 281
  Spicy Fajitas, 222
  Tex-Mex Beans and Rice, 158
Milk, soy, 55
Monounsaturated fats, sources of
  avocados, 10
  nuts, 36
  olives and olive oil, 39
  salmon, 51
  sea vegetables, 53
  seeds, 54
  soy foods, 56
Mortality, alcoholic drinks and, 71
Muffins
  Cherry Corn Muffins, 90
  Fruit and Bran Muffins, 87
  Lemon Blueberry Muffins, **88**, 89
Mushrooms
  cleaning, 34
  dried, soaking, 34
  shiitake, 34–35
    alternate names for, 139
    Beef and Vegetable Stroganoff, 223
    Penne with Roasted Autumn Vegetables, 174

Piled-High Nachos, **279**, 281
  Sautéed Mushrooms and Spinach, 138
  Sugar Snap Peas with Shiitakes, 139
  Vegetable Noodle Bowl, 182, **183**
  Vegetable Quinoa, 146, **147**
Stuffed Mushrooms, 271
Mustard, Dijon
  Herb-Dijon Vinaigrette, **261**, 262
Mustard seed, 29
Myocardial infarction, ix–x

N

Nachos
  Piled-High Nachos, **279**, 281
Niacin, in tomatoes, 63
Noodles
  Peanut Noodle Salad, 116
  Quick Chicken Noodle Soup, 104
  Soba Noodle Salad, 117
  Vegetable Noodle Bowl, 182, **183**
Nori, 53
Nutrients, heart health, 2–7. *See also specific nutrients*
Nutrition, government Web sites on, xviii
Nuts, 36–37, 213
  Brussels Sprouts Amandine, 136, **137**
  Chocolate Almond Biscotti, **238**, 239
  Chocolate Almond Pudding, 243
  Chocolate Almond Scones, 84, **85**
  Fruit 'n' Nut Coffee Cake, 249
  Linguine with Walnut Pesto, 180
  omega-3 fatty acids in, 36
  Orange Pistachio Cake, 247
  Pumpkin Pie in Nut Crust, **275**, 277
  Simple Salmon with Almonds, 190
  soy, 55, 55, 56
  Toasted Trail Mix, 233
  Wild Rice with Almonds and Currants, 151

O

Oat cereal
  Peanut Bars, 233
  Toasted Trail Mix, 233
Oats, 38
  Baked Oatmeal Pudding, 86
  Fat-Free Applesauce Oatmeal Cookies, 237
  Green Tea–Oatmeal Pancakes, 80, **81**

Obesity
    health risks from, xviii, 73
    yogurt for reducing, 73–74
Olive oil, 39–40, 39
Olives, 39, 39
Omega-3 fatty acids
    heart health benefits of, 2
    sources of, 2, 2
        fish, 51, 51
        flaxseed, 23
        plant-based, 51, 51
        salmon, 51
        sea vegetables, 53
        soy foods, 56
        spinach, 58
        tea, 61
        walnuts, 36
        winter squash, 60
        yogurt, 72
Omega-6 fatty acids, in yogurt, 72
Onions, 41–42
    antioxidants in, 125
    Beef and Vegetable Stroganoff, 223
    Chicken and Vegetables in Cream Sauce, 204
    chromium in, 41
    Curried Vegetables with Beans, 162
    Piled-High Nachos, 279, 281
    quercetin in, 5
    Roast Chicken and Vegetables, 209
    Spinach Salad with Warm Onion Dressing, 112
    storing, 101
Oral contraceptives, increasing blood pressure,
        xiv
Orange juice
    Citrus Vinaigrette, 260, 261
Oranges, 42–43. *See also* Orange juice
    French Toast with Orange Cream, 82
    as "golden apple," 43
    hesperitin in, 5
    Orange-Ginger Pork Chops, 227
    Orange-Glazed Broccoli, 135
    Orange Pistachio Cake, 247
    Tofu Citrus Salad, 113
    Warm Steak and Orange Salad, 128, 129
Oregano, 29
Orzo
    Orzo Pilaf, 178
Overweight, health risks from, xviii, 73
Oxidative stress, antioxidants reducing, xvi
Oxygen, antioxidants and, 178

P

Paella, 188, 189
Pancakes
    Green Tea–Oatmeal Pancakes, 80, 81
Papayas, 66
Parsnips
    Mashed Root Vegetables, 278
    Roast Chicken and Vegetables, 209
    Roasted Winter Vegetables, 141
Party foods
    for spring cocktail party, 268
        Indian Chicken Skewers, 268, 269
        Stuffed Mushrooms, 271
        Warm Artichoke Dip, 268, 270
    for summer barbecue celebration, 272
        Best Burgers, 272, 273
        Creamy Potato Salad, 272, 274
        Frozen Yogurt with Fruit Wine Sauce, 274
    for Super Bowl blowout, 279
        Chocolate Snack Cake, 282
        Piled-High Nachos, 279, 281
        Slow-Cooked Chili Con Carne, 280
    for Thanksgiving feast, 275
        Herbed Bread Dressing, 276
        Mashed Root Vegetables, 278
        Pumpkin Pie in Nut Crust, 275, 277
Pasta
    Baked Pasta and Spinach, 171
    Chicken and Eggplant Pasta Salad, 130
    Chicken-Zucchini Pasta Toss, 212
    Greek-Inspired Pasta, 176, 177
    Happy Heart Pasta Primavera, 175
    Linguine with Walnut Pesto, 180
    Mediterranean Pasta with Shrimp, 184
    Orzo Pilaf, 178
    Peanut Noodle Salad, 116
    Penne with Alfredo Sauce, 181
    Penne with Roasted Autumn Vegetables, 174
    Quick Chicken Noodle Soup, 104
    Quick Vegetable Mac 'n' Cheese, 172, 173
    Soba Noodle Salad, 117
    Spaghetti with Puttanesca Sauce, 179
    Spinach Linguine with Fresh Tomatoes and Pork,
        185
    Tortellini Salad, 118
    Vegetable Noodle Bowl, 182, 183
Peaches
    Frozen Yogurt with Fruit Wine Sauce, 274
    Peach-Blueberry Shortcakes, 244, 245

Peaches (*cont.*)
    Peach Melba Smoothie, 94
    Summer Fruit Compote, 257
Peanut butter
    Peanut Bars, 233
    Peanut Noodle Salad, 116
Pecans
    Pumpkin Pie in Nut Crust, **275**, 277
    Toasted Trail Mix, 233
Pectin, in apples, 8
Penne
    Chicken-Zucchini Pasta Toss, 212
    Penne with Alfredo Sauce, 181
    Penne with Roasted Autumn Vegetables, 174
Peppermint, 29
Peppers
    bell, 44–45
        Beef and Vegetable Stroganoff, 223
        Bulgur-Stuffed Roasted Peppers, **168**, 169
        Chicken and Vegetables in Cream Sauce, 204
        Happy Heart Pasta Primavera, 175
        Peppered Couscous, 149
        Piled-High Nachos, **279**, 281
        Quick Vegetable Mac 'n' Cheese, 172, **173**
        Spicy Fajitas, 222
        Vegetable Quinoa, 146, **147**
        Vegetarian Gumbo, 157
        vitamin C in, 122
    chile, 46–47
        Spicy Fajitas, 222
        types of, 46
Pesto
    Linguine with Walnut Pesto, 180
Phyllo dough
    Tropical Phyllo Cups, 253
Physical activity. *See* Exercise
Phytoestrogens
    lignans as, 55
    in soy foods, 56
Phytosterols, sources of
    nuts, 36
    seeds, 55
    spinach, 58
    tomatoes, 63
Picadillo
    Turkey Picadillo, 217
Pie
    Pumpkin Pie in Nut Crust, **275**, 277
Pilaf
    Broccoli-Barley Pilaf, 154
    Edamame Pilaf, 150

    Fruited Rice Pilaf, 150
    Orzo Pilaf, 178
Pineapples, 66
Pistachios
    Orange Pistachio Cake, 247
Plaque, arterial. *See also* Atherosclerosis
    effects of, viii, ix
    flavonoids and, 5
    increasing blood pressure, xii
    omega-3 fatty acids and, 2
Poblano peppers, 46
Polyunsaturated fats, 2
    sources of
        olives and olive oil, 39
        salmon, 51
        sea vegetables, 53
        seeds, 54
        soy foods, 56
Pomegranate spritzer, 268
Pork
    Balsamic-Rosemary Pork Kebabs, 230
    Ginger-Roasted Pork with Sweet Potatoes, 228, **229**
    Orange-Ginger Pork Chops, 227
    Quick White Bean Stew, 231
    Spinach Linguine with Fresh Tomatoes and Pork, 185
Port
    Beef Tenderloin with Cranberry Port Sauce, **220**, 221
Portion sizes, increase in, xvii–xviii
Potassium
    heart health benefits of, 6–7
    for high blood pressure, xiv–xv
    sources of, xv, 7
        apples, 7
        asparagus, 9
        avocados, 10
        bananas, 11, 12
        beans, 13
        carrots, 18
        cherries, 26
        chile peppers, 46
        dark leafy greens, 27
        flaxseed, 23
        garlic, 24
        grapes, 26
        kiwifruit, 30
        lentils, 33
        onions, 41
        oranges, 42, 43

salmon, 51
soy foods, 56
spinach, 58
sweet potatoes, 48
tea, 61
tomatoes, 63
tropical fruits, 66
winter squash, 60
yogurt, 72
Potatoes
Chopped Niçoise Salad, **124**, 125
Creamy Potato Salad, **272**, 274
Garlic Smashed Potatoes, 144
vs. sweet potatoes, 143
sweet (*see* Sweet potatoes)
Potpie
Revamped Chicken Potpie, **210**, 211
Poultry. *See* Chicken; Turkey
Pretzels
Toasted Trail Mix, 233
Processed foods, sodium in, xiii–xiv
Puddings
Baked Oatmeal Pudding, 86
Chocolate Almond Pudding, 243
Lemon-Lime Pudding Cake, 246
Quick and Easy Rice Pudding, 243
Pumpkin, 59, 60
Harvest Cookies, 236
Pumpkin Pie in Nut Crust, **275**, 277
Pumpkin seeds, 54, 55

Q

Quercetin, 7
sources of
apples, 5, 7
bell peppers, 44
cruciferous vegetables, 21
onions, scallions, and shallots, 5, 41
red wine, 5
tea, 61
Quinoa, 49–50
cooking, 50
as "mother of all grains," 49
Quinoa Florentine, 148
Vegetable Quinoa, 146, **147**

R

Ragout
Chicken Ragout, 205

Raisins
Cinnamon-Raisin Quick Bread, 91
Fruited Rice Pilaf, 150
Raspberries
Chocolate Berry Crepes, 256
Peach Melba Smoothie, 94
Raspberry Buckle, 248
Summer Fruit Compote, 257
Red pepper, ground, 29
Red wine. *See* Wine, red
Resveratrol
reducing blood clots, 5
sources of
berries, 14–15
red wine, 70–71
Rice. *See also* Wild rice
brown, 67, 68
Black Beans and Rice, 155
Brown Rice with Greens and Feta, 151
Curry Chicken and Rice Salad, 127
Edamame Pilaf, 150
Quick and Easy Rice Pudding, 243
Fruited Rice Pilaf, 150
Paella, **188**, 189
Tex-Mex Beans and Rice, 158
Vegetarian Gumbo, 157
Rogan josh, 29
Rosemary
Balsamic-Rosemary Pork Kebabs, 230
Rutin, in asparagus, 204

S

Sage, 29
Salad dressings. *See* Dressings, salad
Salads
Apple and Jicama Slaw, 108
Asparagus Salad with Goat Cheese, 111
Barley Edamame Salad, 119
Black Bean Salad, 120, **121**
Chicken and Eggplant Pasta Salad, 130
Chopped Niçoise Salad, **124**, 125
Coleslaw with Lemon Dressing, 108
Creamy "Egg" Salad, 114, **115**
Creamy Potato Salad, **272**, 274
Curried Chicken Salad, 213
Curry Chicken and Rice Salad, 127
Gingered Fruit Salad, 93
Grape and Fennel Salad, 109
Greens with Strawberries and Kiwifruit, 110
Healthy Chef's Salad, 126

Salads (*cont.*)

    Italian Three Bean Salad, 122

    Peanut Noodle Salad, 116

    Quick Arugula and Shrimp Salad, 126

    Sesame Salmon with Spicy Cucumber Salad, 191

    Soba Noodle Salad, 117

    Spinach Salad with Warm Onion Dressing, 112

    Tofu Citrus Salad, 113

    Tortellini Salad, 118

    Warm Kale Salad, 109

    Warm Steak and Orange Salad, 128, **129**

    Zesty Succotash Salad, **106**, 107

Salmon, 51–52

    omega-3 fatty acids in, 2, 51, <u>52</u>

    Salmon Cakes, 199

    Sesame Salmon with Spicy Cucumber Salad, 191

    Simple Salmon with Almonds, 190

    Spiced Salmon Tacos, 192, **193**

Salsa

    Corn Salsa, **264**, 265

    Grilled Shrimp with Mango Salsa, **194**, 195

    Turkey Cutlets with Avocado Salsa, 214, **215**

Satiety, from spinach, 58

Saturated fats, xii, 2

Sauces

    Basic Tomato Sauce, 266

    Beef Tenderloin with Cranberry Port Sauce, **220**, 221

    Frozen Yogurt with Fruit Wine Sauce, 274

    Penne with Alfredo Sauce, 181

    Spaghetti with Puttanesca Sauce, 179

    Updated Cheese Sauce, 263

Scallions, 41–42

    Spicy Fajitas, 222

    Vegetable Quinoa, 146, **147**

Scallops

    Paella, **188**, 189

    Scallops Fra Diavolo, 190

Scones

    Chocolate Almond Scones, 84, **85**

Sea vegetables, 53–54

    Asian Slaw with Chicken, 123

    types of, <u>53</u>

Seeds, 54–55

Sesame seeds, 54, 55

    "open sesame" inspired by, <u>165</u>

    Sesame Salmon with Spicy Cucumber Salad, 191

    Sesame-Seared Tofu, 165

Shallots, 41–42

Shellfish

    Coquille St. Jacques, 187

    Crab Cakes, 198

    Grilled Shrimp with Mango Salsa, **194**, 195

    Mediterranean Pasta with Shrimp, 184

    Paella, **188**, 189

    Quick Arugula and Shrimp Salad, 126

    Scallops Fra Diavolo, 190

    Sweet-and-Sour Shrimp Soup, 102

    Zesty Clam Chowder, 103

Shiitake mushrooms. *See* Mushrooms, shiitake

Shortcakes

    Peach-Blueberry Shortcakes, 244, **245**

Shrimp

    Grilled Shrimp with Mango Salsa, **194**, 195

    Mediterranean Pasta with Shrimp, 184

    Paella, **188**, 189

    Quick Arugula and Shrimp Salad, 126

    Sweet-and-Sour Shrimp Soup, 102

Side dishes

    grain

        Arugula Tabbouleh, **152**, 153

        Black Beans and Rice, 155

        Broccoli-Barley Pilaf, 154

        Brown Rice with Greens and Feta, 151

        Curried Couscous, 149

        Edamame Pilaf, 150

        Fruited Rice Pilaf, 150

        Peppered Couscous, 149

        Quinoa Florentine, 148

        Vegetable Quinoa, 146, **147**

        Wild Rice with Almonds and Currants, 151

    vegetable

        Apricot Asparagus and Carrots, **132**, 133

        Brussels Sprouts Amandine, 136, **137**

        Carrot and Sweet Potato Puree, 140

        Curry-Roasted Cauliflower, 141

        Garlic-Roasted Sweet Potatoes with Arugula, **142**, 143

        Garlic Smashed Potatoes, 144

        Herbed Bread Dressing, 276

        Mashed Root Vegetables, 278

        Orange-Glazed Broccoli, 135

        Roasted Winter Vegetables, 141

        Sautéed Bitter Greens, 134

        Sautéed Mushrooms and Spinach, 138

        Sugar Snap Peas with Shiitakes, 139

Slaw

    Apple and Jicama Slaw, 108

    Asian Slaw with Chicken, 123

    Coleslaw with Lemon Dressing, 108

Sloppy joes
  Souped-Up Sloppy Joes, 225
Smoothies
  Berry Smoothie, 94
  Peach Melba Smoothie, 94
Snacks
  Chocolate Almond Biscotti, **238**, 239
  Fat-Free Applesauce Oatmeal Cookies, 237
  Frozen Berry Pops, 240, **241**
  Fruit with Creamy Chocolate Dip, 234, **235**
  Harvest Cookies, 236
  Mocha Coffee, 236
  Peanut Bars, 233
  Quick No-Bake Apple-Cherry Crisp, 234
  Toasted Trail Mix, 233
  Tropical Fruit Pops, 240, **241**
Soba noodles
  Soba Noodle Salad, 117
Sodium
  on food labels, xiv, <u>xiv</u>
  potassium for eliminating, 6, 7
  recommended daily intake of, xiv
  restricting
    with high blood pressure, xiii–xiv, 6–7
    in meal makeovers, <u>xvii</u>
Soups
  Broccoli Rabe and Chickpea Soup, 101
  Creamy Carrot Soup, 96, **97**
  Escarole and Bean Soup, 100
  Quick Chicken Noodle Soup, 104
  Rich Tomato Soup, 98
  Spicy Red Lentil Soup, 99
  Sweet-and-Sour Shrimp Soup, 102
  Zesty Clam Chowder, 103
Soy milk, 55
Soy nuts, 55, <u>55</u>, 56
Soy products, 55–57. *See also* Edamame; Tofu
Spaghetti
  Peanut Noodle Salad, 116
  Spaghetti with Puttanesca Sauce, 179
Spaghetti squash, <u>60</u>
Spice blends, <u>29</u>
Spices. *See also specific spices*
  old, discarding, <u>29</u>
Spinach, 58–59
  Baked Pasta and Spinach, 171
  Braised Lentils with Spinach, 159
  Greek-Inspired Pasta, **176**, 177
  iron in, <u>58</u>
  Quinoa Florentine, 148
  Sautéed Mushrooms and Spinach, 138

Spinach and Cannellini Beans, 160, **161**
  Spinach Salad with Warm Onion Dressing, 112
  types of, <u>159</u>
Spreads
  Garlicky Hummus, 266
  Soy Delicious Guacamole, **264**, 265
  Tofu Mayonnaise, 259
Squash
  planted with corn and beans, <u>174</u>
  winter, 59–60
    Harvest Cookies, 236
    Penne with Roasted Autumn Vegetables, 174
    Pumpkin Pie in Nut Crust, **275**, 277
    Roasted Winter Vegetables, 141
    types of, <u>60</u>
  yellow
    Happy Heart Pasta Primavera, 175
Stews
  Better-for-You Black Bean Chili, 163
  Chicken Ragout, 205
  Quick White Bean Stew, 231
  Slow-Cooked Chili Con Carne, 280
Stir-fries
  Beef and Asparagus Stir-Fry, 224
  Tofu and Bok Choy Stir-Fry, 166
Strata
  Broccoli and Cheese Strata, 77
Strawberries
  Berry Smoothie, 94
  Chocolate Berry Crepes, 256
  Frozen Berry Pops, 240, **241**
  Gingered Fruit Salad, 93
  Greens with Strawberries and Kiwifruit, 110
Stroganoff
  Beef and Vegetable Stroganoff, 223
Succotash
  Zesty Succotash Salad, **106**, 107
Sudden cardiac death, omega-3 fatty acids
    preventing, 2, 51
Sugar snap peas
  Sugar Snap Peas with Shiitakes, 139
  Vegetable Noodle Bowl, 182, **183**
Sunflower seeds, 54, 55
Super Bowl menu, 279
  Chocolate Snack Cake, 282
  Piled-High Nachos, **279**, 281
  Slow-Cooked Chili Con Carne, 280
Sweet potatoes, 48–49
  Carrot and Sweet Potato Puree, 140
  Garlic-Roasted Sweet Potatoes with Arugula,
    142, 143

Sweet Potatoes (*cont.*)
    Ginger-Roasted Pork with Sweet Potatoes, 228, **229**
    Mashed Root Vegetables, 278
    Oven-Fried Fish and Chips, 200
    vs. potatoes, 143
    Roast Chicken and Vegetables, 209
    vs. yams, 143, 228
Swiss chard, 27, 27
Systolic blood pressure, xii, xiv

T

Tabbouleh
    Arugula Tabbouleh, **152**, 153
Tachycardia, x
Tacos
    Spiced Salmon Tacos, 192, **193**
Tart
    Flavorful Fruit Tart, 254, **255**
Tea, 61–62
    Green Tea–Oatmeal Pancakes, 80, **81**
    legend of, 62
    types of, 61
Tetrazzini
    Tuna Tetrazzini, 197
Tex-Mex-style dish
    Tex-Mex Beans and Rice, 158
Thanksgiving menu, 275
    Herbed Bread Dressing, 276
    Mashed Root Vegetables, 278
    Pumpkin Pie in Nut Crust, **275**, 277
Thyme, 29
Tofu, 55, 56
    Creamy "Egg" Salad, 114, **115**
    Sesame-Seared Tofu, 165
    Tofu and Bok Choy Stir-Fry, 166
    Tofu Citrus Salad, 113
    Tofu Mayonnaise, 259
Tomatoes, 63–65. *See also* Tomato juice
    Basic Tomato Sauce, 266
    colors and shapes of, 64
    Greek-Inspired Pasta, **176**, 177
    lycopene in, 4, 63, 63, 64
    Rich Tomato Soup, 98
    for ripening bananas, 11
    scientific name of, 64
    Spicy Fajitas, 222
    Spinach Linguine with Fresh Tomatoes and Pork, 185
Tomato juice
    Tomato-Basil Vinaigrette, 260, **261**

Tortellini
    Tortellini Salad, 118
Tortillas
    Piled-High Nachos, **279**, 281
Trail mix
    Toasted Trail Mix, 233
Triglycerides, xii
    lowering, with
        grapes, 26
        kiwifruit, 31
        omega-3 fatty acids, 2
        shiitake mushrooms, 34, 35
        soy foods, 56
Tropical fruits, 66
Tuna
    Chopped Niçoise Salad, **124**, 125
    Grilled Tuna with Wasabi Cream, 196
    Tuna Tetrazzini, 197
Turkey
    Healthy Chef's Salad, 126
    Herb-Roasted Turkey Breast, 218
    Slow-Cooked Chili Con Carne, 280
    Turkey Burgers, 216
    Turkey Cutlets with Avocado Salsa, 214, **215**
    Turkey Picadillo, 217
Turmeric, 29, 30

U

Ulva lactuca, 53
Unsaturated fats, xii

V

Veal
    Makeover Veal Marsala, 226
Vegetables. *See also specific vegetables*
    Beef and Vegetable Stroganoff, 223
    Chicken and Vegetables in Cream Sauce, 204
    cruciferous, 21–22 (*see also* Broccoli; Brussels sprouts; Cabbage; Cauliflower)
        introducing children to, 22
        preparing, 21
    Curried Vegetables with Beans, 162
    fiber in, 3
    Mashed Root Vegetables, 278
    Penne with Roasted Autumn Vegetables, 174
    Quick Vegetable Mac 'n' Cheese, 172, **173**
    Roast Chicken and Vegetables, 209

Roasted Winter Vegetables, 141
sea, 53–54
    types of, 53
Vegetable Noodle Bowl, 182, **183**
Vegetable Quinoa, 146, **147**
Vegetarian main dishes. *See* Main dishes,
    meatless
Ventricular arrhythmia, x
Vinaigrettes
    Citrus Vinaigrette, 260, **261**
    Herb-Dijon Vinaigrette, **261**, 262
    Tomato-Basil Vinaigrette, 260, **261**
Vindaloo, 29
Vitamin A
    caution about, 4
    sources of
        bell peppers, 44
        carrots, 18
        chile peppers, 46
        cruciferous vegetables, 22
        garlic, 24
        oranges, 42
        seeds, 55
        spinach, 58
        sweet potatoes, 48
        tomatoes, 63
        tropical fruits, 66
        winter squash, 60
        yogurt, 72
Vitamin C
    heart health benefits of, 5–6
    sources of, 6
        bell peppers, 44, 44, 122
        cherries, 26
        chile peppers, 46
        cruciferous vegetables, 22
        garlic, 24
        grapes, 26
        kiwifruit, 30
        lemons, 32
        limes, 32
        onions, scallions, and shallots, 41
        oranges, 42, 42
        seeds, 55
        shiitake mushrooms, 34
        spinach, 58
        sweet potatoes, 48
        tomatoes, 63
        tropical fruits, 66
        winter squash, 60
        yogurt, 72

Vitamin E, sources of
    kiwifruit, 30
    seeds, 55
    spinach, 58

W

Wakame, 53
Walnuts
    Linguine with Walnut Pesto, 180
    omega-3 fatty acids in, 36
    Pumpkin Pie in Nut Crust, **275**, 277
Wasabi
    Grilled Tuna with Wasabi Cream, 196
Web sites, health, xviii
Weight loss, xvi–xviii
    foods for
        hot red peppers, 44
        nuts, 36
        sweet potatoes, 48
    for reducing diabetes risk, xvi
Whole grains, 16–17, 67–69. *See also* Grains
    fiber in, 3
    gluten-free, 68
    parts of, 17
Wild rice
    Wild Rice with Almonds and Currants, 151
Wine
    recommended consumption of, 70
    red, 70–72
        flavonoids in, 5
        Frozen Yogurt with Fruit Wine Sauce, 274
Winter squash. *See* Squash, winter
Women, heart attack symptoms in, ix, x

Y

Yams, 143, 228
Yogurt, 72–74
    Frozen Yogurt with Fruit Wine Sauce, 274
    Tandoori Chicken, 202

Z

Zeaxanthin, sources of
    bell peppers, 44
    spinach, 58
    winter squash, 59
Zucchini
    Chicken-Zucchini Pasta Toss, 212

Conversion Chart

These equivalents have been slightly rounded to make measuring easier.

Volume Measurements

U.S.	Imperial	Metric
¼ tsp	–	1 ml
½ tsp	–	2 ml
1 tsp	–	5 ml
1 Tbsp	–	15 ml
2 Tbsp (1 oz)	1 fl oz	30 ml
¼ cup (2 oz)	2 fl oz	60 ml
⅓ cup (3 oz)	3 fl oz	80 ml
½ cup (4 oz)	4 fl oz	120 ml
⅔ cup (5 oz)	5 fl oz	160 ml
¾ cup (6 oz)	6 fl oz	180 ml
1 cup (8 oz)	8 fl oz	240 ml

Weight Measurements

U.S.	Metric
1 oz	30 g
2 oz	60 g
4 oz (¼ lb)	115 g
5 oz (⅓ lb)	145 g
6 oz	170 g
7 oz	200 g
8 oz (½ lb)	230 g
10 oz	285 g
12 oz (¾ lb)	340 g
14 oz	400 g
16 oz (1 lb)	455 g
2.2 lb	1 kg

Length Measurements

U.S.	Metric
¼"	0.6 cm
½"	1.25 cm
1"	2.5 cm
2"	5 cm
4"	11 cm
6"	15 cm
8"	20 cm
10"	25 cm
12" (1')	30 cm

Pan Sizes

U.S.	Metric
8" cake pan	20 × 4 cm sandwich or cake tin
9" cake pan	23 × 3.5 cm sandwich or cake tin
11" × 7" baking pan	28 × 18 cm baking tin
13" × 9" baking pan	32.5 × 23 cm baking tin
15" × 10" baking pan	38 × 25.5 cm baking tin (Swiss roll tin)
1½ qt baking dish	1.5 liter baking dish
2 qt baking dish	2 liter baking dish
2 qt rectangular baking dish	30 × 19 cm baking dish
9" pie plate	22 × 4 or 23 × 4 cm pie plate
7" or 8" springform pan	18 or 20 cm springform or loose-bottom cake tin
9" × 5" loaf pan	23 × 13 cm or 2 lb narrow loaf tin or pâté tin

Temperatures

Fahrenheit	Centigrade	Gas
140°	60°	–
160°	70°	–
180°	80°	–
225°	105°	¼
250°	120°	½
275°	135°	1
300°	150°	2
325°	160°	3
350°	180°	4
375°	190°	5
400°	200°	6
425°	220°	7
450°	230°	8
475°	245°	9
500°	260°	–